PRAISE FOR *AM I GOING TO BE OKAY?* (AND IS *"Okay"* ENOUGH?)

Patti Brennan's *Am I Going to Be Okay?* is the book I've been waiting for my entire adult life. She leads the reader effortlessly through the maze that is personal finance, one in which many of us, myself included, had long felt hopelessly lost. And, along with a treasure trove of crucial information, she gives us her own remarkable life story. She understands that the facts of a life, anyone's life, are intricately interwoven with the facts about money, and how to manage it. It's a book I'd never expected to read—a page-turner about personal finance. It's a significant accomplishment.

—Michael Cunningham
Pulitzer Prize winning author of The Hours, Day, *and others*

Money matters can be hard to grasp, especially when trying to plan a future that can, itself, be hard to grasp. One's eyes cross. Patti Brennan's clear and carefully considered guidelines provide a way to see and plan with calming foresight.

She marshals her thirty years of experience to tell entertaining hands-on stories to make finance personal, meaningful, and fun.

—Ken Corbett, Ph.D.
Clinical Assistant Professor, New York University; author, Boyhoods: Rethinking Masculinities and A Murder Over a Girl: Gender, Justice, Junior High

Patti Brennan knows people and she knows money. This book is for every person who has ever worried about money. Written with compassion, common sense and humor, this book is the financial adviser everyone needs and it gives every reader the chance to understand the world of money and to do well in it.

—Amy Bloom
NY Times best-selling author, In Love, White Houses, Lucky Us, Away, *and others*

Patti Brennan has written an extraordinary book: lively, practical, clear, and enormously helpful for anyone who has the need for financial planning. Her approach is client centered and outcome oriented. She focuses on client needs, and is able to quickly separate what is important from all the noise and jargon that surrounds most discussions of investing and financial planning. Whether you're a professional yourself, or simply someone who wants to know whether they'll "be Okay," this book is for you.

—John Emerson
Vice Chairman, Capital International, Inc.

In *Am I Going to Be Okay?* Patti Brennan guides readers through the complex world of personal finance with warmth, wisdom, and actionable advice. Drawing on her decades as one of Barron's top-ranked U.S. advisors, she goes beyond numbers to show how money is inextricably linked with our fears as well as our values, goals, and dreams. Whether you're starting out or nearing retirement, Patti provides the tools and insights to navigate life's challenges with clarity and confidence. Her passion shines through as she empowers readers to make smart choices, build wealth, and create meaningful legacies. In a world where finances are a source of anxiety for nearly everyone, this book gives the reader reassurance and hope, proving that with the right plan, you will be more than okay.

—**Susan Theder**
Chief Marketing and Experience Officer, FMG Suite

AM I GOING TO BE *Okay?*

(AND IS *"Okay"* ENOUGH?)

MONEY: Timely Intelligence, Actionable Ideas, Answers to the Questions that *Really* Matter

AM I GOING TO BE *Okay?*

(AND IS "*Okay*" ENOUGH?)

PATTI BRENNAN, CFP®

Forbes | Books

Published by Forbes Books, Charleston, South Carolina.
An imprint of Advantage Media Group.

Forbes Books is a registered trademark, and the Forbes Books colophon is a trademark of Forbes Media, LLC.

Printed in the United States of America.

10 9 8 7 6 5 4 3 2 1

ISBN: 978-1-94663-356-9 (Hardcover)
ISBN: 979-8-88750-013-3 (eBook)

Library of Congress Control Number: 2024908605

Layout design by Ruthie Wood.

Since 1917, Forbes has remained steadfast in its mission to serve as the defining voice of entrepreneurial capitalism. Forbes Books, launched in 2016 through a partnership with Advantage Media, furthers that aim by helping business and thought leaders bring their stories, passion, and knowledge to the forefront in custom books. Opinions expressed by Forbes Books authors are their own.

ACKNOWLEDGMENTS

Who supports the decision of a young woman to leave a stable nursing career and start a financial planning firm out of the laundry room while he grew his business out of the dining room? Who jumped in with advice and encouragement while four young children crawled around our ankles and his two brothers lived in the guest room? Only Ed Brennan, who has enthusiastically been at my side every step of the way, putting me on a pedestal I did not deserve. In addition, I couldn't have done it without our four supporting cast members—Michael, Kelly, Carrie, and Jack—who sometimes found themselves filing and answering phones or stuck somewhere because their mom was always running late. For them, resilience was born at a very young age.

Speaking of resilience, I want to thank my friend Mary Nakajima, who spent countless hours poring over each draft of this book, tearing it apart. In addition to her agile mind and eye for detail, *her wit is like none other.* She was brutally honest and expected perfection, *repeatedly reminding me how far I was from that goal.* Writing a book is a grueling task, yet in a weird sort of way she made it fun for me.

Even so, there were many days—and months—when I would get so discouraged writing this book that I almost abandoned the project altogether. It was much more difficult than I realized at the outset, and I've felt the need to start from scratch many times during the process. I could not have finished without the support of the incredible group of professionals who work at Key Financial, whose tendencies toward perfection rivals my own, and whose efforts helped to get this book over the finish line. This process and the concepts in this book are the result of years of tweaking, refining, and perfecting the experience we give our clients, and many of the ideas came from learning with my team along the way. As professionals, they've never stopped learning, and I couldn't be more grateful for their loyal support and encouragement.

I also want to acknowledge the industry professionals who have helped me along the way. Where possible, I have tried to acknowledge the person who may have said something or taught me a technique I am sharing with you, yet so many came from brainstorming conversations, study group meetings and conferences over the years. Just know that the financial model and most of the concepts in this book are the culmination of thirty-four years of learning from others. It is my hope that they will be proud that they shared their wisdom with me. If you are one of them and are reading this book, thank you for making a difference in my life ... *so that perhaps* ... I can do the same for others.

One more note: Writing this book has been an incredible journey, and I am excited to share these insights with you. *While no book is ever completely free from minor errors*, I want to assure you that **the concepts here are what truly matter**; you can put the calculator away. *Eventually, even my dear friend Mary* understood that my goal is to provide **clarity, not perfection**, and to give you the tools to navigate your financial life with confidence.

CONTENTS

INTRODUCTION

The Question That Changed Everything

"Am I going to be okay?"

That was the question my mother asked me as we sat in her living room not long after my father's death. Dad had suffered a long decline before he died of bladder cancer. As a former ICU nurse and the only person in my family with healthcare experience, I spent a lot of time helping with his care and interpreting what doctors were saying. On the last day of his life, with all of his seven children and his wife of forty-two years gathered around his hospital bed in our childhood home, Dad took his final breath. I checked for his pulse, looked at my mother, and said, "Mom, he's gone."

There was a stunned silence. We were expecting it, and were relieved that his suffering was over, but there is still a finality that sends shock waves through your body. Eventually we zombie-walked into action. Someone called the undertaker, others began tidying up.

As we were swirling around each other, trying to process what we had just witnessed, I heard Mom calling my name from the living room— always a sign that I was in trouble when I was a child. I wondered what I might have done. Did Mom think Dad had suffered too much? Had I called his death too quickly? Was I not there enough for her?

Mom took my hands, looked at me face to face, and said, "Patti, when your Dad and I were in your office, and we were talking about what I should do if something were to happen to him, and you were giving us options and making suggestions . . . I was nodding my head and acting like I understood what you were saying, but I want you to know right now, I didn't have a clue."

And that was when, with that wide-eyed, panicked look I saw so often growing up, she said, "I don't have the financial brain you and your dad have[1] and need you to tell me the truth. *Am I going to be okay?*"

I don't have words to express the emotion that rises in your chest when, as a daughter, you can look your own mother in the eyes and say, "Mom, you're going to be fine. This is going to be seamless. You are going to be more than okay."

---

1   Please note, this is a word-for-word quote, and what often happens: *Dad was still alive to her.*

> Then she asked a question that was even more consequential for me
> and that gave me life-changing insight into the phrase *peace of mind*:
> **"Patti . . . what do people do whose *daughters* <u>aren't</u> CERTIFIED**
> **FINANCIAL PLANNERS™?"**

That one question was an epiphany. Even though I had been a CFP® for almost 10 years, I'm not sure I realized how important a trusted relationship with a financial planner could be. That conversation with my mom at the lowest point in her life would change my perspective forever.

From ICU to CFP®

You may be wondering why and how I made the transition from Intensive Care Unit nurse to CERTIFIED FINANCIAL PLANNER™. It does seem an unexpected career move, but I did it the same way most of us do anything—through a series of small steps that led to a much longer journey. The answer starts with why I became a nurse.

Growing up, I was the fifth of seven children, all born within eight years. We weren't poor, but Mom and Dad lived paycheck to paycheck, and were sometimes just a little bit short of having enough money to cover all the bills. Life could get emotional and chaotic, and while some people thrive on uncertainty and drama, I craved order and security, and found that order in numbers. I believe there is great value in using objective metrics to make rational choices. It's also important to recognize the powerful influence of emotion on decisions. Let's face it, when cash flow is tight and there's not a lot to fall back on, *the entire family feels it.* Parents are on edge and the kids feel anxious, sometimes not even knowing why. One unexpected bump in the road can destroy the entire car, creating havoc with everyone's schedules. We all know the feeling of panic that comes with unexpected events, the hold fear can have on a situation or an outlook. As a result, I learned the value of hoping for the best but knowing that a backup plan is imperative. If Plan A doesn't work, we'll go to Plan B, never allowing failure to be an option and always aiming for a solution. Numbers and plans were my solace.

As I reached my senior year in high school, I began to think about what type of career I would like. Back in the day, the more popular choices open to women were teacher, nurse, secretary, and stay-at-home mom. Our next-door neighbor, who was a doctor's wife, told me she thought I would be a good nurse, so that was the path I chose.

Then, during my senior year at Georgetown University, I took a financial planning course and absolutely loved it. If I had known that such a career existed when I started school, there is no question that financial planning would've been my number one choice. Yet I was so far along in the nursing program that it didn't make sense to change, so I spent the next several years as an oncology nurse and then worked in the ICU.

Night shifts in intensive care involved sitting by a patient's bedside making sure they remained stable and being ready to jump in at any moment. On those rare occasions when things were quiet, usually on breaks, most of us passed the time grabbing a quick bite and reading magazines. There were a lot of copies of *Glamour, Cosmopolitan*, and *People* being passed around. Everyone used to make fun of me because I always had *Forbes* and *Fortune* by my side. It was simply what I was drawn to.

One night, while things were quiet, I was listening to a medical resident named Scott complain about having to do his taxes. I said, "I love doing taxes, it's like solving a puzzle." Could I find one more deduction? Could I save twenty more dollars? I started to ask him some questions.

"Don't you moonlight in urgent care, Scott? If so, you can really save a lot of money on taxes."

"What do you mean?" he asked, puzzled.

"Well, when you moonlight, you are an independent contractor, so you're in business for yourself. That means you get to deduct certain things, such as a portion of your home expenses because you have a separate office. You can also write off your car mileage because you have to go back and forth to the hospitals where you moonlight."

"Whoa, no kidding?"

"Get me your paperwork, and we can go over it together."

I helped Scott fill out his tax return that year, and he got thousands of dollars back as a refund. To him, that felt like winning the lottery. Then as now, residents can work fifty to sixty hours in a hospital, then moonlight for another shift or two to pay off their huge student loan debt, and the government, through the tax code, is willing to reward and encourage that work ethic—but with a hitch. You have to know you can take those deductions[2]! The year before, when my friend Scott did not take them, Uncle Sam didn't come knocking on his door with a $3,000 check. What you don't know can cost you money—sometimes a lot of money.

It wasn't long before word got around to others in the hospital who began lining up to have me look at their taxes. I understood the rules, loved saving money, and could help people I cared about. It was a win-win all the way around.

---

2   A word of caution: Tax laws have changed over the years and will certainly continue to do so; if you are an independent contractor, be sure to consult a qualified tax advisor or CPA when considering certain deductions.

About a year later, there was a "Help Wanted" ad in the classifieds of the Sunday newspaper for a position as a financial planner. I told my husband Ed that if I had to do it all over again, this was what I'd choose. I loved my nursing career, but it wasn't completely satisfying for me. It was like buying an off-the-rack suit compared to a tailored one. Both looked fine on the outside, but they didn't feel the same. Ed encouraged me to apply: "What have you got to lose? You're probably not going to get the job, so a phone call won't kill you." Eleven interviews and three personality tests later, I was offered the position.

The founder of that firm, Roy, was in the forefront of developing a *real* financial planning model, one that recognized the fact that each person is unique, with his or her own goals and resources. Both he and my direct manager, Ray, were willing to listen to my ideas and were open to a different approach. I was used to asking my patients questions to get to the bottom of how they felt, both physically and emotionally. Similarly, as I gained experience, I learned how to zero in on what my financial clients wanted, while determining the best way to get there. As it turned out, not having a financial background actually worked in my favor. Both men appreciated the fact that I didn't have to unlearn approaches that were common at the time; with me they had a clean slate to help them forge a model of how a *real* financial planner can make a difference.

In hindsight, I can say I was fortunate that I didn't learn about financial planning until my senior year at Georgetown. Those years spent in the hospital provided a solid foundation for my future career as a CFP®. Nursing involved working side by side with brilliant surgeons and specialists, and always circling back to what mattered: the health of the whole patient. It is not just what we say to people but how we say it that matters. With that experience under my belt, I was never intimidated by anyone, no matter what their specialty was. If I believed someone was missing something or was going to make a mistake, I gently and tactfully spoke up. If you or someone you love is ever in the hospital, just remember: *Nurses advocate. So do financial planners.*

Over the years I've learned that the two things people worry about most are their health and their money (and the same for the people they love). Opinions regarding both topics can vary tremendously, and the wrong advice, or no guidance at all, can lead to unfortunate and even fatal consequences.

Financial planning and wealth management are hard, especially *if* they are done right, and sometimes people just don't know where to turn or whether they're missing something. It might surprise you that the skills learned at the bedside translate quite easily to wealth management. *Healthcare is hard too*, and knowing everything about every organ in an intricate system as the human body is daunting, especially during a crisis like a cancer diagnosis or a visit to the ICU. The nurse focuses first on the patient, addressing each part of the body that needs to heal only after understanding what's going on holistically. Then the task is to help coordinate all the specialists, organize the treatment plan, and monitor the patient to make sure the plan is working. Just as there is so much to know about the human body and how each approach affects the health outcome and how the patient feels, financial affairs are often equally complicated. Changes in approaches in the areas of retirement planning, cash flow, tax laws, wills and trusts, and even what you want in life can affect your financial future and what is left to the people you love. This book will tie it all together.

Is This Book for You?

My goal in these pages is to come as close as I can to sitting with you in your living room and having the same kind of conversation I had with my mother. A deep and personal one: a conversation about whether you'll be okay **and what you mean by "okay"** with a focus on your goals for (and during) your lifetime and what you want to leave after you're gone.

When I was preparing the outline for this book, everyone kept asking me, "Patti, who is your audience?" I kept dodging the question because I don't believe I should be picking the audience. *I believe you should pick yourselves.*

I'm not sure where you are in life or what might resonate with you. It's often assumed that all of us, especially those who have achieved financial success, have a certain level of knowledge, yet I've learned that just because people might be excellent surgeons, run a company, or have a high net worth for other reasons, *that doesn't mean they are adept at optimizing their own financial affairs.* Even worse, sometimes people hesitate to ask questions for fear of betraying a lack of knowledge. **This can happen to anyone,** especially those who were so hyper focused on their professions or careers that they didn't have the time or inclination to learn about personal finance.

Whether you have a hundred dollars or a hundred million, there is something here for you. If you are in the latter category, you may not be inclined to read this book, and I totally get it. I'll just say that many wealthy people still feel the need for financial advice or a financial planner because they've learned that financial confidence about their own future and less worry about intergenerational wealth are not the same thing. A person's or family's net worth is one of several byproducts of a life of work, sacrifice, and probably more than a few sleepless nights. (Other outcomes might include mentoring future generations, a pristine reputation, and creating lifelong relationships.) Wealthy people *often recognize that they may not have all the answers,* and so they seek appropriate guidance from professionals who might. They understand that there is always something to think (and worry!) about, laws that may be changing, and charitable organizations where their efforts can leave a true mark for generations to come.

No matter what your financial status is, there is ample evidence that when it comes to big life goals, most Americans could be doing better.

Results from the Federal Reserve 2022 Survey of Household Economics and Decisionmaking (SHED) indicate a decline in peoples' financial well-being over the previous year. The survey, which was fielded in October 2022, found that self-reported financial well-being fell sharply and was among the lowest observed since 2016. The share of adults who said they were worse off financially than a year earlier rose to 35%, the highest level since the question was first asked in 2014. Housing had something to do with that: Nearly two-thirds of renters said that their inability to afford a down payment to buy a home was a reason they rent (Board of Governors of the Federal Reserve System, *Economic Well-Being of U.S. Households*).

37% would not have been able to cover a $400 expense completely with cash or its equivalent, while 28% of adults went without some form of medical care in 2022 because they could not afford it.

Progress toward retirement savings goals declined in 2022. Only thirty-one percent of non-retirees thought their retirement savings plan was on track, down from 40% in 2021.

Although almost three-fourths of non-retired adults had at least some retirement savings, about 28% did not have any.

According to a 2022 survey released by Schroders, the participants thought on average that it would take $1.1 million to retire comfortably but only 24% expected to reach that mark; 56% expected to have saved less than $500,000, including 36% who forecast less than $250,000 in savings (Welsh, *GenXers will not Retire Comfortably*).

How did we get to this point? It's not for lack of information. In fact, there is so much information available that you would think everyone would know what they should be doing. The problem is that having access to information and knowing what to do with it are two different things.

My intention in this book is for you to find ideas that will help you protect, grow, and use your assets to lead a *great* life: *the one you want*. You'll find concepts explained in terms anyone at any level can understand. You could be looking for a plain and simple explanation of a concept such as wealth management, or for ideas about retirement planning, college planning, healthcare insurance, or when to take Social Security. You might want to learn how to avoid estate taxes while exploring what constitutes not only an inheritance but a real legacy. Or maybe you're just curious about the fifteen mistakes people make over and over again. Some of what is in the book may apply to you, some of it may not. I have written it in the way I would want to read something like this, by a person who knew nothing in the beginning and just wanted to understand.

The one thing I didn't want is another boring book on finance that is filled with unrelatable words and drones on about the *shoulds*. There are very few shoulds here, just lots of concrete examples and stories to make it easier to understand and apply the ideas. There are lots of those here too.

To help you decide if this book has something for you, a brief look at the key concepts that inform it and are woven throughout might be useful. They are as follows:

KEY CONCEPTS

(Learned from experience and others)

True financial security doesn't happen accidentally.

There are certain Key Force Multipliers. You can get where you want faster than you ever thought, and further than you ever dreamed.

There are also wealth destroyers that will lead to financial demise.

Anyone can be rich; not everyone will be wealthy.

Everything changes. No exceptions.

Start where you are; the past is history.

Over-confidence is usually fatal.

Humility is the key to financial success. Life, too.

There is always hope, but hope is not enough.

Goals coupled with executed strategies (inspired action steps) and constant monitoring will work over time. Figure out what is working and what isn't and adjust as necessary.

An inheritance is what you give to someone. A legacy is what you put into someone. You can make both last for multiple generations.

Pain is inevitable. Suffering is *optional*.

Trust and respect are earned.

You can't recycle time. Once it's gone, it is gone.

It's never too late... until it is.

These key concepts will become clearer as you see them in action in the pages that follow. Some of them may seem unusual in a book about financial planning, *but I mean this to be an unusual book.*

Anyone Can Be Rich. Not Everyone Will Be Wealthy.

The difference between a rich person and a wealthy person is that a wealthy person has sufficient assets to maintain their standard of living without a salary; *they have sustainable wealth.* Someone can earn $500,000 per year, but what happens when the earning power is gone—how long do the savings and investments last? If financial confidence is the ultimate goal, most people want to be wealthy.

Financial Planning is a Verb, Not a Noun

You are going to hear the term "*real* financial planning" used many times in this book.

A plan is not planning. Real financial planning is an active process, not a set-and-forget stack of spreadsheets or a calculator you pull off the internet. **It is a set of action steps integrated to accomplish the things most important to you.** Don't get me wrong. A financial "plan" is nice to have, but it's static. What happens when the kids decide they want to go to a private university when you were thinking state school? Or when one of those bear markets happens to occur the year of retirement? How about when that job you thought would support your family for the next ten years suddenly disappears, or one partner in a two-income family decides to stay home with the children? What do you do when you have a plan, but *life* happens?

You might ask the question: *Why bother* planning and setting goals if you know things are probably going to change? That is a *great* question. Research has shown that something happens to us when we take the time to create the image of an ideal future, rich with specifics. Our subconscious minds don't know the difference between things we imagine and reality, especially if you factor in some emotion like fear[3].

---

3   Just ask someone who has worked themselves into a panic before public speaking.

Instead, develop a habit of looking forward and asking important questions as you envision the progress you want to make. And when priorities change, no big deal. That achievement muscle is strong, flexible, and resilient.

There will always be a new President, a change in tax law, opportunities for growth and financial landmines to avoid. Things change. Priorities do too.

Financial checkups are similar to medical checkups. Using a set-and-forget system for your money is a recipe for trouble—just as it would be if you did not return to the doctor periodically even after receiving a clean bill of health. Even worse, we have many Americans in their sixties and seventies who aren't getting regular financial physicals at a time when going back to work may not be an option. Retiring from work is one thing; *staying retired* despite market fluctuations, tax law changes, and—for many people—physical and cognitive decline is quite another. Over the years, it is important to monitor progress and evaluate strategies the same way nurses monitor a patient's vital signs and adjust the financial medicine when necessary.

You may be wondering about the difference between financial planning and wealth management. Financial planning creates the framework; wealth management executes the steps and manages the plan over time. The idea of "wealth" is subjective, and therefore managing that wealth is also very personal—the key is having a process to *build wealth sustainably and remain wealthy*. In other words, think of the phrase "financial planning" as the process of *creating* a plan and "wealth management" as the *execution and ongoing management* of that plan.

To compound wealth over time—and to preserve what you've accumulated to pass on to your heirs—*the key is to have a simple, repeatable process* with a few levers thrown in to multiply your efforts and resources. The levers can turbocharge the process and provide momentum so that success is almost inevitable. To lock it in place, keep yourself accountable by monitoring your progress toward the goals you've articulated as most important to you.

Whether you have $20,000, $2,000,000, or $200,000,000, there is always room for improvement. The outcome can show up in the form of lower taxes, freer cash flow and more confidence along the way. This is achieved by understanding—and applying—tax benefits available to you, avoiding uncompensated risk, achieving target rates of return, not overpaying for insurance, avoiding retirement plans that fall short, and sloppy wills or trusts. Outcomes are different for everyone.

Equally as important, financial planning *with* wealth management can build a framework to withstand the uncertainty that comes with any crisis, including a worldwide economic lockdown caused by a lethal virus. Long after COVID-19, the world may look different, but the life you want should not. This book will present actionable strategies to help you make the vision you have of your future a reality. *It is not intended to replace your adviser, if you have one, but to make that relationship even more powerful than it already is.* You've probably heard the saying "ignorance is bliss." When it comes to your financial life, it isn't. You can certainly continue doing what you've done in the past. Or you can find out if there's something more you can do to create a rock-solid foundation and a tax-efficient legacy for generations to come. Let's be smart with your money.

How to Read This Book, and How *Not* To

If you're looking for a surefire guarantee of financial security and untold wealth, *you may as well close the book right now*. That said, please allow me to bore you with some cautionary—*but important*—words. This is not a manual of advice about specific investments, though you will find throughout sample investment portfolios showing performance based on types of investment and various indices. The figures I quote in these are for illustrative purposes only and are not necessarily indicative of past or future results of any specific investment. They do not include consideration of the time value of money, inflation, fluctuation in principle, or in many instances, dividend rates and taxes. You'll see a glossary of terms in the back of this book that many of us (often wrongly) assume you already understand. For example, an index is a hypothetical portfolio of specific securities (common examples of indices are the Dow Jones Industrial and the S&P 500), the performance of which is often used as a benchmark in judging the relative performance of certain asset classes. Indices are unmanaged portfolios and should only be compared with securities with similar investment characteristics and criteria. Investors cannot invest directly in an index.

When viewing the data in some of the examples, readers should understand the difference between certificates of deposit (CD's), T-Bills, and equity investments, such as stocks. A CD is a timed deposit offered through banks and is insured by the Federal Deposit Insurance Corporation. T-Bills are short term instruments (52 weeks or less) issued by U.S. Treasury and are backed by the full faith and credit of the U.S. Government. While they are not FDIC insured, they are considered one of the safest instruments you can invest in. A

CD has a specific, fixed term (often three months, six months, or one to five years) and usually a fixed interest rate. It is intended that the CD (or a T-Bill) be held until maturity, at which time the money may be withdrawn together with the accrued interest If held until maturity, the return/performance provided through CD's and T-Bills will not be subject to the fluctuation experienced in equity markets. CD's offer a fixed rate of return and FDIC insurance, which guarantees deposits up to a standard amount of $250,000. Unlike CD's and T-Bills, stocks and other equity investments are not deposits, are not FDIC-insured, and can fluctuate in value. They are subject to risk, including possible loss of principal. Unlike CD's, stocks can be sold and purchased at any time within trading hours. Investors need to be aware of the difference in risk associated with CD's and equities, as well as other investments that can and will fluctuate in value.

You'll see that I also have a lot to say about tax strategies, but I must say as well that any tax advice contained in this book is not intended to be used, and cannot be used, for purposes of illegally avoiding taxes or penalties imposed under the United States Internal Revenue Code, or for promoting, marketing, or recommending to another person any tax-related matter. Always consult a CPA or other tax professional before implementing any concept. That goes for estate planning and any legal advice as well; please consult a qualified attorney.

I'd like to suggest that the best way to read this book is to take from it what best applies to your own situation and your particular goals. I started with the idea that you can be your own financial planner, and that you can do this by yourself. That is the purpose of this book, organized into three major sections:

1. Section One: "Strategies…" will give you a timeless process to build the financial life you want and *enjoy the process*. My

goal is to help you feel in control, empowered, and confident with the progress you are making.

2. Section Two: "Tactics…" digs deeper into specific ideas to grow and preserve your wealth, including what to do when the next crisis hits (…and the next one, and the one after that, too).

3. Section Three: "Hijacks." This is where you'll get to learn from the mistakes of others, so you don't have to make them. I'm going to show you where the landmines are and how to avoid stepping on them.

Please note: You might be tempted to go directly to Section Two that discusses specific ideas, and maybe skip to the chapter outlining the most common mistakes. (*Sometimes, I just want the answers, too!*).

Try not to do it. You can peek, but there are important reasons why we don't want to put the cart before the horse, most notably that *this is what many people do already.* In medicine, prescription before diagnosis is considered malpractice. The same principle applies to your money.

To Delegate or Not

Some people don't care to monitor their financial affairs or have the resources to do so. Yet, for most people, the ultimate goal is quality of life and peace of mind. To be clear, a CFP® or other financial advisor can't *give you* peace of mind; that's why I refer to it as financial confidence… maybe even an overall sense of financial well-being. To me, this means you aren't a pie chart, so managing a portfolio may not be enough to show that you are making real progress. Financial planners are not just for the wealthy; people of all financial means often choose to have an adviser because they've realized that their time and talents are better spent elsewhere. Others see finances as fun and prefer to do their planning themselves because they find it empowering. *Either decision can be the right decision for you.* If you do choose to work with a professional, you can think about the relationship as a journey that might be understood as follows:

> Your goal is a vacation of a lifetime,
> someplace sunny and warm with lots of fun things to do.
> To get there, you could fly direct, stop off in Chicago,
> or take the redeye, flying all night.
> Good financial planners are like pilots.
> They make sure you get up in the air,
> land safely,
> arrive on time,
> and when the going gets rough,
> they help you weather the storm.
> Your investments, insurance, wills, and trust(s) are like the airplane,
> simply a means to an end.
> The pilot is the person there to make sure
> you're not on a flight to Alaska
> when you expect to be on the beach by noon.
> — Patti Brennan, CFP®

May your journey be fulfilling, and may you find in these pages something useful, informative, and perhaps even entertaining. I thank you for your time in staying with me this far.

PART ONE: STRATEGIES

Preparing for Takeoff

CHAPTER 1

The Four Keys for Life Financial Planning System

True financial confidence doesn't happen accidentally.

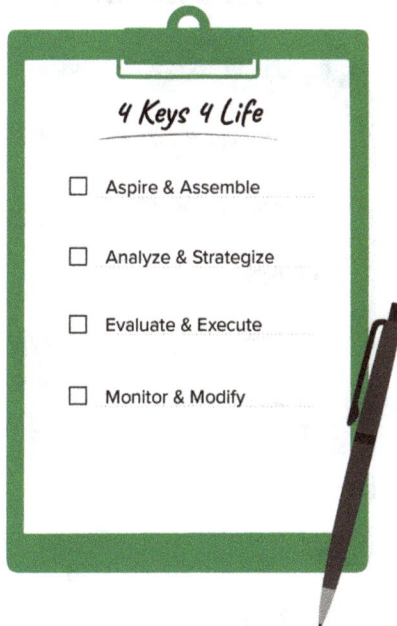

4 Keys 4 Life

☐ Aspire & Assemble

☐ Analyze & Strategize

☐ Evaluate & Execute

☐ Monitor & Modify

How do you know where you stand, how you compare, and if you can do better? The Four Keys for Life is a repeatable system that can give you those benchmarks and can work for anyone. It has evolved from my years of being a CERTIFIED FINANCIAL PLANNER™ (CFP®), and from the standards that the CFP® Board has laid out for the profession. My goal here is not to teach you how to be a CFP® but to boil the planning process down into a digestible format, with comprehensive steps that can be grouped into distinct categories.

The Four Keys for Life, when taken together, form a real financial planning process that you can use whether you are twenty years old or seventy, and whether you have $1,000 to start or $100,000,000 accumulated. Priorities may be different, but the principles apply to everyone. The process works at all levels of net worth to *customize integrated strategies and tactics, so redundancies are eliminated, money is saved, and nothing is missed.*

Key 1: Aspire and Assemble

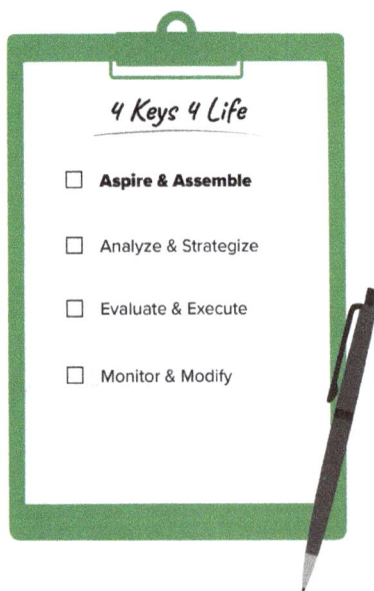

4 Keys 4 Life

☐ **Aspire & Assemble**

☐ Analyze & Strategize

☐ Evaluate & Execute

☐ Monitor & Modify

The first Key for Life is a visualized future or, in other words, a wish list that is rich in specifics. Instead of simply stating that you wish to retire someday or hope to leave your grandchild money, you need to get to the specifics of your goal. This involves really digging down, envisioning what you want to do with your life, and taking into account the money you've saved along the way. One specific goal might be, "I'd like to retire in seven years and have $8,000 per month deposited after taxes. I'd ideally have my mortgage paid off and be able to take one long international trip a year, as well as several others within the country. I want to have enough disposable income to be able to help the grandchildren. And I'd like all of this to last at least thirty years after retirement. Our parents lived into their nineties, and they were always worried about running out of money."

Another goal might be, "I want to pay for 75% of my children's college and 100% of their weddings, with a cap of $40,000 for each objective. I also want to buy a large family vacation home on a lake so that there will be a place for my children and grandchildren to gather for holidays. Let's assume I've got $650,000 with no mortgage at first, then a scenario with 50% going toward a mortgage. And because I've seen what end-of-life care can do to finances, I want to be able to cover any long-term nursing care I might need so I don't burden my children."

These are very specific goals. And because they're so specific, you can run scenarios to see how you're tracking toward that beautiful future you yearn for. Pursuing a goal also gives you your why. In her book *Grit*, Angela Duckworth[i] talks about the parable of the bricklayers (Duckworth, *GRIT*).

> Three bricklayers are asked: "What are you doing?"
>
> The first says, "I am laying bricks."
>
> The second says, "I am building a church."
>
> The third says, "I am building the house of God."[4]

In the end, it comes down to purpose; doing what you were meant to do. That does not have to be lofty or career-oriented, by the way. It could mean spending more time with family and friends, serving on a board, or contributing your intellectual capital (or good old-fashioned labor) to a cause you believe in.

8,000 Days

Let's start by taking the pressure off; you don't have to know what you want thirty years from now. When thinking about your future, keep in mind that everyone's priorities will be different, and each person's goals will undoubtedly change as life progresses.

Dr. Joseph Coughlin, director of MIT's AgeLab, is working to redefine retirement by focusing on longevity planning. Dr. Joe has divided a person's life into four 8,000-day (roughly twenty-two-year) segments. Depending on which season of life you are in, there will be questions to ask and decisions to make. Sometimes, the same questions apply in every decade of life. The first 8,000 days comprise *the learning phase*, which covers birth through college. As a parent of four children, I recognize that this phase isn't usually associated with massive wealth accumulation. Piggy banks and summer jobs may not lead to significant savings, but you can make a huge difference in a child's financial education by exposing them to some of the fundamentals. Think of it as the missing semester of college, life lessons that aren't taught in the classroom.

---

4   *Big* difference.

Then we reach *the growing phase* which spans our twenties to mid-forties. During this time, people are usually focusing on their careers and starting families. Saving money for a down payment on a home tends to be prioritized over retirement; the latter is too far off. In this phase, it is common to be living in the here and now, and just trying to get your feet planted.

Some of the questions to ask in your twenties and thirties:

What issues should I consider...

If I'm starting a new job?

If I'm getting married?

If I'm choosing whether to buy or lease a car?

If I'm considering investing in a retirement plan with my employer?

If I get a promotion or raise at work?

If a new job requires me to move?

If I lose my job?

If I'm having (or adopting) a child?

If I'm funding my child's college education?

If I'm buying a home?

If I'm paying off my student loans?

When I'm reviewing my tax return?

When I'm determining what insurance to buy, and how much?

If I'm refinancing my mortgage?

If I'm deciding whether to contribute to a Roth IRA or Roth 401(k) versus a traditional IRA or 401(k)?

When reviewing my paystub, am I making sure to pay for disability insurance with post tax dollars?

The following twenty-two years—about 8,000 days in our forties and fifties—encompass *the maturing phase*, when we're in the peak earning and spending years. Kids are often part of the picture, and the chaos of activities and schoolwork needs to be balanced with career pressures and getting ahead.

For many people, the fifties are the most expensive decade. Many reach this stage and it suddenly hits them—they're underfunded. The kids are teenagers, college is right around the corner, and retirement is not far off. They have that "Oh, my goodness, what are we going to do?" moment. It's important to know all is not lost, but it didn't have to be this way. If those in their fifties haven't been doing financial planning, this is the time to drill down and seriously ask, "What's the highest priority, and how do we get there?" The answer might involve being more aggressive with the portfolio than their comfort zone would normally permit and maximizing every tax planning strategy available. Others might take on a high-deductible health insurance plan coupled with a Health Savings Account (HSA), which would decrease premiums while increasing tax-sheltered income. This is a great option for a healthy person, but it might mean taking on more healthcare costs if there is a crisis. We'll talk more about this later.

Some of the questions to ask in your forties and fifties:

In addition to those mentioned above, what issues should I consider...

If I lose my job at this age?

If I want to save more?

When I'm determining if a backdoor Roth IRA contribution is right for me?

If I'm taking a distribution from my child's 529 plan.

If I'm planning for my aging parents?

If I'm doing a Roth conversion[ii]?

If I'm thinking about refinancing my mortgage?

If I'm purchasing a larger home, or a second home (what's the impact on other priorities)?

When I'm determining the tax and other implications of a rental property?

If I'm deciding whether to own real estate outright or through an LLC or corporation?

If I'm consolidating dormant 401(k)s?

If I'm exercising stock options?

If Restricted Share Units (RSUs) vest?

If I'm meeting with an attorney to prepare a will and/or a trust?

The final 8,000 days make up *the exploring years*, which begin in our mid-sixties, when many people enter retirement. By this age, the large expenses of raising a family and building a net worth are largely behind parents, while others are exploring other priorities.

Sometimes it is easier for couples in the midst of raising a family to agree on priorities than it is for those facing retirement. "I want to move closer to the kids," is one person's objective, while the other spouse says, "We don't want to move too close. Otherwise, we're going to become babysitters and do a lot of the running around, and I don't want to spend my retirement that way." Having that conversation is critical. In fact, having more than one retirement conversation is essential, *because retirement isn't one monolithic stage of life.*

Some of the questions to ask in your sixties, seventies, and beyond:

In addition to the above, what issues should I consider...

When I retire (or ideally, before)?

In determining various ways to supplement cash flow in retirement?

In deciding which account I should withdrawal from first?

If I want to invest to keep pace with inflation while keeping the portfolio resilient to risk?

If I'm deciding whether to consolidate my dormant 401(k)s into an IRA at retirement?

When I'm making my pension election: take it as a monthly payment or a lump sum?

In deciding the age to claim social security? What about my spouse? What if I'm divorced?

In choosing my Medicare coverage during open enrollment?

In evaluating how my tax picture changes when I retire?

In establishing my charitable giving strategy?

If we need to provide care for a loved one, or if a parent passes away?

In determining if surcharges on Medicare Part B and Part D apply to me?

If I experience a sudden wealth event (inheritance, profits from selling a business, etc.)?

In determining how healthcare costs will change as I transition
into retirement?

If I am on Medicare Part D and my prescriptions change?

When I'm taking Required Minimum Distributions (RMDs) from
multiple IRAs, 401(k)s and 403(b)s?

If my spouse has been diagnosed with a terminal illness?

If I have been diagnosed with a terminal illness?

If my spouse passes away?

As you read the questions above—which certainly aren't exhaustive—you might note *the absence of a question* many people start out with: Which mutual fund (or exchange-traded fund), cryptocurrency, one of those sophisticated sounding investments only available to certain investors[iii] should I pick? That's *backwards*. Once you have answers to the above questions and a clear path to your financial future, then you can focus on how to get the highest rate of return with the least amount of risk. While it is important, portfolio management is just one of many ways to help you along life's journey. Stay tuned.

The Four Phases of Retirement: A New Narrative

According to Dr. Joe, the last 8,000 days—often referred to as "retirement"—also tend to fall into four very distinct phases.

Phase One: Managing Ambiguity

This phase includes the first few months after retirement, the honeymoon phase, filled with projects, activities, and trips. It's not unlike freshman year in college, a time to explore and test boundaries. Retirees have worked and been responsible all their lives, and now it's time to cut loose. They want to travel, play golf every other day, and try new restaurants.

Unfortunately, anxiety can creep in because their cash flow needs will likely increase just as their income goes down. As you think about this phase for yourself, rather than pretend your expenses will decrease in retirement, let's acknowledge that you want to go a little wild during the first season of retirement. Define what that looks like and have fun with it.

Phase Two: Making Big Decisions

In this second phase, you've traveled to the places you wanted to travel, and you've golfed as much as you wanted to golf, and you're now ready to settle into a less exciting life. Priorities change. This is the time when spending usually trends downward and there is often a move or a downsize[5].

There is no question that cognitive changes can begin to occur during this phase. For all you youngsters out there, be warned: according to Dr Joe, the ability to process and retain new information begins to decline starting at age thirty! That's the bad news. The good news is that as we get older, crystallized intelligence improves. Have you ever had one of those "gut feelings"? You don't know how you know; *you just know.* That's because our brains have processed years and years of data in our subconscious minds, and we've developed unconscious pattern recognition over time. Experiences locked away deep in our brains help us come to conclusions almost effortlessly. It seems there really is a connection between brain activity and gut instinct.

---

5   Downsizing used to mean moving to a smaller, less expensive home. In today's real estate market, a better term might be "rightsize": a smaller footprint for about the same amount of money.

Phase Three: Managing Complexity

During the third phase, it is important to acknowledge that health issues can begin to accelerate. Many retirees find that moving into retirement communities where they can age in place is a great solution to the difficulties of the normal aging process. Irrespective of what the issue is—health or otherwise—there is no one way that is right for everyone.

For example, I know one couple who had their retirement completely figured out. They had spent their marriage moving around the world as one spouse climbed the corporate ladder. They found they loved Europe and planned on retiring to their favorite city. They saw themselves enjoying the cafes, the museums, the opera, the ballet, and all the other cultural activities the city offered. They planned to use their new European home as a jumping-off point for all the traveling they wanted to do around the Continent. Then the first grandchild came on the scene, and suddenly priorities shifted. They realized they wanted to be more involved with this child than living and traveling in Europe would allow them. No big deal—the Four Keys for Life allowed them simply to run new numbers to see what was possible. Their vision still isn't completely clear, but they are looking at moving to a warm-weather city in the United States, with annual vacations to Europe.

Phase Four: Living Solo

It is a near certainty that one member of a couple will precede the other in death. Yet, too many couples do not plan for that eventuality. According to the Federal Reserve Bank of Chicago, the average annual income in the three years before a spouse died dropped from $75,000 to $47,000 after the spouse's death, a drop of almost 40% (Fadlon et al., *Financial Life After the Death of a Spouse*). This could impact future social security income, ability to cover expenses, or save for the future. You need to plan for life alone, even if you're married now. Think ahead to what you would need if your partner wasn't there. Would you need help around the house or caregiving at some point? Would you need help paying bills? Whatever it is, be prepared and organize your financial affairs accordingly.

Important: *The Solo Phase forces the survivor to go through the first three stages that began at retirement* (Ambiguity and Uncertainty, Making Big Decisions, Managing Complexities) *all over again, often when those cognitive synapses aren't firing off like they used to.* Whether the loss of a partner was expected or sudden, there is a period of uncertainty about living alone, managing household tasks, and handling finances. Then there are new decisions and complexities to manage. The goal is to make this as seamless as possible. *Like it was for Mom.*

In all stages of life including the four phases of retirement, remember to set both "drop-dead" priorities and "nice-to-have" rewards. Nearly everyone says that their financial objective is to have a retirement that preserves their wealth, but people who have only one priority may find it hard to keep up the momentum. A better approach is to have several smaller interim targets—some necessary, some fun—that will continue to motivate you as you reach them. Little wins lead to big wins.

Here's an example of a big win. One of our clients dreamed of buying a Jaguar convertible. He was still young, married with three children, and just in his forties. Before broaching the subject with his wife, he wanted to see if this was really a possibility, and we could tell that driving a new sports car represented his ability to work hard and succeed. So we ran the numbers and included the Jag to see what it would do to their financial plan. It turned out that this purchase didn't interfere with achieving their long-term financial goals, but it would require a bit of rethinking some of the shorter-term priorities and how we earmarked certain resources.

In the meeting to discuss potential outcomes, I told him that if he wanted to get the Jag, he and his wife could pull it off. They had two choices. Get it right away and put off the basement renovation for a little while, or not renovate at all. Or save extra for the Jag and keep the other objectives on track.

He decided that it would be better for the whole family to delay the purchase and save extra for the car. All of a sudden, earning the money took on new meaning. We set a timeline of one year, eliminated service-related costs around the house for things he could do himself, and acted like he had the car payment now by setting aside the money each month. When he got that car, he was so jazzed up because he generated more money than he had ever earned before—multiples of what the car payments added up to!

He'd start our first conversation by saying, "This probably isn't doable, but..." It was an incredibly rewarding experience for him to realize that with a little bit of leverage and the right process, based on realistic benchmarks, he could achieve this goal.

The last step was just selling the idea to his wife.

When the planning process is done effectively, goals often change. Goalsetting is not a once-and-done exercise. A person at age forty may have one set of objectives that will change when they are fifty. Hopefully that's because they've already hit the earlier goals or are on track to exceeding them. You laid the groundwork ten years before, adjusted along the way, and now have the freedom to think bigger—and maybe sooner!

Key 1 - Part 2: Assemble

Thus far we've been discussing the first part of Key 1, Aspire. Now let's turn to the second part: Assemble. Aspiring is the fun part. Assembling is the hard-work part, but if done properly, it is a form of cathartic organization.

This is where you pull together all the pieces of paper that tell you where you stand right now. You'll want to know actual amounts—savings, investments, debts, income, household expenses, retirement accounts, insurance policies, and everything else that will help model where you are and project where you can be in the future. Approach this task bearing in mind that there is no judgment here; ideally this isn't the time to guess. Try to use real numbers.

For the record, I am not a fan of the word "budget." It sounds like the word "diet" and immediately makes me think that I need to sacrifice something. Cutting your standard of living is a last resort, so for now, let's just define what your expenses are[6]. Enlighten yourself. Once you have some insight into your cash flow, you might find yourself making different decisions. Then, instead of wondering where your money went, *you're going to tell it where you want it to go.* If you work with a professional, they will probably want you to define your

---

6   *Don't worry*—you are not alone. Most people have no idea. No judgement.

financial life as it is today or even better, with a few fun things thrown in the mix.

While assembling is probably the most time-consuming part of the whole process, it lays the foundation for an accurate projection and a realistic financial plan. Most of the questions below can be answered by looking at statements from investments and retirement plans, 401(k)s, and Social Security statements. And don't forget employee benefits. The goal is to organize your financial affairs to give you a clear path forward.

Organizing Questions to Consider

What is the value of your real assets—primary residence/ investment properties?

How much do you currently have in savings/equities/fixed income/alternatives?

What is the cost basis on non-retirement investments?

How much do you expect to receive monthly from retirement accounts, deferred compensation plans, and other employee benefits?

How much do you expect to receive monthly from Social Security/pensions?

If you retired today, how much income would you receive from income-producing investments/savings/part time work?

In other words, what are your cash flow needs now, and how much do you think you'll need for some of the bigger ticket items (cars, weddings, travel, and maybe even furniture for kids moving out) in the future? Just figure out what you need today, add some buffer for fun stuff, and most programs will figure out inflation for you.

It's even better when those expenses are itemized out. When you list everything that you tend to spend money on today, you'll be surprised how quickly it adds up. You might think you need $8,000 but find that $8,000 isn't quite going to cut it. That's where monitoring can help. Let's be sure to stay in the *no judgment zone;* just define how you live now and how you *want* to live later.

Key 2: Analyze and Strategize

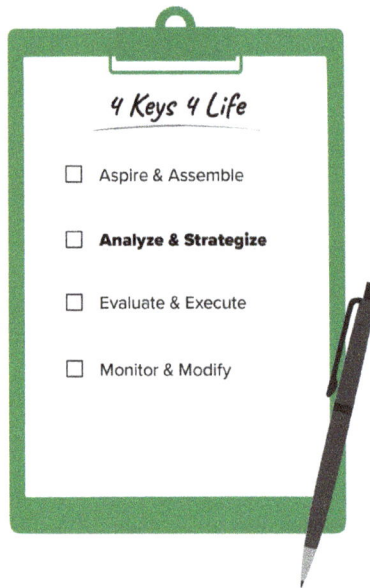

Start where you are, the past is history. Now is the time to begin bringing your ideas and hopes to life. There is always hope, but hope is not enough, and you need to execute a plan.

Once you've put real numbers to your wish list, you're ready to evaluate what you can do and set up steps to get there. Be careful about relying on some of the calculators you might find on the Internet, or even in accounting programs and spreadsheets. For example, if the program or plan you are using asks, "What is your tax bracket?"

instead of calculating that out for you, projections are not going to be very realistic. Here's another hint: If a program doesn't separate mortgage payments so that when the mortgage is paid off, your cash flow needs decrease, chances are it's going to overestimate what you could actually require and make you work longer than necessary. Projecting what you'll need in retirement is as much art as science, but it is important. Don't assume life will be cheaper when you retire. Don't tell yourself, "I won't be commuting to work, buying work clothes, incurring tuition expenses, or making mortgage payments, so if I'm spending $8,000 a month now, I'll probably just need $5,000 a month after I retire." It's this magical thinking that gets so many people in trouble. The $5,000 is pulled out of the air without any basis in fact.

For many people, the retirement years are just as expensive as their pre-retirement years, if not more so. Yes, many retirees have paid off their mortgage, or are close to doing so. But they also might turn around and buy a second home. And maybe they aren't commuting to work, but they are taking international vacations. They join a country club and play golf every day. A big expense often missed is support for children and grandchildren. And healthcare expenses grab a bigger share of the pie, so a confident retirement is not without its costs.

I've had reasonably comfortable people with seven-figure assets tell me, "We have $2,000,000, we're going to be fine," but they were just guessing. Initially, they thought they were tracking well, but when we ran the numbers, they realized that based on their lifestyle and the things they wanted to do, $2,000,000 was not nearly enough. *They were rich, but they were not wealthy.*

To determine if you can afford the life you envision, the key is to determine first where you are now. You can't map out the best route to your destination if you don't know your starting point. Have you ever stood in front of one of those maps at the mall to figure out what direction you need to head in to get to the store you want to go to? If you can't find *the "You Are Here"* sticker, those maps don't help a lot. Even if you do see the sticker, you need to look at where you're standing in relation to the stores surrounding you so you know which way to begin walking. How often do we all start off, only to have to turn around after we get our bearings?

Perhaps an example will help. The graphics on the next page give a snapshot of Luke and Jen Sample's long-term financial picture based on where they are now. The charts and graphs represented below are from eMoney Advisor, LLC, a comprehensive financial planning system used by professional advisors. There are several companies offering software to advisors today; this is the one we rely on. My goal here is not to endorse software; it's simply to demonstrate the power of using technology to help model potential outcomes. You've probably heard the saying: garbage in… garbage out. Even professionals can misunderstand or misuse software, creating unrealistic expectations. *Trust but verify.*

Back to the Samples. When they were growing up, they dreamed of being millionaires. They are now in their early sixties and have saved almost $3,000,000 in their portfolio. They are hugely successful financially, with a beautiful home where they raised their family, and a vacation home at the beach. Luke would like to retire next year at age 62; Jen is already retired and receiving her pension. They plan on taking Social Security at their full retirement age instead of waiting until age 70. Education is an important value to Luke and Jen, and they would like to be able support their children's and grandchildren's educational pursuits. While this would be nice, their primary goal is never to be a burden on their family.

Cash Flow *Base Facts in First Year (2021)*

The Cash Flow report illustrates your income, savings, expenses, and resulting net cash flow on an annual basis.

Based upon the levels of income and spending in the *Base Facts*, you will deplete your portfolio assets in 2046 (age 86/88).

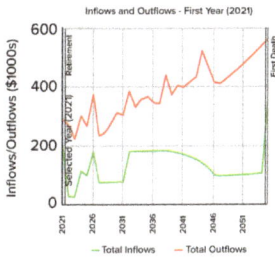

CASH FLOW SUMMARY:

Year/Age:	2021(61/61)
Income Flows:	$200,000
Investment Income:	$0
Planned Distributions:	$0
Other Inflows:	$0
Total Inflows:	**$200,000**
Total Expenses:	$263,610
Planned Savings/Investment:	$26,000
Total Outflows:	**$289,610**
Net Cash Flow:	**($89,610)**
Total Portfolio Assets	$2,985,943

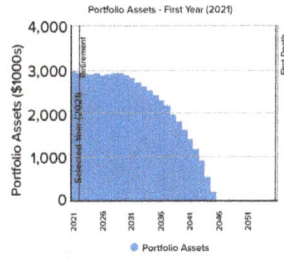

Courtesy of eMoney advisors, LLC[i]

We will explore what goes into a *real* financial plan in Chapter 2, as many online systems can lull people into a false sense of security. A financial analysis and plan with concrete action steps is the first of the six Key Force Multipliers discussed in that chapter and can be used to determine where you stand based on what you've done up until now. It is the "You are Here" sticker on that map in the mall. This is not to say that the projections are going to be perfect, but you do want to consider inflation, changes in taxable income and rates, healthcare costs, and higher Medicare premiums. It is also important to include those important yet random life events like cars, weddings, and travel. Since helping children and grandchildren is a goal, we can integrate that into the financial plan *once we know that Luke and Jen are tracking well.*

Luke and Jen are like a lot of Americans: they *can* retire, they just *can't* maintain their standard of living for the rest of their lives. *Had they continued unchecked*, based on the assumptions in the plan, they could run out of money. Worse yet, Luke and Jen wouldn't realize this until they were dipping into their principal in their mid-seventies, when going back to work is not an option for most people.

> It's never too late, until it is.

Key 3: Evaluate and Execute

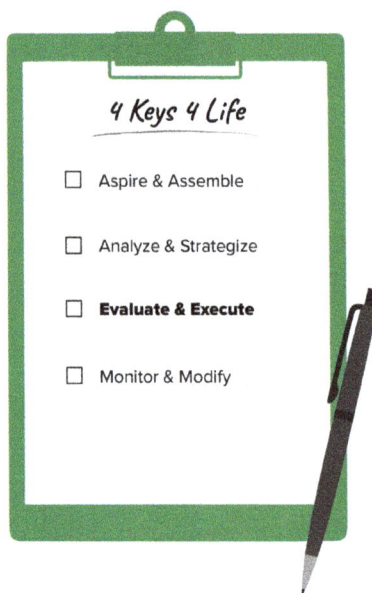

Every plan is like putting together a puzzle; while most people start out searching for the corners, the first step is to focus on the picture on the top of the box. Once you've established where you are, where you want to be, and what your incremental goals are, you have the foundation for a plan—the picture you are going to create. Then the corners of the puzzle serve as the foundation to fill in the rest of the straight edges, the perimeter of the future you are creating for yourself.

A word of caution about prioritizing your priorities: When you made your wish list, we assumed money was no object, but that's just not realistic. Money is a finite resource, no matter how much you have. As with everything that has a limit, it's important to prioritize your needs and wants so that your capital covers all your needs and as many wants as possible.

Work-Life Choices with Consequences

Career advice and financial planning often go hand in hand because money touches so many things in our lives. The late Jack Welch, former chairman and CEO of General Electric, once said, "There is no such thing as work-life balance. There are work-life choices with consequences." In other words, *when we make one goal a priority, we have less time, money, energy—less something—to focus on another.*

It's important to remember that we aren't seeking to acquire everything on that wish list today. You may be able to have it all, but maybe not all at once. Priorities and real numbers give you hope and confidence, and eventually the things you really want are achievable. One client had a daily countdown to retirement, and on days when she felt especially overworked and underappreciated, she would send me an email with just one number in the subject line. We both knew what it meant. Just knowing that there was an endgame and that the finish line wasn't as far off as she thought it was made a huge difference. It was still measured in years, but she made it. She's now living the life she dreamed of.

We had a relatively new client who had been laid off in a corporate restructuring of a pharmaceutical company. He was interviewing other companies in his field, though he wasn't very enthusiastic about it. I said, "Jim, if money wasn't an object, what would you really *like* to do?" That question unleashed something inside him. He talked for twenty minutes about a nonprofit organization he was involved with. He was passionate about it and said he would love to work for it full-time. However, in a soft voice he said, "My wife, Barbara, is a stay-at-home mom, and we have a daughter in college. We put the other two kids through school as well, and we don't have enough for retirement. It's probably not a possibility because I'd have to take a significant pay cut."

I said, "I don't know whether that's feasible or not, but let's run some numbers. Would you be willing to work longer? Instead of retiring at sixty-two, which was your goal, would you be willing to work until you're sixty-five or sixty-eight if you were working for the nonprofit?"

And Jim responded, "Absolutely."

Sure enough, it turned out that he could still accomplish his objectives, as long as he worked longer than originally planned. So, he accepted the position with the nonprofit, earning significantly less than he had at the pharmaceutical company. But he loved it; it didn't feel like work to him. In a meeting a few years later, I showed Jim and Barb their numbers from five years prior and compared them to where they were today. They were tracking far ahead of where we thought they would be, and Jim could retire if he so desired. *Just to be careful not to get ahead of ourselves*, we ran numbers on their current plan assuming a bear market, and another assuming much lower returns going forward. In both cases, it was clear that Jim could still retire. He said, "That is wonderful to know but I love what I do; it's fun for me." And he continued to do what he loves.

This didn't happen magically. Jim hadn't changed his priorities, but he realized he had to change his tactics. While he was open to working five more years, that would not be enough. We also had to be a little bit more aggressive on the portfolio, more conscious of taxes, and monitor progress along the way. In the end, a combination of strategies allowed him to do work that he truly loved.

Just like the choice regarding work-life balance, every decision comes with a consequence. For example, if you buy a new car every three years, you will have less capital to put toward school tuition. If you prioritize both cars and tuition, you might have to reduce retirement savings. In order to make an educated decision on which priorities are most important, you need to work with real numbers. You need an integrated analysis[7] to help you see the impact of various decisions and what happens when you tweak here and there. A comprehensive system that projects potential outcomes into the future can help you decide exactly how important each priority is.

---

7   Forecasting may be another way to describe this. There is one thing that is almost certain: Much can and will change over your lifetime. Keep in mind: These are projections, not guarantees. Just set it up so it's easy for you. This does not mean that aggregating or consolidating account values onto a dashboard is planning; *that's just accounting*! Spreadsheets that simply project values out at a level rate of return aren't great either. Too many factors such as taxes, inflation, and random cash flow needs are left out, leading to conclusions that could be a fairy tale. *Please be careful.*

COMPETING GOALS			
Priority:	Retirement	Comparison	Retiring at 60, 65, or 70
Priority:	Send children to college	Comparison	Public vs. Private 100% funded or partially?
Priority:	Protect Family	Comparison	Term life vs. Whole life How much?
Priority:	Purchase car	Comparison	Used vs. New Lease or Buy?

Most people want to retire, educate their children, protect their families from sickness or premature death, and leave a legacy, but everybody has a different vision of what that looks like. Once you see the side-by-side comparisons that project potential outcomes into the future, you can decide what you are willing to do—or give up—to create the life you want.

For example, based on the projections, it might turn out that you are not going to be able to pay for college for your kids and save for retirement at the same time. In that case, the goals will need to be adjusted, at least for now. Maybe, instead of funding four years at a private college, you commit to cover half the cost and your child can cover the rest with work, scholarships, and loans. Or instead of funding a private college, you commit to covering a public, in-state university. You might want your child to have some skin in the game and have them work for a portion of he cost. This approach also works for retirement, second homes, and other big purchases. The thing to remember when setting priorities is that it is a rare goal that can't be tweaked to make it more achievable. You'll see some examples in the next chapter.

Key 4: Monitor and Modify

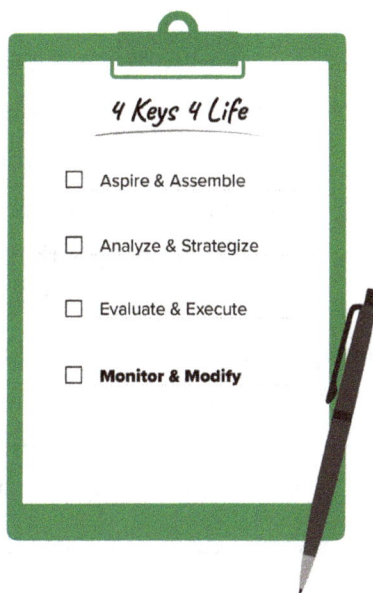

It's one thing to have a vision of where you want to go; it's another thing to have concrete steps to get there. *Then you need to make sure the steps are working!* The base plan and scenarios hold the plan accountable, tracking your progress. Let's face it: You might have a teenager who wants to go to an Ivy League college, but if they aren't focused on their schoolwork and keeping their grades super high, it's just not realistic. The same logic applies to your financial affairs. Magical thinking is one thing, actually doing something proactive is quite another.

It can be empowering to witness a financial plan that's working; the momentum builds along with it. Don't wing it! If your goals are clear, specific, and time-based, you have a good chance of achieving them. Seeing your progress and reaching the targets you set along the way releases invisible problem-solving energy *and makes this fun.*

The Difference Between a Map and GPS

Also, because life can be unpredictable at times, chances are that you're going to be thrown some curve balls. You may not make the income you originally anticipated. There may be job losses. You may think you and your partner are going to work until you're sixty-five years old, and then when you have kids, you go to Plan B and say, "Maybe one of us should stay home." That changes the financial landscape, and you have to figure out a new strategy. This is reminiscent of a time when we used maps, only to find that a road we were travelling on had a four-hour traffic jam due to construction. That's why a more accurate way of framing the monitoring process is to think of it as more like a GPS system. When you want to take the scenic route, hit a roadblock, or make a wrong turn, it updates the directions to get you back on track *before* you've gone an hour out of your way.

Checkups: New Meds and Different Strategies

If you have a financial plan that was done more than three years ago, what you have is the equivalent of a physical exam of a person three years younger. Is it possible that a chest X-ray might reveal something new? How about blood tests, or that mole on the back of your leg that looks a little different? The earlier you catch an issue, the easier it is to correct. And keep in mind that things could change for the better! You may have lost some weight, so the dosage of your medicine can be lowered, or you can even stop taking it. You also need to monitor your plan to see what may have changed. This process also reinforces the actions you are taking and helps to build confidence over time. Think of caring for your financial health the same way you do your physical health.

Just as patients require regular check-ups to catch any new conditions, your financial plan needs regular fine-tuning and oversight. This prevents small issues from becoming major ones over time. Even people who would be considered affluent can have a financial projection that may not look great. A couple in their late fifties with over $4,000,000 in savings and investments who wanted to retire at age sixty were projected to run out of money in their late seventies. Like Luke and Jen, they dreamed of being millionaires when they were kids and not only did they make it, they made it fourfold! It was a rude awakening to learn that it wasn't enough for them. If they had followed the Four Keys for Life process, they would have known long ago how much they really needed to retire early and could have made minor changes to ensure they didn't run out of money.

We have a crisis in America today, and it is only going to get worse. There are too many Americans who are going along thinking that they're doing fine, but they don't really know. They may even have an advisor managing the portfolio, but without a comprehensive, *integrated* analysis based on their cash flow situation, ability to save, resources, and corporate perks, the advisor may not understand what the portfolio needs to earn. To me, real value is not just in prescribing a path to achieve important objectives but in helping with the ongoing—and often grinding—journey along the way. In order to deal with inevitable complexities, stress tests are a way of modeling the baseline plan against the unpredictable. What if rates of return on investments are lower, or you experience a bear market[8] at retirement, or you need more cash flow due to a long-term health care issue?

---

8   Bear markets—losses of 20%, 30%, or even 50%—are predictably unpredictable. If you have money in stocks or funds that invest in equities, understand that bear markets happen. They are completely unpredictable in terms of when they will occur, how deep they will be, and how long they will last. *The key is knowing how they might affect you financially.*

This approach helps you to understand where your financial future is vulnerable so you can manage, transfer, or avoid such risks altogether.

Failing to monitor your financial plan is like taking a drug that doesn't quite keep the blood pressure down consistently. It may not be a huge deal now, but the patient probably won't live as long as they would with a more effective drug. Just as the right medicine can add years to your life, the right financial approaches observed and tweaked over time can add years to your wealth. For most people, this not only enhances psychological wealth but can also make a huge difference for your heirs.

The Secret Sauce: Enjoy and Share What You Have Today.

Monitoring progress is crucial, but we don't want to hyperfocus and lose sight of the precious moments along the way. Rewarding yourself from time to time can help keep you on track. When we were first starting out, Ed and I bought a blue Chevy for one dollar. Essentially, the seller saved the cost of having the car scrapped. It had roll-down windows, ripped-up cloth seats, and no air conditioning. Still working out of the laundry room with a part-time employee, we set a goal to work and save to the point where I could hire someone full-time and move to a basement office. We drove that car until I hired my first employee (who worked for me for 34 years until he retired) and we could afford a very used Volvo that had leather seats and air conditioning. Every time we got in that car and turned on the AC, we were reminded (completely subconsciously) that we were able to do something we weren't sure we could do. Reaching interim goals is empowering. It builds momentum and confidence that what you are doing is working.

I believe sharing wealth builds more of it, and I'm not just talking about money. There is a lot to be said for sharing your time and knowledge, and for the impact you can have on another human being. At one point in time, I realized that I didn't have a lot of work-life balance. I had four children and about 150 families counting on me. There was absolutely no money to "give back," yet it occurred to me that I wasn't setting a great example for my kids.

So, I started teaching CCD—a religious education program for the Catholic Church—to kindergartners. The best part was that each week one of my children was my "student teacher," which gave me some one-on-one time with each of them. Every class included three things I wanted the kids to learn, and we always ended with a game of "trash ball" to reinforce the lesson. Two teams would line up, and each child got one point for correctly answering a question from the class that day. Then they took a wadded-up piece of paper and threw it into a trash can six feet away. If they got it in, they got another point. Even today, grown-up kindergartners come up to me and tell me how much fun CCD was, *especially* trash ball.

Here's the point: *Don't forget the value of your own human capital and the impact you can have on others.* Ed and I could not afford to donate money—we were barely scraping by—but giving can come in many forms. It's the secret sauce.

CHAPTER 2

The Six Key Force Multipliers (KFMs)—Riding the Tailwinds

There are certain Key Force Multipliers (KFMs) that will get you where you want to go faster than you ever thought and further than you ever dreamed.

In February 2020, a British Airways passenger plane took off from New York City and landed in London less than five hours later, breaking the record for the fastest subsonic flight between the two cities and reaching London *almost two hours early*.

The short flight time was not planned. The plane was the same as always. The pilots and crew were the same as always. The number of passengers on board was the same as always. So what was different?

The tailwinds.

The flight was riding a much stronger than usual jet stream, with winds over 200 miles per hour propelling the aircraft.

At times the plane reached speeds of 825 miles per hour. The pilots didn't need to do anything different except take advantage of what nature was providing, keep the plane on course, and hold on for the ride.

The Key Force Multipliers outlined in this chapter are a lot like those tailwinds. They are ways to boost the effectiveness of the Four Keys for Life Financial Planning System, helping you hit your targets faster. At their core, these multipliers automate and motivate you to get past the inertia that is so detrimental to reaching the goals you've set. They also acknowledge that we're all just human, and sometimes painfully so.

When the financial planning profession was born in the late seventies, it was not where it is today. Instead, financial planning focused on selling investments and insurance, without a whole lot of thought about the client as an individual. But as Ed and I were working our way out of debt, I kept asking myself how I would want to be treated if I were a client. I didn't want to have to be afraid like my parents were. I wanted things to be easier, with a clear path and thought this was probably how everyone else felt too. I believed that if I could figure out a system or a process that worked for us, those same techniques and strategies could work for others as well.

While getting my own family on a solid financial footing, I found six strategies that made saving and investing not only easier but also more productive. The KFMs can turbocharge the process and provide the tailwinds that work for anyone in any situation. They provide clarity and motivation to be strategic, and that momentum makes success almost inevitable.

My husband and I did not start out wealthy—far from it. We drove old cars, put off buying new clothes, and cut corners wherever we could. We tried out a few jobs before getting it right, and we even had a financial crisis or two (*okay, maybe five or six*). We bought our first house just before the crash of 1987. When the recession hit, we nearly lost everything. At the time, financial advisors were paid on a commission basis sometimes with a modest draw to be used to even out the lumpy months. At one point, there was no income coming from me, and Ed lost his job. As the recession lingered, we were using credit cards to pay our mortgage. We had a small baby, and it was so scary I almost left the industry.

To get through, I returned to my roots working twelve-hour night shifts on weekends in a local ICU. On Monday mornings, I changed out of my scrubs, kissed our son and my (very depressed) husband, and drove into the city, *feeling like a complete fraud*. Yet somehow we managed to overcome this season of our lives. Ed and I never lost sight of our values and found new meaning in the phrase "divide and conquer." We needed to crawl out of the pit of debt by increasing our opportunities for income and cutting costs. It didn't happen overnight, but life turned around. Failure just wasn't an option.

Please don't underestimate the power of the Key Force Multipliers no matter where you are in the wealth spectrum; the leverage occurs when you apply them consciously and consistently. If you make a habit of applying the six KFMs once a year, you can achieve what you want sooner than you think possible, *and actually enjoy the process.* The end result for most people is a feeling of being organized and in control, with immeasurable clarity and confidence.

KFM 1: Customized tools to model and stress-test your financial future.

Among the most important of these tools is the use of powerful software to track your progress and help you see the impact of certain strategies. The first step in the Four Keys for Life process is to aspire, and this Key Force Multiplier (KFM) puts numbers behind those aspirations to make them more concrete. For example, when you think about a new house, you want the picture of your amazing new home to flash instantly into your mind—but you also need to see how it plays out financially. Run the numbers, and make sure you understand what is being assumed for various expenses such as the amount of a down payment, the mortgage term and the interest rate. Items such as furniture, moving costs, and landscaping should be included, and while you might not know exactly how much to allocate to these expenses, estimating works just fine. The same applies to your retirement: what do those years look like for you?

The key to this KFM is *customized* tools and brainstorming. Earlier we applied the Four Keys for Life System and the second key, Analyze and Strategize, to Luke and Jen Sample's financial life. While their near-term financial picture looked fine, their plan was not sustainable, even though they had amassed millions of dollars. The analysis showed that without changes, they would run out of money.

Ideally, in a *real* financial plan, each analysis is integrated with the others. When one assumption is changed, you can see the implications in other areas as well. I think we can all agree that an EKG verifies your pulse and the health of your heart much more accurately than a watch and the touch of a finger. The financial planning process leverages technology in the same way to provide a measure of the health of your household. It can also provide insight into where your financial future might be vulnerable if sudden disruptions occur. Equally important, you can see the impact of various solutions *before* implementing any of them.

Let's begin with a five-year cash flow report[9].

---

9   The financial planning charts you see on this page and the pages to follow have been used with permission from the folks at eMoney, a company we have relied on for many years to provide comprehensive financial planning projections and scenarios. Please note that this is not an endorsement of one company; there are many providers in this space. What you don't want is a calculator with pretty graphs modeling out fairy tales. Please be careful to look under the hood.

5-Year Cash Flow Base Facts in First Year (2021)
The 5-Year Cash Flow report illustrates your income, savings, expenses, and resulting net cash flow on an annual basis.

Year/Age	2021 (61/61)	2022 (62/62)	2023 (63/63)	2024 (64/64)	2025 (65/65)
Portfolio Asset Balances (Beginning of Year)					
Taxable Investments	1,124,860	1,143,759	973,560	845,519	709,795
Retirement Accounts	1,579,962	1,709,202	1,823,376	1,945,178	2,075,116
Cash Accounts	81,900	61,926	62,975	64,045	65,139
Insurance Accounts	25,000	25,660	26,337	27,032	27,746
Stock Options/Grants	33,319	45,396	58,162	71,705	47,270
Total Portfolio Asset Balances (Beginning of Year)	**2,845,041**	**2,985,943**	**2,944,410**	**2,953,479**	**2,925,066**
Cash Inflows					
Salary					
Luke's Salary	175,000	0	0	0	0
Social Security	0	0	0	0	9,125
Deferred Income					
Jen's Pension	25,000	25,000	25,000	25,000	25,000
Stock Options/Grants Sale	0	0	0	85,421	61,425
Total Cash Inflows	**200,000**	**25,000**	**25,000**	**110,421**	**95,550**
Cash Outflows					
Living Expenses	124,300	121,992	126,872	131,947	137,225
Liabilities	25,776	25,776	25,776	25,776	25,776
Education Expenses					
Jessica's College - Penn State	35,758	0	0	0	0
Jimmy's Grad School	0	0	0	10,000	10,000
529 Plan Withdrawals	(35,758)	0	0	0	0
Stock Options/Grants Purchase	0	0	0	46,624	35,253
Insurance Premiums	7,200	7,200	7,200	7,200	7,200
Taxes	63,334	20,181	12,220	23,382	14,635
Other Expenses					
Extra Vacation in Retirement	0	12,500	0	12,500	0
Jen's Medicare Part B + Supplement + Dental	0	0	0	0	6,196
Jessica's Wedding	0	65,000	0	0	0
Jimmy's Wedding	0	0	0	25,000	0
Luke's Medicare Part B + Supplement + Dental	0	0	0	0	6,196
Luke's New Car	0	0	26,337	0	0
Master Bathroom Renovation	25,000	0	0	0	0
Vacation property expenses - Util, taxes, etc.	18,000	18,475	18,963	19,464	19,978
Planned Savings	26,000	0	0	0	0
Total Cash Outflows	**289,610**	**271,124**	**217,368**	**301,893**	**262,459**
Total Inflows	200,000	25,000	25,000	110,421	95,550
LESS: Total Outflows	289,610	271,124	217,368	301,893	262,459
EQUALS: Net Cash Flow	**(89,610)**	**(246,124)**	**(192,368)**	**(191,472)**	**(166,909)**
Total Portfolio Asset Balances (End of Year)	**2,985,943**	**2,944,410**	**2,953,479**	**2,925,066**	**2,929,271**

Chart courtesy of eMoney Advisors, LLC.

Here you can see that Luke and Jen Sample begin with $2,845,041 in Total Portfolio Assets. This figure is also referred to as "working capital" and includes bank accounts, brokerage, stock plans and retirement assets. This is important in forming the basis of a financial plan's assumptions. Earlier we discussed the difference between being rich and being wealthy; these projections help you determine whether your spending and savings habits lead to sustainable wealth over your entire lifetime. It is especially important when you are retired, because like that football team on the five-yard line trying to score a touchdown, you have a much shorter field. *While the risks are still present, the options are more limited.*

The five-year cash flow also pins down a household's investment objectives because it reveals whether the rates of return are sufficient to sustain the working capital over a lifetime. This is where the Assemble step in the Four Keys for Life begins to pay off: up-to-date statements and other relevant financial data would reveal the amount and nature of assets held. Since it is an integrated analysis, the five-year cash flow projection also helps to anticipate an unforeseen event (such as a new roof) that could trigger a much higher income tax bill because something had to be sold to pay for it. Once you have your household's holistic financial position organized and up to date, a surprise expense such as an unexpected tax bill will be a thing of the past. While some people tend to focus on rates of return, a feeling of empowerment and control is just as important even if it is far more difficult to measure.

The Net Cash Flow (inflows minus outflows) makes understanding your financial future easier. It's the figure you'll find on the bottom of each column of Luke and Jen's projections, arrived at on the basis of the figures preceding it, starting with a summary of the portfolio at the beginning of each year, categorized by type. For example, the data flowing into their website each night to keep the projections relevant also flow over to this page which summarizes their Taxable Investments (brokerage and mutual fund accounts), retirement funds such as 401(k)'s and IRAs, cash accounts, insurance cash values and stock plans from their employer. This is *not* a summary of their net worth—that can be found on another tab on their website. For example, we don't include a primary residence in this projection because we don't want them to have to rely on the equity in their home as a source of capital or income. We know it's there, but they'll always have to live somewhere, so let's steer away from relying on it.

As you move down the page, you'll see Cash Inflows. The Samples can expect $175,000 in income from Luke's salary and bonus plus an additional $25,000 from Jen's pension distribution, totaling a pre-tax inflow of $200,000. Income taxes are calculated separately for each year because the amount of taxable income is going to vary significantly during their lifetime, as it does for most people. This becomes clear as you move down to the next category, cash outflows, and the line item: Taxes.

Cash Outflows include regular recurring household expenses, scheduled liabilities such as mortgage and car payments, as well as a one-time expense for their daughter Jessica's last year of college. Fortunately they have a 529 plan[iv.] so there is a direct offset to the cost of her education, and their year-by-year net worth statement shows how much is left in the account after each withdrawal. You'll also see staggered expenses such as new cars every six years and an extra special vacation expense every other year in retirement. They would also like to renovate a bathroom and plan for weddings for their two children.

In this example, in year one we can see that Luke and Jen have $289,610 in total outflows, which results in a negative Net Cash Flow for the year of ($89,610). In other words, they don't have enough income coming into the household, so they'll have to sell some investments.

Money In	$200,000
Money Out	-$289,610
Net Cash Flow	($89,610)

We subtract that net cash flow figure of ($89,610) from the initial $2,845,041 Total Portfolio Asset Balance **and they have an end-of-year value** of $2,985,943.

You may be wondering how Luke and Jen had a negative cash flow of almost $90,000, withdrew all of it from their after-tax account, and ended up with a greater total portfolio balance in year one (2021). This was possible because Luke was still saving and getting a match in his 401(k), and the compounded returns on invested assets were greater than the amount they needed to withdraw. While the Samples can sleep soundly for 2021, if we look to the next year, we see a troubling pattern that begins with Luke's retirement and the accompanying drop in income, which leads the annual negative net cash flow to increase substantially. Even though Social Security will kick in when they reach age sixty-six, the household's anticipated expenses combined with intermittent costs such as home improvements and weddings are just too much, and their working capital depletes over time. Unfortunately, they aren't going to realize this until Luke is already retired and the money has already been spent. In other words, they are not ready for retirement.

It is far better to understand that earlier so that alternative scenarios can be considered. What if Luke worked a few more years, or if they cut their spending? What will provide more relief, downsizing in ten years or Luke working for six more years?

As you will see in the next pages, various potential scenarios can be dropped in to see which alternative might provide an optimal outcome. They can also be compared to the baseline, and even to each other.

Cash Flow Scenarios

Report:	Cash Flow ⌄		First Year ⌄		Show:	⌄

| Base Facts |
| Downsize Residence in 10 years |
| Estate Plan |
| Reduce Spending 20% |
| Sell Shore Property |
| New Scenario |
| Higher Expenses $10K |
| Estate & Financial Plan |
| Advanced Plan - Jul 2018 |

Chart courtesy of eMoney Advisors, LLC

This sets off some alerts that will signal what type of care plan is required. Sometimes it may be as simple as diet and exercise (cutting back on expenses and restructuring debt) or even just monitoring cash flow to make sure the household expense information accurately reflects their reality. In other words, a projection is just that: a projection. It is not unusual to find that people just aren't sure what their cash flow needs are, or will be, in retirement. That's okay! This is where a system can really help.

Let's assume that you run the numbers for yourself and—*unlike Luke and Jen*—the projection suggests there is excess cash flow of $24,000 per year. The first question to ask is: Do you feel like you can save $2,000 per month, over and above what you are contributing to the 401(k)? Or when the bonus comes in, what do you tend to do with it? If there is very little money in the bank or in non-retirement accounts, then it's a good bet that this money has not been saved, at least historically. This happens when people look at the numbers in bewilderment, wondering where that excess cash flow is really going. It almost doesn't matter how it is being spent at this point, we just don't want fairy tale projections. It might just mean adding an appropriate amount—in this example $24,000—as a miscellaneous expense buffer to soak up that excess cash flow and replicate what has probably been happening in the past more accurately. Otherwise, the software is going to assume that money will be saved and invested going forward (which has not been the case historically), resulting in projections that are not going to reflect your potential financial future with any degree of accuracy.

This is why some of the online calculators and robo-advisors *scare me:* Without the benefit of human interpretation and experience, important decisions may be made based on what might be that fairy tale, and drastic changes may have to be considered later in life.

This is an example of having a process that keeps the numbers accurate going forward. It can be powerful if accounts are consolidated and account values are automatically updated every night on one dashboard. It doesn't take long to see what's happening on an ongoing basis, or if unanticipated expenses are occurring. The key is to understand reality as early as possible while adjusting the numbers to be sure the chosen strategies are still appropriate.

There are many ways to solve a problem. For example, Luke and Jen could reduce expenses, work part-time, or align the portfolio's asset allocation[v] with the goal of achieving higher returns. They could run scenarios and model different outcomes to determine which course of action will provide the benefit most aligned with their goals and investment objectives.

In the following chart, we have elected to illustrate two additional scenarios for Luke and Jen: **Downsize Primary Residence in 2025 compared (side by side) with Sell Shore Property**[10], which seeks to solve the problem of the accelerating withdrawal rate growing negative.

---

10   There is a long list of considerations when making this comparison, including the cost of each transaction, the tax implications and most importantly: whether the Sample family would even be open to these solutions! In the Sell Shore property scenario, for example, we included an annual expense to rent a home at the beach for 6 weeks, which could be used to travel anywhere else instead.

It is clear from the left side of the graphic below that while downsizing could help, it doesn't solve the problem. Choosing to sell their vacation home and renting is a far better outcome for Luke and Jen, while allowing for flexibility. In this scenario they are free to spend their vacations wherever they want to go.

Cash Flow Scenario: Downsize Vs Sell Shore Property

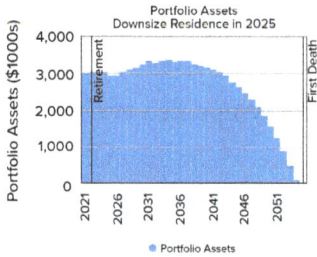
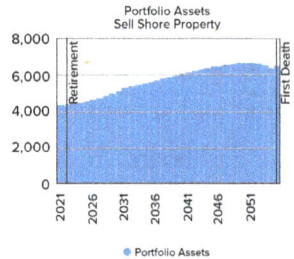

Chart courtesy of eMoney Advisors, LLC

Below you can see a drop-down example of various "what ifs" that can be toggled in to stress test different scenarios:

Cash Flow What if's and Stress Tests

Report: [Cash Flow ⌄] [First Year ⌄] Show: [Sell Shore Property ⌄] [⌄]

- 4% Rate of Return
- 6% Rate of Return
- 7.5% Rate of Return
- Bad Bear Market (2022 -40%)
- Disability Occurs - Jen
- Disability Occurs - Luke
- Downsize Residence
- Expense buffer of 10k/yr
- Expense buffer of 20k/yr
- Expense buffer of 30k/yr
- Inflation rises to 6%
- Lower Rate of Return 3.43%
- Lower Rate of Return 4.56%

Chart courtesy of eMoney Advisors, LLC

Once a scenario is found to work, we have the option to modify and stress test it by toggling in some of the "what ifs." This is like a fire drill and helps to illustrate the simulated effects of different market conditions such as a lower rate of return or a bear market. This way, if one of these does happen, everyone knows what to do and no one panics[11]. As you can see in the following chart, even if Luke and Jen are willing to make changes to their housing situation, they are still walking that fine line of not being able to afford to be too conservative with their portfolio allocation. An example of this would be if they chose a target return of 4% with a portfolio allocation (left graph) and not so aggressive as to expose themselves to a wicked bear market (right graph) at retirement. Their working capital would not survive either scenario, *even if they were willing to sell their beach house:*

---

11   Okay, people might still panic but that's usually because of hyped up headlines and other clickbait.

Cash Flow Scenario

Report: [Cash Flow ▾] [All Years ▾] Show: [Sell Shore property ▾] [4% Rate of Return ▾] vs. [Sell Shore property ▾] [Bear Market 2023/for 3 yrs/-15% ▾]

View: [With Total Portfolio Assets Only ▾]

Based upon the levels of income and spending in the *Sell Shore Property with 4% Rate of Return*, you will deplete your portfolio assets in 2052 (age 92/92).

Based upon the levels of income and spending in the *Sell Shore Property with Bear Market 2023/for 3yrs/-15%*, you will deplete your portfolio assets in 2045 (age 85/85).

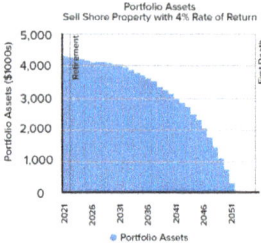

Portfolio Assets
Sell Shore Property with 4% Rate of Return

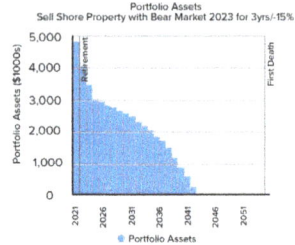

Portfolio Assets
Sell Shore Property with Bear Market 2023 for 3yrs/-15%

RELEVANT FACTS:	
Luke's Retirement:	2022 (62)
Jen's Retirement:	2019 (59)
First Death (Luke):	2055 (95/95)
LIVING EXPENSES	
Current:	$124,300
Retirement:	$117,300
Indexed at:	4.00%
Inflation Rate:	2.64%

RELEVANT FACTS:	
Luke's Retirement:	2022 (62)
Jen's Retirement:	2019 (59)
First Death (Luke):	2055 (95/95)
LIVING EXPENSES	
Current:	$124,300
Retirement:	$117,300
Indexed at:	4.00%
Inflation Rate:	2.64%

Chart courtesy of eMoney Advisors, LLC

Fortunately, this does not mean the Samples are doomed to a beachless life strapped for cash. It just means that they will have to continue to monitor their plan and identify opportunities to improve the flow of cash and increase financial assets. They'll do this by applying some of the strategies discussed in Part Two and avoiding the hijacks and mistakes listed in Part Three.

The above charts and graphs will give you a sense of what financial planning can look like. It doesn't have to be overly complicated, and the graphs will provide you with important insights into the results of decisions *before* you act on them. It is important to be able to explore options that can be used to change course as events unfold. I have purposely not included the detailed charts that go along with the graphs, primarily because you might close this book right away. But if it looks too simplified, it is right to wonder how meaningful the projections are and ask questions about the underlying assumptions. When it comes to projecting your potential future, details are important. The output needs to be understandable, relatable, and straightforward if something needs to be updated or corrected. The technology is getting better every year, but unfortunately there are still a lot of misleading online calculators out there.

The Importance of Progress

You may have heard successful management consultant Peter Drucker's quote "What gets measured gets managed." In other words, if you don't measure it, you can't improve it. It *almost* doesn't matter what system you use, (note the emphasis on the word *almost*) as long as you have a system that is easy to use and specific to your needs. Monitoring your progress also creates accountability. It's one thing to have a goal; it's another thing to take concrete steps to get there. The key is to find an easy way to make sure you are getting closer—and staying there—because otherwise, your goal is just a wish.

Here's where the real power comes from: You can look back at where you were when you started and make sure your plans are in motion, guiding you on the path to success. It's very easy to sabotage a plan if you don't feel you're making progress. Consider a person who is diagnosed with adult-onset diabetes. A comprehensive care plan will include diet, exercise, and perhaps a prescription. Eventually the lab results improve, making the life changes worthwhile. Financially, there is just nothing like that feeling you get when you can look back at where you first started and confirm that what you are doing is actually working.

Aggregation Is <u>NOT</u> Portfolio Management, and Portfolio Management Is <u>NOT</u> Real Financial Planning.

Be careful. Many online tools allow you to consolidate accounts onto one dashboard so you don't have to log into (and remember passwords for) *umpteen* different websites. *This may give better visibility into a household's portfolio,* but it is *not* portfolio management, and it *certainly is not* financial planning! I am dipping into topics in Part Two here, but this is also important under the discussion of Key Force Multiplier (KFM) #1. *Customized tools* to model, stress-test, and keep track of your financial future help to remind you of your "why," motivating you to continue along the path that you know is working.

Don't get me wrong. Aggregating your accounts onto one site or dashboard is a neat way to keep things organized, *but that's just an accounting function.* If the accounts are scattered in different places or with different advisors, the left hand probably doesn't know what the right hand is doing on any given day. For example, if you are managing one account, an advisor is managing a second, and one of those robo-advisor platforms is managing your 401(k), then you and your advisors may not realize where there are gaps, overlaps, or unnecessary tax consequences.

To take this one step further, it is also essential to understand that portfolio management is not wealth management. *It's a means to the end.* Managing the portfolio is just one of many strategies that can be used to optimize your financial affairs and complement your investment objectives. Having real-time account values populate an integrated suite of cash flow, tax, retirement, and estate projections is crucial to keeping the plan relevant. Then, as things change—new jobs, cars, kids in private vs. public school—your plan continues to be a reliable measure of potential opportunities, you can consider different approaches, and your portfolio remains aligned with your objectives.

Remember: Clumping account values onto a client portal (aggregation) is not portfolio management, and portfolio management is not real financial planning. And while we are at it, portfolio management is not true wealth management either.

It might sound silly and a bit like pop psychology, but research has shown that visualizing your goals—whether it's an Olympic medal, the car of your dreams, or the job of a lifetime—can make achieving them more attainable. This is the time to articulate them, whether these hopes are for you, your children, or your grandchildren.

Automate Your Blueprints

You can't just talk about goals; you need a blueprint, ideally one that is updated every night, automatically, based on changes in account values. It's like building a home. Project what you want and when you want it, stacked on top of other priorities. Run the numbers; play it out. *Then think about everything that could go wrong*: loss of a job, a wicked bear market (or two!), inflation, higher taxes, even a premature death. It's your home; build exactly what you want. *Just make sure it has a solid foundation and the roof doesn't leak.*

Let it rip: Dream.

KFM 2: Specific Strategies For Execution

Keep in mind that financial products like mutual funds, insurance, exchange traded funds (ETFs), and hedge funds[vi] are **tools**, *not strategies.* They are like the carpet, appliances, heating, and air conditioning system (HVAC) for a home. But similar to how the items installed in a home are not the same, your financial tools can vary, based on your needs and how you implement them. That's why strategies are far more powerful when they are congruent with your personal situation: your resources, cash flow needs, and tax situation.

I understand that the cost of insurance can seem like a detractor—not a multiplier. The right kind of insurance is *simply a tool used to transfer risk*, and the "cost" of not having it is uncertainty. Insurance is there to remove the possibility of an unexpected incident derailing wealth accumulation in a short period of time. Therefore, in the end, having insurance can actually be a multiplier in terms of providing options a family might have if the unthinkable occurred.

Tax laws seem to change with every administration, so it's important to understand what you can do today, what it might look like in the future and always stay informed and in touch with your tax advisor. For some, it makes sense to pay taxes now. For others, it is better to wait. This is where a robust tool that can run yearly tax projections integrated with annual income and expenses can make a difference. When you apply customized projections based on your goals, it removes the stress of having to guess about what your future holds.

Knowledge Is Not Power. Execution Is.

Think about structures that are designed for strength. A builder can take one hundred bricks and arrange them into ten columns to create a wall with six columns of twenty bricks each. It will look solid and do an adequate job of dividing a room in half, but if that builder wants a wall strong enough to withstand gale force winds and hold a roof up over the house, he or she is going to have to use a staggered pattern so the bricks in each row overlap the gaps in the row below them. The new wall contains the *same* number of bricks as the first, has the *same* amount of mortar, and is the *same* height and width, *but it's exponentially stronger.* All it took was a fresh perspective and a change in how the bricks overlapped to make a huge difference in function.

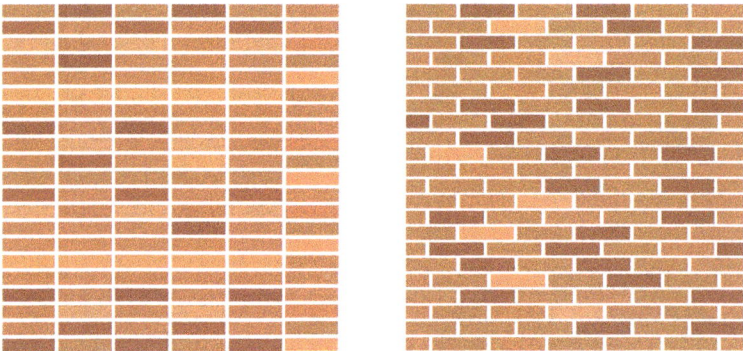

A strong financial plan with a portfolio of staggered bricks is similar to that strong wall. How the bricks are put together makes all the difference.

It's not unusual for people to save and invest diligently, but still be in a relatively weak position. They use their savings account for whatever is needed—new tires on the car, a child's tuition, house renovations, vacations, and lots of other random expenditures. Their retirement vehicles—401(k), Roth IRA—all have similar investments, such as exchange traded funds (ETFs) and mutual funds. The rest of their financial picture is similar too—money in various accounts but no effort to make each of those savings and investments work with the others to build momentum.

A better way is to rearrange those accounts into Three Pools of Money, each with a specific purpose and investments matched to that purpose. Just as a bricklayer staggers the rows to create extra strength, consider a Three Pools of Money system with staggered time frames. This allows you to populate each pool with short-, medium-, or long-term investments, depending on the time period each pool is expected to cover. The pools intersect and support each other, making the entire investment structure stronger, and are actively rebalanced[vii] and reallocated as goals and circumstances change (which we know happens all the time). Just be careful not to jump in and out of investments on a whim.

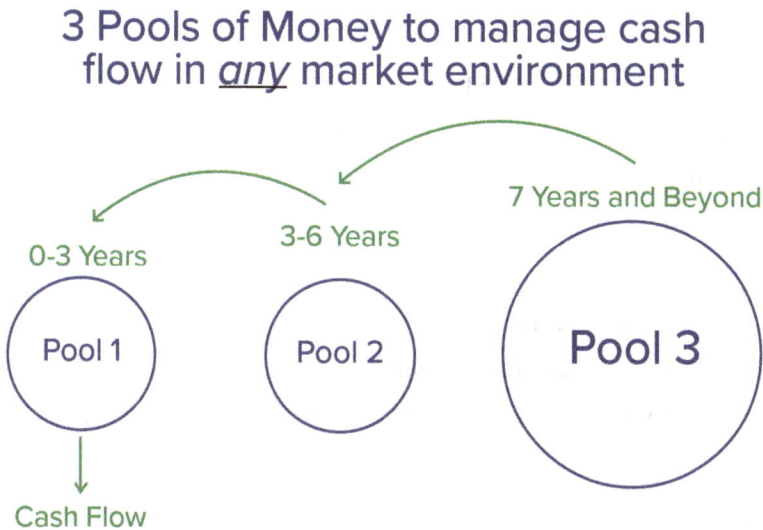

3 Pools of Money to manage cash flow in *any* market environment

7 Years and Beyond

3-6 Years

0-3 Years

Pool 1

Pool 2

Pool 3

Cash Flow

To set up the pools, take a piece of paper and draw three circles (similar to what you see above), one for each pool of money. Pool 1 is relatively small, representing the total amount of money you expect to pull from your savings and investments within the next three years. If you're already retired, this pool could cover day-to-day household expenses or other short-term cash flow needs. If you're still working and have an income to cover daily expenses, the pool could cover extras such as tuition, vacations, and home repairs. The assets in this pool would be relatively reliable and liquid, such as cash, cash equivalents, and money market funds. You may have a separate emergency fund as well. If it's unlikely you will need to pull from savings in the next three years, a portion of the assets in Pool 1 can be invested for higher interest, such as in CD's or short-term bonds.

Pool 2, which is the same size as Pool 1, is your three-to-six-year money. These assets are not quite as safe as those in the first pool, but they're not as volatile as investments in the stock market. Assets in the second pool could include government, municipal, and even corporate bonds, or (depending on your age and income), floating-rate or high-yield vehicles to boost long-term potential returns. Deciding which assets belong in this pool is a moving target, because it's more art than science to try to anticipate which of today's assets will retain their value over three to six years, and maybe even grow over this period. Do we expect double-digit returns? No. This might surprise you, but after the financial crisis in 2007-2009, we actually had a portion of Pool 2 assets in blue chip dividend-paying stock funds. At the time, we couldn't imagine that three to six years after 2009 those equities wouldn't be higher than they were when we were coming out of such a deep recession. Before COVID-19, Pool 2 assets became much more conservative because stocks and stock funds in this pool had recovered from those deep lows. Even that decision depended on each person's age and financial resources. The capital in Pool 2 isn't absolutely guaranteed, but at the very least, these assets should keep pace with inflation and hopefully do even better.

What you do with the Pool 2 allocation in the midst of any global crisis varies based on your needs and preferences. That's the beauty of this system: You can leave things as they are or adjust based on new needs, *but you aren't reacting to headlines.* In other words, this system can prevent you from being a victim of circumstances. Without it, panic can set in, and you can liquidate at an inopportune time. Some people never recover.

Pool 3, which is ideally larger than the other two, is your seven-plus-year money. This is the pool that contains inflation hedges, as well as equities such as large and small company stocks[viii] and international equities. Depending on your risk tolerance, this pool could also include alternative investments such as real estate, natural resources, and commodities. The reason to add alternatives is that they can provide additional diversification[ix], that yin-yang effect where complementary forces interact to form a dynamic system in which the whole is greater than two halves.

Think of your portfolio as a garden—you want something blooming throughout the year so you always have something wonderful to admire. In the same way, when one area of the portfolio is down, you'd ideally want to have something that is holding its own or benefiting from the catalyst that caused a particular market segment to fall in value. Please don't get me wrong. Diversification is no guarantee against losses; the goal is to reduce the size of the losses to make it easier to recover.

To illustrate how these pools work, let's look at a sixty-two-year-old client who wants to retire from a job that gives her $60,000 per year, after taxes. She doesn't qualify for full Social Security for another four years, so we have to replace her income with the first pool of capital assets. That means we need to be able to pull $5,000 a month from the portfolio to create her "mailbox money," which is the monthly direct deposit into her bank account.

To set her up, we are going to need to have at least $180,000 to $200,000 in Pool 1—that's three years' worth of distributions with a bit of a buffer. Pool 2 is going to be populated with another $200,000 of assets so that it is relatively the same size as Pool 1. Pool 3 could contain the balance of her portfolio.

Once you have your three pools populated, the real work begins. These are not set-and-forget portfolios. You'll want to monitor them to make sure you're getting the results you hope for and rebalance to stay ahead of bear markets. I believe it's good practice to go into every day of every year assuming that the next bear market is beginning tomorrow, because you want to know that when (*not if*) it does happen again, you won't have to sell assets that were meant to be long-term investments to cover cash flow.

To be clear, you are not moving everything in anticipation of what could be a bear market—nobody can predict that. It's just reassuring to know that when it does happen, you don't have to change your portfolio.

So how does this work? During the year, you take gains from Pool 2 to replenish assets that have been spent from Pool 1. Then take returns from Pool 3 to replenish Pool 2. If you are in your accumulation years, any additional savings are allocated to Pool 3 to continue to grow your long-term assets. Setting up your portfolio in this way keeps your life savings six years ahead of the next bear market.

I'm not sure there is ever actually a "good" time for investments to lose market value, but some seasons of life are much worse than others. For example, retirees and those facing near term tuition payments or big-ticket items will often have investment money that fluctuates, and in some cases the market is down right when they need to take a distribution from the portfolio. If they don't have a system in place when they learn they'll need the money soon, they'll justifiably panic when the market starts falling. This leads many investors to sell at the wrong time, sabotaging their financial future because they have to sell more shares to create the same amount of cash.

It might seem *odd* that panic is sometimes justified. This heightened state of anxiety occurs when people realize that they might be in over their heads. They might have taken a shortcut such as trying to be too aggressive for their own comfort level. Determining risk tolerance is tricky, and unfortunately most people don't really know until they are in it. Fear and greed are the two enemies of real wealth accumulation over time. Fear cuts both ways: fear of losing more and fear of missing out (FOMO). As with forgoing a doctor appointment because you are limited on time, shortcuts like having too much money in cash accounts or in one asset class (and ignoring all the others) to capture oversized gains can lead to an early death.

Keep it rational.

By using the Three Pools of Money system, monitoring, and rebalancing as necessary, you will be far less likely to be in a position where you *have* to sell low. You are seven years ahead of the next bear market, so if (when) that happens, you have seven years before you have to worry about having to sell low. And based on historical averages, that seven years should be plenty of time to ride out a market decline.

The next chart demonstrates this powerfully, with a historical perspective on the duration of bear markets (and their depth) compared to the length of bull markets and what the S&P 500[x] earned[xi]. As always, please remember what they always say about past history: It is no guarantee of future results. But it's all we have to manage expectations, and there are some pretty nasty periods in here:

As of June 30, 2022. S&P 500® (gross dividends reinvested) in USD. Bear markets represented peak-to-trough price declines of 20% or more in the S&P 500®Index. Bull markets reflect all other periods. Past performance is no guarantee of future results. 1Monthly returns are shown for S&P 500®Index, except for the COVID-19 Crisis, which is daily.

Graphics can be enlightening. Here is another way to look at the same information (AMG Funds, *A Long-Term Perspective*):

AMG Funds: Keep Calm and Remain Diversified, FactSet, S&P Dow Jones Indices as of June 30, 2023. The indices are unmanaged, are not available for investment, and do not incur expenses. Past performance is no guarantee of future results.

By the way, percentages can be deceiving, especially when looking at these beautiful green mountain charts. During the financial crisis that started in 2007, $1,000,000 in the S&P 500 was worth less than $500,000 by March of 2009 with headlines speculating (screaming) about further declines. Having lived through more than a few major downturns, I will tell you that they can test the patience of even a seasoned investor.

The prime advantage of the Three Pools of Money system is that it allows you to manage much of the risk inherent in timing withdrawals needed for cash flow. Don't get me wrong—you are not "timing" the market, *that's a loser's game.* Market timing occurs when an investor thinks they can predict whether the market is going to go up or down and tries to trade ahead of their "hunch."

For the record, I can't look you in the eyes and tell you market timing never works, because that's just not true. Sometimes it does! But just as a gambler can sit at a poker table and win, we know that if he stays there long enough, eventually the house will clean him out. It is well understood that when taking taxes and transactions costs into consideration, market timers and traders tend to remember only their winners, especially—when re-telling their story to others! No one engaging in market timing has demonstrated an ability to achieve outperformance over a buy-and-hold approach with proactive rebalancing[xii] over time.

KFM 3: Purposeful Savings with Tax Efficient Compounding That Can Blow Your Mind

Key Force Multipliers (KFM)

☐ Customized tools to model and stress-test your financial future

☐ Specific strategies and execution

☐ **Purposeful savings with tax-efficient compounding that can blow your mind**

☐ Accountability checkpoints that optimize your resources and human capital

☐ Sidestepping mistakes that sabotage progress

☐ A reward for your follow-through from time-to-time

The third Key Force Multiplier involves purposeful, realistic savings aligned with your vision, actual actions born out of the first two KFMs. This means you aren't just randomly saving 6% or 10% of your income in some bottomless bucket. Instead, your purpose in saving is to reach a visualized future you have articulated. If you want to pay for your children's education, how much is that really going to cost? From there, you work the numbers and set up a savings and investment plan that achieves your purpose.

When our son Michael was born, Ed and I decided that paying for our children's college was an important priority. My parents paid for our tuition, room, and board, so when I graduated from Georgetown, I had no student loans. Ed, on the other hand, did. It certainly affected our launching pad when we started our life together, coloring what each of us was able to do.

I ran the numbers and determined that if we saved $387 every month and the return averaged 8% per year, we could afford any college Michael wanted to attend.

We continued to do this for each of our four children every time we got pregnant, and when it came to our unborn youngest, we were still struggling to make ends meet. When I told Ed about our little "surprise" baby, the first words out of his mouth were *not*, "Oh, Patti, this is such wonderful news." Or, "Oh, Patti, now we won't have a middle child." Or even, "Patti, thank you for being willing to go through another nine months of water retention, backaches, and excruciating labor."

Nope. Ed's first and immediate response was,

"Where in the world are we going to find another $387 every month!?"

My response:

"I have no idea, but we are going to do it anyway."

When our kids got to college, thanks to the combined magic of automatic investing, dollar cost averaging[xiii], and compound returns, each one had enough money to cover their costs, and there was also money left over. The financial confidence this gave us was well worth the vacations we might have given up along the way.

Maybe paying for college isn't a priority for you and instead you'd really like a home at the beach. How much—including upkeep and taxes—will that cost? Can you drive there, or should you build in the cost of flights? Again, you're working with important and measurable goals, so you run real numbers and set up a savings and investment plan that gets you there.

Here's the part that a lot of people miss—The goal you're saving toward makes the process more rewarding. It doesn't seem like such a big sacrifice. When the savings are just set up as a random percentage of income, it is too easy to cheat and use that money and use it for today's self rather than your future self. Specific goals, with purposeful savings to get you there, create both accountability and momentum that keep you motivated and moving forward.

A corollary to purposeful savings—*or maybe a mini-KFM*—is to take advantage of compound interest. Albert Einstein is often credited with saying, "Compound interest is the eighth wonder of the world." What he observed is something anyone can benefit from; although especially in years when interest rates are low, we should probably replace the words "compound interest" with "long-term compound growth." (More on how to create a compounding machine in Part Two.)

What's so miraculous about compounded returns? If you start early enough, most of your later savings come from appreciation that is earned on *already-earned* growth. It's like free money that just keeps accumulating. Eventually, you can create a salary from your portfolio when you stop earning one. Compounded returns with strategic tax and estate planning are the secret to generational wealth.

In his book *The Geometry of Wealth*, Brian Portnoy presents three graphs that illustrate this point (Portnoy, *The Geometry of Wealth*). This book makes so many good points that I'd encourage any student of personal finance to read it cover to cover.

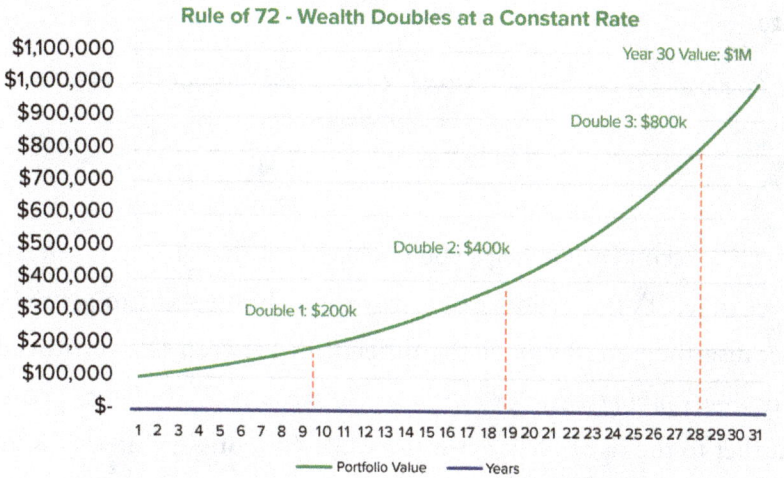

Rule of 72 - Wealth Doubles at a Constant Rate

The first chart (above) shows what happens when you have $100,000 doubling at a constant rate[12] $100,000 becomes $200,000; $200,000 becomes $400,000; $400,000 becomes $800,000. In thirty years at a constant rate of 8% growth, the initial deposit of $100,000 grows to $1,006,266[13].

---

12   Which doesn't really exist, even in bank accounts. For example, money market accounts went from paying about 1% to over 5% in just a few short years, and they will probably change again. Bank accounts, bonds, stocks and pretty much anything you put your money in will have fluctuating returns over time. The graph is simply demonstrating an average at a constant rate to illustrate the power of compounding—and how illusive it can be in the beginning.

13   It's important to note that the graphs on these pages are hypothetical examples to demonstrate a mathematical principle. It does not illustrate any investment products and does not show past or future performance of any specific investment.

Months to Accrue Next $100,000 at 8%

The second graph helps you visualize how that growth accelerates over time. It's the major reason why the rich just seem to get richer, because they *are.* Look at the differences between the vertical red lines—*it's taking a lot less time to make the next $100,000* as you go further to the right. Why? Because while your original deposit is just $100,000, the *earnings are growing at 8% too.*

Here's where Portnoy breaks it down into months:

"Scale" of Wealth Creation Accelerates for Each Incremental $100,000

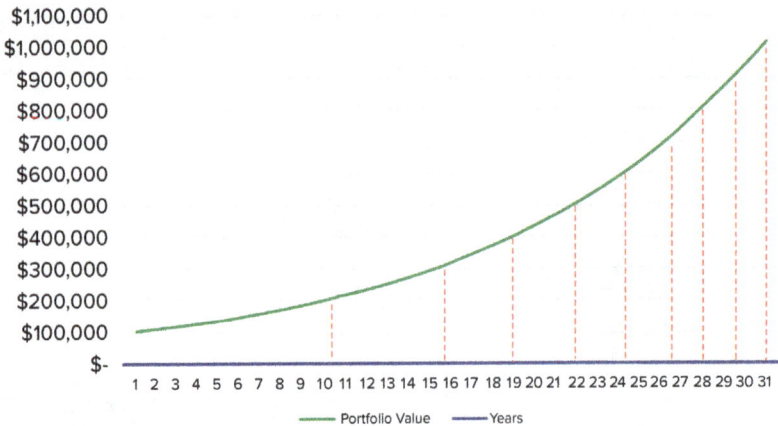

Most of your results come in the final third of this time horizon. According to the Rule of 72, when you divide a rate of return into 72, money will compound at a constant rate. For example, 8% divided into 72 means that a portfolio would double approximately every 9 years, but the scale at which growth occurs accelerates with time. We call this the hockey stick phenomenon. In the beginning, *it feels like you're not really making much progress*—it takes about nine years to make the first $100,000—but then the growth rate shoots up at the end. Imagine making $100,000 in just over a year—without any additional effort on your part. The effort comes at the front end—to save the money in the first place and to keep it invested in spite of scary headlines, portfolio volatility, and other temptations.

"HOCKEY STICK" ASSET GROWTH

ASSET

The Miracle Happens Here

TIME

When we talk more about purposeful savings in a later chapter, I'll include graphics that illustrate the strength of compounding. Knowing that your money is growing exponentially—as long as you don't touch it—is incredibly motivating, and you'll likely want to continue executing the recommendations in your financial plan.

KFM 4: Accountability Checkpoints That Optimize Your Resources And Human Capital

Key Force Multipliers (KFM)

☐ Customized tools to model and stress-test your financial future

☐ Specific strategies and execution

☐ Purposeful savings with tax-efficient compounding that can blow your mind

☐ **Accountability checkpoints that optimize your resources and human capital**

☐ Sidestepping mistakes that sabotage progress

☐ A reward for your follow-through from time-to-time

Sticking to a financial plan takes discipline, but eventually it becomes a habit. An example of this fourth "hack" might be an annual review of your financial plan with your spouse, a significant other, or the professional who helped you build it. Accountability checkpoints serve two purposes. First, they keep you on track. Think how hard it is to stick to a diet if you never weigh yourself or try on those clothes that used to be too tight. You don't know if you're progressing, so you don't know if what you're doing is working. Checkpoints also serve as motivators. As you reach each one, you get a rush of adrenaline, which gives you the energy and enthusiasm to dig in and keep going.

Optimizing your human capital means deciding whether financial planning is an area of your life you have the time (or even want) to manage and whether you are capable of doing so. Otherwise, you can delegate it to a professional who can provide ongoing advice and checkpoints.

KFM 5: Sidestepping Mistakes That Sabotage Progress

Key Force Multipliers (KFM)

- [ ] Customized tools to model and stress-test your financial future
- [ ] Specific strategies and execution
- [ ] Purposeful savings with tax-efficient compounding that can blow your mind
- [ ] Accountability checkpoints that optimize your resources and human capital
- [ ] **Sidestepping mistakes that sabotage progress**
- [ ] A reward for your follow-through from time-to-time

Thus far, I have focused on strategies that work over-time, but we all also need to be aware of the mistakes that can derail even the best plan. In the beginning of this chapter, we learned how tailwinds can carry an airplane to its destination much faster than stagnant air. The opposite phenomenon is headwinds, which make it more difficult for the airplane to make progress toward its destination. Mistakes are headwinds that can hijack your plan and put your most important objectives at risk. I'll dig into the fifteen mistakes people make over and over again in Part Three to make sure you don't destroy all your hard work.

KFM 6: A Reward for Your Follow-Through from Time to Time

Why is this one so important? Because you will never stick to your financial plan if you don't build in some rewards along the way. I'm not necessarily talking about huge purchases like a house on a beach—

at least early on! The rewards can be small tokens reminding you of your progress, or shared experiences with people you love. They will be different for everyone. For me, it was a used car with air conditioning, and a nice outfit from time to time. A colleague has a list of landscaping and gardening equipment, something I could care less about. In fact, it would make me feel guilty I wasn't working on the lawn. Make it meaningful for you. Your subconscious mind will form a powerful link between what you do and the outcomes you receive. Rewards lock in a powerful reinforcing mechanism that builds on your momentum and makes it sustainable.

The Domino Effect

Think of how a lever allows you to lift much more weight than you could on your own. In their book *The One Thing*, Gary Keller and Jay Papasan do a brilliant job of helping us visualize the huge impact one small gesture can have (Keller and Papasan, *The One Thing*). Have you ever set up a line of dominoes and lightly tapped the one on the end so it fell, and all the others clapped down, one after another? *Such a small action for such a large result.* Key Force Multipliers act the same way.

Compounding dominoes are even better. When it comes to money, compounded returns mean that your dominoes *aren't* the same size. They get larger and larger over time, just as in this picture.

The Key Force Multipliers help to reframe your mind-set so you can consistently recognize what's working and what isn't. From there, you can follow through on the actions that make a difference. Some multipliers involve a bit more legwork than others, but even relatively small things like KFM #4 (accountability checkpoints) and KFM #6 (token rewards) can make a huge difference. The Key Force Multipliers don't just help to magnify your efforts and accelerate your financial success, they provide the soil for enjoying the process along the way.

If you use them with the Four Keys for Life process, *you essentially engineer results*. They also work well because they are geared to the individual—you. They aren't a set of generic steps that try to fit everyone into the same box. Rules of thumb are fine for people wanting shortcuts, but all too often shortcuts leave people—short! If you are using someone else's rule of thumb, how will that apply to you?

KFMs provide leverage to a repeatable process. The six strategies work because they simplify and automate your financial plan. Together, they make the financial house fit with your unique needs and lifestyle, making the steps engaging and meaningful throughout, even when things change.

When is the Best Time to Use KFMs? (And Why Bother?)

You might be wondering if it's too late to begin using Key Force Multipliers or if you need to use all of them or any at all. Wouldn't just using time-tested strategies be enough?

Sure, you could, but you would be back to facing the issue of "prescription before diagnosis" and the malpractice that often results. The key is to apply action items within the structure of the first KFM—a customized financial plan—with ongoing wealth management to monitor your progress and tweak as needed. This will help you enjoy your progress along the way. KFMs are based on principles and values, which is why they're so powerful. It doesn't matter whether you have $10,000, $1,000,000, or $100,000,000. Applying a particular idea might be *efficient* but the Key Force Multipliers make that same idea truly *effective. In other words, you are solving the right problems and capitalizing on opportunities only as they apply to you in real time* and only as they present themselves.

Of course, certain people might get more value out of some of these ideas than others, in terms of absolute numbers. If someone gets a 10% return on $100,000, it's one thing. If another person gets a 10% return on $10,000,000, that's quite another. While the dollars involved might be different, $10,000 to someone who has $100,000 can actually have more impact on their quality of life than an extra million would have on the life of someone who already has several million dollars in hand. It isn't all about absolute dollars. It's about what your financial life looks like now and what can be done to preserve it *and* improve it *exponentially.*

What you have is what you have. *It's your everything.*

PART TWO: TACTICS

Buckling Up, Dealing with Turbulence

CHAPTER 3

The Realities of Risk (Obvious *and* Obscure)

The *Obvious* Risks: Market Fluctuations

This is the risk that sells newspapers, the one everyone worries about: a wicked bear market with declines approaching 30%, 40%, 50%, or even more.

When you invest in the stock market, it is important to realize that *your investment can lose value at any moment in time*. How much? A decline of 10% or more is considered a market correction, while a bear market is defined as a loss of 20% or more. Markets tend to be volatile every year; the average intra-year decline of the S&P 500 has been -14% historically (J.P. Morgan Asset Management, *Guide to the Markets*). They went down, and recovered so that investors looking at annual returns from January to December may never know it even happened! And while wicked bear markets of 50% on the S&P 500 are rare, they do happen.

In downturns like that, what should you do?

Let's say you invested in the S&P 500 four years before the financial crisis:

> **If you invested $100,000....**
>
> | In January 2003: | By January 2007 you would have: | But by Januay 2009: |
> |---|---|---|
> | $100,000 | $182,863 | $115,208 |

Data supplied by American Funds and analyzed via YCharts on 8/8/2023.

Please keep in mind that the chart above is not as dramatic as what actually occurred. (This is the problem with looking at history and calendar-year returns). The chart reflects a loss of approximately 37%, but the two charts in the prior chapter reflected peak to trough—October 7, 2007 through March 9. This is the time period when investors witness the well-diversified *S&P 500* index lost 51% of its value. Some of the companies in the index certainly lost more than others.

As headlines warned of a looming depression and cable TV featured prominent money managers predicting further declines, even the most patient investors were tested. The Federal Reserve had cut interest rates to near zero, and Treasury Secretary Hank Paulson was on his knees begging Congress to pass a fiscal stimulus. At that point, you had two choices: sell your equities, or ride things out.

2 OPTIONS: PULL OUT VS. STAY THE COURSE

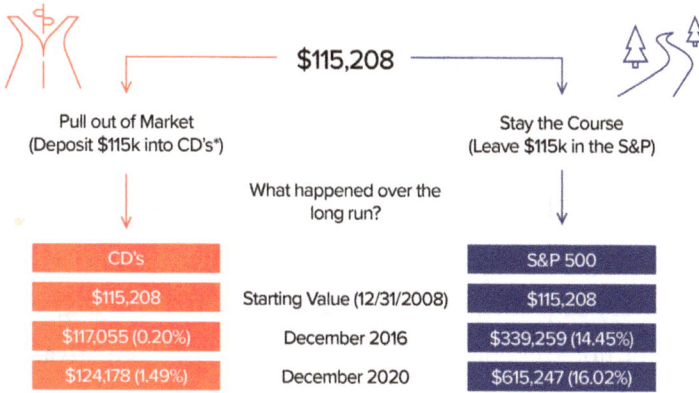

$115,208

Pull out of Market
(Deposit $115k into CD's*)

Stay the Course
(Leave $115k in the S&P)

What happened over the long run?

CD's		S&P 500
$115,208	Starting Value (12/31/2008)	$115,208
$117,055 (0.20%)	December 2016	$339,259 (14.45%)
$124,178 (1.49%)	December 2020	$615,247 (16.02%)

*Please note: Since bank rates can vary, six month T-Bill was used as proxy for CD's.
Source of data: Ycharts.com (S&P 500: Assumes reinvestment of dividends); American Funds/Citi Group 6-month treasury bill

As you can see in the table above, those who put their money in "safe" CD's (or in the case above, 6-month treasuries) barely recovered nine years later. Meanwhile, those who held on for the ride recovered and ended up exceeding five times more money in the same time period.

This phenomenon of recoveries in the stock market isn't new. Let's compare two investors, Nellie and Joe, both in their mid-twenties. Suppose they both invested $100,000 in the S&P 500 at the end of 1964. Just eight years later, by December 31, 1972, they would have seen that $100,000 grow to $180,220. That's a pretty good return, right? But we all know that equities markets are volatile, and by September 1974, the value of their investment would have fallen to $113,055—pretty much back to where they started ten years before.

Now they had two choices—get out or stay in. Every nerve in Nellie's body was probably screaming, "Get out! Find something safer!" In the seventies, when interest rates on CD's were significantly higher than they are now, Nellie just couldn't take it anymore and capitulated at the bottom of that 50% bear market in 1974. She was very content with the 6% interest rate she was getting on her six-month CD (or treasury bill) at the time *and thrilled when they started paying 12% a few years later.* She could sleep at night again.

But how did that flight to safety work out? In this example, Nellie recovered her losses in about eight years (in 1981). Joe just ignored what was going on while the S&P 500 took less than two years to return to its pre-bear high, and by December 31, 1976, it was worth $192,264.

Recovery to prior values is just one aspect of investing, and that is certainly not the end of the story. Long term, the advantage of staying in the equities markets and riding out bear markets is evident. Throughout her life, Nellie's first scary experience never left her; and she could not tolerate even the thought of losing money again. As a result, she simply rolled over her T-Bills (just as one might do with CD's) at maturity to remain conservatively invested over the next forty-six years. Joe remained fully invested throughout, even in his sixties, in the midst of the great financial crisis (2007-2009).

Here's where "performance" can be deceiving. By December 31, 2008, Nellie's investments in these very safe, guaranteed investments grew to $786,814 (averaging almost 6% annualized return—not bad!). During the same timeframe, and even despite the 37% loss in 2008 alone, Joe had earned double Nellie's return—about 11%—but thanks to the power of compounded returns he amassed $4,341,642 – *not* double the amount of money as Nellie. Both started with the same $100,000 but ended up—even despite a tech bubble, a worldwide financial crisis and everything in between—*with very different outcomes.*

Markets have volatility risk, but fluctuation is just that: *fluctuation.* It isn't real loss unless the investor actually sells the investment. Nellie moved her principal out of the market trying to avoid stock fluctuations, but she suffered an opportunity cost that was far greater in the long run, *one that even a 37% loss at the worst possible time—in the very last year—couldn't erase.* For her, that added up to a $3.5 million difference over the 34 years from 1974 to 2008. Even in the midst of that bear market Joe had amassed sustainable wealth, so his risk *capacity* was still quite high. He could have left his S&P 500 account alone, living on the dividend (about $100,000 per year), or continued to reinvest and watch it grow.

Let's fast-forward to December 2020, when they were both 70 years old. Nellie was earning an average annual return of 4.45%—again, not too bad! Joe, on the other hand, slept through the significant volatility *and* four more wicked bear markets yet still earned 12.26%, meaning that the S&P earned about three times Nellie's return (4.46% vs. 12.26%). *So, did Joe have three times the account value of Nellie's?*

I hope you're sitting down: Nellie's bank statement showed a total value of $836,331 while Joe had amassed an account value of $23,064,533[14]. The comparison is almost surreal, but it is real.

Note that I am not comparing apples to apples. As long as they are held to maturity, T-Bills are safe and guaranteed by the U.S. Government. CD's are also FDIC-insured. The S&P 500 does not have any of these attributes. The story of Nervous Nellie is simply an example of what people tend *to do* when markets begin to go into a seizure, which can get so uncomfortable that it's just plain human to want to do *something*. It feels right to avoid those things that can do the most harm while they're happening, but in this context, permanent harm usually occurs when you sell in the midst of the plunge, as Nellie did.

---

14 Joe had amassed something else as well: an estate tax issue, but this is one of those problems you kind of want to have, and there are several options to mitigate or eliminate it. Stay tuned for Chapter 6.

You might wonder why anyone in their right mind would want to invest in the stock market, knowing that they could lose 50% or more within months. Further, returns on diversified portfolios are often choppy and unpredictable, and performance often seems completely unconnected to economic reality. Over short periods of time, you would be correct to think that investing in the market is like gambling. When someone tells me they want to avoid the risk of the market, I quickly learn that what they really want to avoid is *uncertainty.*

To understand why investing even just a portion of your money in the stock market still might make sense, we need to discuss some fundamentals. The total value of a company (measured by the number of outstanding shares multiplied by the stock price on any given day) reflects the *opinions* of analysts and traders regarding its earnings in the future and the sustainability of its profits over the years. Remember: they are just opinions, *educated guesses* at best, and as smart as the rationale might sound, no-one knows for sure. All too often, even the CEO of a company cannot predict its earnings of the company they run—*day to day*—over even just the next three months. In fact, they get it wrong all the time!

The reason diversification is so powerful is that the risk of uncertainty dissipates when you spread it across different industries that might react differently to an economic event during different time periods. Recall that garden concept discussed in the previous chapter, but keep in mind that diversification is not a guarantee against loss. It is important to acknowledge that storms can and will occur. *Realistically, nothing is going to grow during a storm, and if it's a tornado, some plants may be completely wiped out.* If the design of your landscape recognizes this inevitable fact, when the sun eventually comes out again, your garden will flourish. The same is true of a well-designed portfolio invested in various asset classes and great companies around the world.

The stock market is considered a leading indicator, often reflecting economic expectations nine to twelve months ahead of time. For example, because of positive expectations, and contrary to what you might think, a diversified index can increase in value even when the unemployment rate is skyrocketing, and company earnings are not growing. The reverse also happens, with declines of 10% or 20% when the economy appears to be roaring ahead. As a leading indicator, the market can provide some value in terms of consumer sentiment, but usually not for the reasons the "experts" give at the time. And just like a meteorologist predicting the weather, the market is not always right.

An example of a lagging indicator is the unemployment rate. During a recession, senior corporate executives realize that the demand for their goods or services has declined, so they look to cut costs to maintain profitability. Widespread layoffs are often the result, which affects the unemployment rate. But obtaining the data often takes time, and executives don't want to overreact by laying off well-trained employees lest they be caught short-handed if demand was not adversely affected. A recent example of this is Amazon during the pandemic. Can you imagine what would have happened to its earnings if Amazon's CEO had announced widespread layoffs during the recession in 2020? Without a sufficient number of employees, the company would not have been able to meet the service demands of consumers shut up in their homes, and its profits would have suffered.

Leading and lagging indicators can be useful, but their predictive accuracy is usually clear only after the fact. What *is* clear is that investing in the stock market almost always pays off in the long term—but how long is that?

In January 2009, I was giving a talk to a group of people in a continuing care community. I presented a slide that showed the comparison of Nellie's and Joe's experience investing in CD's and the S&P 500 during the downturn in the 1970's and beyond. There was a woman named Joan sitting in the front row, with a beautiful head of gray hair. She was listening intently and nodding her head in agreement. Then I put up the slide showing the difference in CD's and equities over thirty years, and Joan was suitably impressed. She said, "Patti, that all makes a lot of sense, but I'm seventy-five years old. I don't have thirty years. I can't afford to keep my money invested in the market, so I've been thinking about calling my broker."

"I totally understand," I said. "Do you think you have five years?"

"Well, I think so."

"How about ten years?"

She paused. "I damn well hope so."

Everyone in the room giggled, but understood that this was serious. Joan might have thought she couldn't afford to ride out a volatile market, but if she lived another ten years, the reality was that she couldn't afford not to ride it out. If she sold, her losses would be permanent, and since her pension did not increase with inflation, *she might need more of her capital to fill a gap that was already there.* I put up another slide that showed the five- and ten-year growth of that $113,055 investment we were talking about, and then I asked the audience if anyone was getting 10% on their CD's. No one moved. I followed up by asking if anyone was getting 6%? Still no response. Then I showed them a 4% CD growth rate compared to the market index. Those investors who moved their capital to CD's earning 4% would have had a portfolio worth $168,390 ten years later, but those who remained invested in the S&P 500 would have had a portfolio worth $392,479, clocking in a rate of return of 14.65%. Joan got the message, put her phone away and kept her investments exactly where they were.

The *Obscure* Risks: (What Sabotages Even Sophisticated and Relatively Rich People?)

Performance vs. Outcomes: Average Annual Returns Can Be Misleading

When choosing an investment, many people look at historical rates of return and pick the Funds that performed "the best." There are several ways to calculate rates of return, some better than others. Examples include arithmetic versus geometric returns and time-weighted versus internal rate of return. Each can arrive at a different conclusion.

HOW and WHEN a Return Is Achieved Matters $100,000 Invested Two Ways:		
	Portfolio A	Portfolio B:
Year 1 Return:	30%	10%
Year 2 Return:	-10%	10%
Year 3 Return:	10%	10%
3 Year "Average" Return:	**10%**	**10%**
Both of these investments could be shown as having a three-year average "performance" of 10%. But which would you rather have?		
	Portfolio A	Portfolio B:
3 Year Outcome:	**$128,700**	**$133,100**
*Notice: I did not say **"return."** The returns were the same. The <u>outcome</u> was quite different.		

A basic approach is to add up the returns each year and then divide by the number of years. This can be misleading because it understates the impact of losses. For example, the chart above illustrates two investments of $100,000. Fund A goes up 30% in year 1, down 10% in year 2, then right back up 10% in year 3. Boring can be better: losses hurt more than gains help. When Fund A lost that 10% in the second year, it needed to earn more than 10% in the third year just to break even.

Let's see how it works out in real dollars. Fund A grows by 30% the first year, so it starts the second year at $130,000. It then has a 10% loss, which takes it to $117,000. The next year, it grows 10%, *but that growth is on a lower dollar amount, so it only reaches $128,700.*

Sometimes, we even find that an investment with a lower three-year average could be accumulating more capital than one with a higher average rate of return. This outcome illustrates that for any individual or family, *when and how you receive the return is potentially more important than the average return you achieve over time.*

The chart below illustrates what it takes just to break even after a loss. For example, if you lose 20% in a given year, you need to earn 25% on that lower dollar value just to get the investment back up to the value it was before the loss.

PERCENTAGE NEEDED FOR RECOVERY	
Loss Incured (%)	Required Gain (%)
5%	5.2%
10%	11%
15%	18%
20%	25%
25%	33%
30%	43%
35%	54%
40%	67%
50%	100%
60%	150%
75%	300%
80%	400%

The Difference Between "The" Return and "Your" Return

One way of comparing performance is Time Weighted Rate of Return (TWR), which is a measure of the compounded rate of growth in an investment or portfolio. This approach eliminates the distorting effects of contributions and withdrawals that may have occurred during the period being measured. For example, what if your investment does really well in the first seven months of the year and you add $15,000 from a bonus on August 1? Markets don't perform in a symmetrical fashion, so let's assume the market stays completely flat for the rest of the year. TWR is designed to eliminate the effect of timing and size of cash flows as if the contribution didn't happen. You'll typically see TWR when reviewing options to invest your 401(k) contributions or on a mutual fund's website. If you are making contributions, TWR is not going to be a relevant measure of how you did.

Internal Rate of Return (IRR) is used to determine your *true* performance, because it includes the impact of additions and withdrawals made during the period being measured. It is the most accurate answer to the question "How much money *have I made* on my investment or portfolio?" *While TWR can reflect an investment or strategy, IRR represents your <u>personal</u> return from implementing the strategy.* One is not better than the other, but it's important to note that there can be a dramatic difference between the two calculations. Also, there is no rule of thumb in terms of which calculation is going to show a higher or lower result. That will depend on what happened during the time period, whether you added or withdrew money, and if so, how much. Therefore, you need to understand which calculation to use when evaluating your portfolio and planning your future. While TWR can be used to compare investments, IRR should be used to evaluate your outcomes. This is even more important when projecting returns on your portfolio in a *real* financial plan.

Volatility Is One Thing, Sequence of Return Risk Is Quite Another

As the wording indicates, sequence of return risk has to do with the *order* of your gains and losses, but here's where the timing of your returns gets deceiving: during your working years, it doesn't really matter. Two portfolios with the same average annual return will end up accumulating the same amount of money, for the simple reason that the returns were just earned at different times *and left to compound irrespective of headlines or other people's investments.* In other words, no changes were made (which is probably *not* realistic).

Let's assume Steven is starting with $1,000,000. We can break his financial life up into two different seasons. The accumulation (or working) years and the retirement years, when distributions from a portfolio are often needed.

In the example below, we are going to assume that Steven invested in three hypothetical portfolios and that he didn't add or take money out during the accumulation years. Even though returns (or losses) were generated at different times, all three achieved an average rate of return of 7%. Sure, when comparing balances at various intervals during Steven's working years, the value of each portfolio may have been very different, but he was a long-term investor. All that mattered was the value of each account when he retired, measuring from point A to point B. What happened in the middle didn't matter to Steven[15]. As luck would have it, all three earned the same average rate of return of 7%. That's a terrific outcome!

AVERAGE RETURNS CAN BE DECEIVING

RETURN PATTERNS	YEAR 1	YEAR 2	YEAR 3	YEAR 4	YEAR 5	AV. ANNUAL
PORTFOLIO A	22%	15%	12%	-4%	-7%	7%
PORTFOLIO B	7%	7%	7%	7%	7%	7%
PORTFOLIO C	-7%	-4%	12%	15%	22%	7%

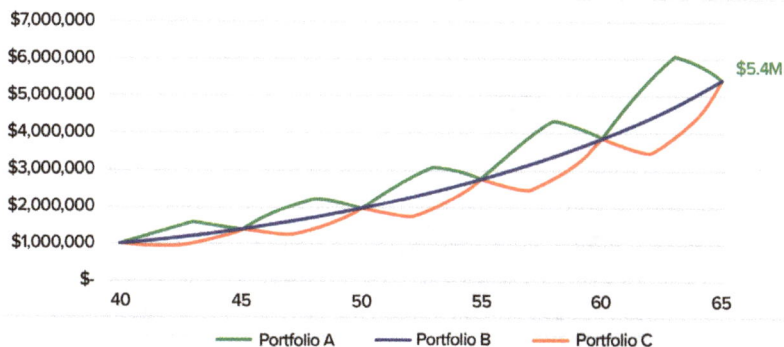

$5.4M

Portfolio A — Portfolio B — Portfolio C

---

15 Although it *always does* to the investor, which is why achieving the same rates of return in all three portfolios is an unlikely outcome. For example, look at the values depicted on the chart around Steven's age 57. If this were his actual investment experience, *chances are he would compare the two outcomes and sell the "loser."*

If no changes are made during the accumulation years, the order of your gains and losses doesn't impact your portfolio, but what about drawdown years?

Let's take those <u>same</u> portfolios, with the <u>same</u> starting value of $1,000,000, and the <u>same</u> average rate of return of 7%. Just as in the first chart, *the only difference is the sequence of returns,* but now Steven is retired. Since he is projected to earn 7%, he is going to take out 6%, or $60,000 per year, adjusted for 3% inflation every year. In year 2 he would receive $61,800 from his portfolio, in year 3 he would receive $63,654, and so on[16].

Note the red line at age ninety, when the only difference between having just a bit less that what he originally invested (about $900,000) or running out of money completely is *when* those returns (or losses) were generated. Portfolio withdrawals compound losses, which means it takes longer to recover from a portfolio decline. Once withdrawals are added to the mix, even similar portfolios with the same *average* return can have very different *outcomes*.

---

16   In reality, most people don't automatically increase their draw from a portfolio at the rate of inflation each year. Additional distribution needs tend to be chunky, when the $5,000 per month just isn't quite cutting it. For example, in year 3, Steven might pull out an extra $4,000 because his savings account balance is depleting. By just year 5, that extra (one-time) withdrawal is closer to $10,000, because that's what Steven needs to maintain his purchasing power. *That's why wealth management is an important extension of the financial planning process; to provide sustainable cash flow for the rest of your life.* The key is to make sure what you planned for is occurring the way you hoped it would.

**SEQUENCE OF RETURN MAY MATTER MORE THAN AVERAGE RETURN IN RETIREMENT
(6% ANNUAL WITHDRAWAL; 3% INFLATION)**

RETURN PATTERNS

	YEAR 1	YEAR 2	YEAR 3	YEAR 4	YEAR 5	AV. ANNUAL
PORTFOLIO A	22%	15%	12%	-4%	-7%	7%
PORTFOLIO B	7%	7%	7%	7%	7%	7%
PORTFOLIO C	-7%	-4%	12%	15%	22%	7%

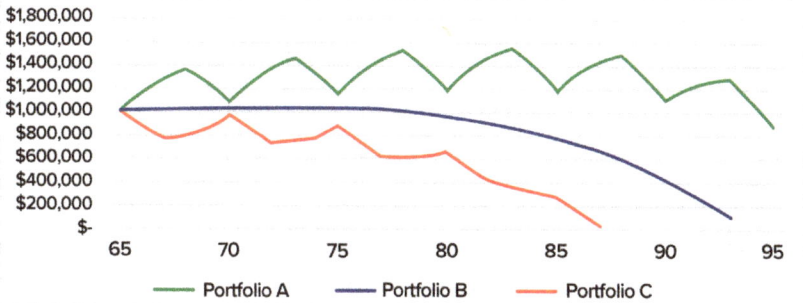

A Critical Period: The Red Zone

Remember that football team trying to score from the five-yard line? They're in the red zone, a term for when a football team gets to the 20-yard line or closer. It's much harder to score a touchdown because the field is shorter, with less room to spread the opposition out and get the ball into the end zone. The coaches have to be even more strategic and creative because the options are more limited. In 2019, the Philadelphia Eagles were great in the red zone, scoring a touchdown 62% of the time. Other teams did not have such a high success rate.

Cash-flow timing risk increases exponentially when people enter the red zone of retirement planning, which spans the five years before retirement to the five years after retirement. The decisions people make during that decade can ultimately determine their standard of living for the rest of their lives, and—if it's a priority—how much they leave to their families. And just as in football, the options become more limited.

Many people think it's too late to plan when they hit their sixties, yet retirement planning is often *more important* when you stop working, because at that point, you have accumulated whatever you're going to have. Then it's just a matter of how that will sustain you for the rest of your life. It is also a time when the Three Pools of Money can carry you into the endzone.

Any robo-advisor or internet site can put together a balanced portfolio for you, but now that you truly understand cash-flow timing risk, it is important to have a system that helps you deal with this risk; otherwise there is a good chance that your portfolio will fail to provide the retirement you envision. You want a system that integrates your investments in a way that creates synergy between your need for income and your need for growth. Such a system can help determine the growth of your cash flow and the time frame in which you are going to need it. That's why the Four Keys for Life financial plan, the Three Pools of Money, and ongoing wealth management are crucial. In retirement, your field is shorter, the options are more limited, and the stakes are much higher.

4%: The Shocking Realities

In his book, *The Geometry of Wealth*, Brian Portnoy brings to light an odd investing conundrum (Portnoy, *The Geometry of Wealth*):

1. The stock market has delivered great returns over the long term, well in excess of returns on cash equivalents such as treasury bills, CD's, and money market funds.

2. Most individual stocks don't outperform cash equivalents over the long term.

In other words, most stocks do just so-so to poorly, but stocks in general do well. I need you to sit down for this one: research by Hendrik Bessembinder in the *Journal of Financial Economics* illustrates that dating back to 1926, 58% of common stocks have a lifetime return less than that of a one-month treasury bill (T-Bills are a proxy for cash and CD's of the same maturity) (Bessembinder, *Do Stocks Outperform Treasury Bills?*). That means about four out of seven stocks did worse than a risk-free investment.

It gets even *worse*. Many people have hunches or sentimental attachments to their stocks, or they simply don't want to pay taxes on a gain. Here's the problem: in terms of lifetime dollar wealth creation, the returns of just 4% of all public companies account for most of the entire net gain for the U.S. stock market since 1926. Collectively, the other 96% of public companies matched (or did worse than) the rate of return on T-Bills (Swedroe, *Individual Investing Involves Risk*).

Let's not stake your financial future on the belief that the company you work for (or the stock you inherited, or the hot tip someone gave you) is one of the 4%. If that's what you're doing, have you asked your spouse if he or she feels the same? Married couples often split the chores of running the household. One spouse takes care of the schedules, shopping, and household repairs, while the other handles financial affairs. It is important that both spouses are aware of decisions involving risk because the entire family will be affected.

Most of the returns you get from the stock market typically come from about ten companies. The problem is that those ten companies change dramatically over time. Just ask anyone who owned Apple or General Electric (GE) in the nineties. Back then, the founder of Apple was booted to the curb, and the company was on fumes, trading at a split adjusted price of under one dollar. Meanwhile, GE was considered one of the greatest enterprises of all time, so well diversified it was practically a no-lose proposition. As of December 1999, GE was trading at about $322 per share. By the end of the tech bubble in October of 2002, it traded at $158. Here's where the head fake comes in: it grew back to $260 by October 2007, and then it really got slammed with the financial crisis of 2008, dropping to about $46 by March 2009. Over 20 years later in December of 2020, this Great American Company—which it is—stood at about $67.42. The total return of this well-respected American enterprise was a loss of over 50%,—4% per year while the company on fumes, that almost went bankrupt, clocked in at almost 28% during the same period. For those people who didn't want to try to guess the future back then, the S&P 500 provided a respectable 6.6% return.

At the risk of making this very painful for you, a $100,000 investment in GE fell to about $44,000, that company on fumes (Apple) grew to almost $17 million dollars, while the same amount invested in the S&P 500 was worth $384,000.

I don't want unrealistic expectations to seep into the pages of this book. Could Apple continue to perform as well into the future? Sure, it's a great company. Just remember what they said about General Electric twenty years ago. You would be wise to wonder which companies are about to tell the same story over the next 20 years.

Yet your financial future does not have to rely on a crystal ball. The good news is that over the past 100 years, and even though the strongest returns came from just a few companies, the S&P 500 has produced a compound return of approximately 10%—about 400 times as much as T-Bills.

Investment Returns vs. Investor Returns

If you look at the chart below, you can see the damage investors do to their portfolios when they make decisions based on emotion rather than logic. This isn't new; investor outcomes are *consistently poor*! Irrespective of which two decades we chart, the outcomes are very similar; the damage done by human nature doesn't change much. For example, over the twenty years beginning in 2001 to the end of 2020, investors suffered three wicked bear markets: the tech bubble, the financial crisis of 2008 and the COVID-19 pandemic. Even so, holding onto the S&P 500 provided an average annual return of 7.5%, while a portfolio comprised of 60% in the S&P 500 and 40% in high-quality bonds had a return a 6.4%. But the average investor earned only 2.9%! That's a huge difference in real dollars! Here's the point: the updated chart below from 2022 (Source of data and chart: JP Morgan asset management *Guide to the Markets*) tells a very similar story!

20-YEAR ANNUALIZED RETURNS BY ASSET CLASS (2002-2021)

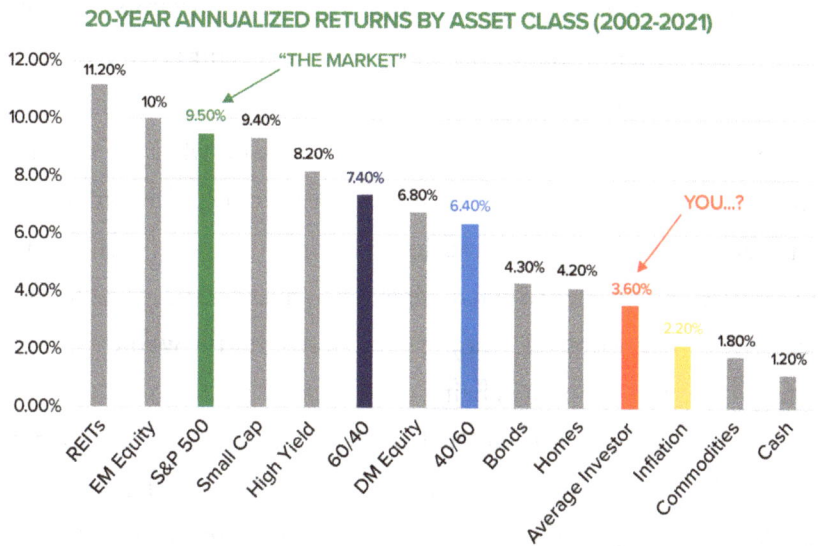

Bar chart with the following values:
- REITs: 11.20%
- EM Equity: 10%
- S&P 500 ("THE MARKET"): 9.50%
- Small Cap: 9.40%
- High Yield: 8.20%
- 60/40: 7.40%
- DM Equity: 6.80%
- 40/60: 6.40%
- Bonds: 4.30%
- Homes: 4.20%
- Average Investor (YOU...?): 3.60%
- Inflation: 2.20%
- Commodities: 1.80%
- Cash: 1.20%

Source: Bloomberg, FactSet, Standard & Poor's, J.P. Morgan Asset Management; (Bottom) Dalbar Inc., MSCI, NAREIT, Russell Indices used are as follows: REITs: NAREIT Equity REIT Index, Small Cap: Russell 2000, EM Equity: MSCI EM, DM Equity: MSCI EAFE, Commodity: Bloomberg Commodity Index, High Yield: Bloomberg HY Index, Bonds: Bloomberg U.S. Aggregate Index, Homes: Median sale price of existing single-family homes, Cash: Bloomberg 1-3m Treasury, Inflation: CPI. 60/40: Reflects a balanced portfolio with 60% invested in S&P 500 Index and 40% invested in high-quality U.S. fixed income, represented by the Bloomberg U.S. Aggregate Index. The portfolio is rebalanced annually. Average asset allocation investor return is based on an analysis by Dalbar, Inc., which utilizes the net of aggregate mutual fund sales, redemptions and exchanges each month as a measure of investor behavior. Guide to the Markets—U.S. Data are as of September 30, 2022.

You can see similar outcomes if you consult Morningstar, which is considered one of the best sources of reliable data on index returns, mutual funds, and ETFs. There you can find the phenomenon of investors not realizing the potential *of their own investments* when you look at what they do with their portfolios. For example, if you look up a mutual fund, you will see annualized returns over various periods such as five years, ten years, or even since the inception of the investment. At the same time, you can look up what the average investor actually realized during those same periods[17]. The difference between investment return and investor return is often significant; investors don't even earn what their own investments provide! It's because of what people *do*. They're not invested for the whole ten—or twenty—year period that is being compared.

It's hard to hang on when the markets are volatile, or when a fund underperforms other investments for a year or two, but research has demonstrated that over time markets recover and those who are patient come out ahead. And it typically takes a surprisingly short time to recover. As you will see in the chart below, the 25 best days in the market came within one month of the 25 worst days (AMG Funds, *A Long-Term Perspective*).

---

17   This is another reason why choosing investments based on their three-, five-, or ten-year performance doesn't tell you much. Remember the example of Steve in the discussion of sequence of return risk? He probably compared the two investments and sold the one that was "underperforming" when he was about 57 years old. The **investment** did just fine, but if he did what so many others tend to do, **he** didn't actually earn the average rate of return of 7% on **his** account.

REMAINING INVESTED IS CRITICAL.

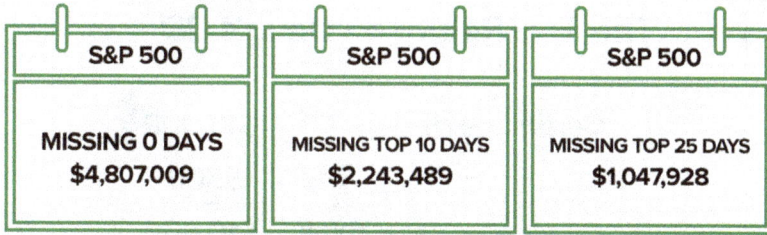

S&P 500	S&P 500	S&P 500
MISSING 0 DAYS $4,807,009	MISSING TOP 10 DAYS $2,243,489	MISSING TOP 25 DAYS $1,047,928

IF $1,000,000 HAD BEEN INVESTED ON JANUARY 1, 1999 THROUGH DECEMBER 31, 2022, MISSING EVEN A FEW OF THE MARKETS BEST DAYS WOULD HAVE DRAMATICALLY IMPACTED RETURNS.

Clouded Memories

Despite a bull market beginning in 2009, most people still believe that it was a down year. It did indeed start off terribly, losing another 15% after plunging 39% just the year before. Yet by the end of 2009, the market actually rose 23% for that entire year. In order to do that, it had to recover the 15% it lost before it could go back up. Investors who still believe 2009 was a down year are "anchoring" to what happened the previous year. This is a common mistake when investors attach themselves to past market performance.

Perception isn't always right. It's been almost 15 years since the financial crisis, yet for many investors, it feels like it just happened yesterday. That's why a financial plan with ongoing wealth management is so important. It keeps you anchored in reality and helps mitigate the negative effects of acting on perception.

The Downside to Stability: It's Riskier Than You Might Realize

The Real Return on Doug's CD	
Certificate of Deposit:	$10,000
5%:	+$500
Total:	$10,500
25% Tax:	-($125)
Net After Taxes:	$10,375
Less 4% Inflation:	-($400)
New After Inflation:	$9,975
Net Purchasing Power LOSS:	= ($25)

Focusing on keeping your money safe can produce riskier results. Let's take the example of Doug, who explained that since he couldn't afford to lose any of his principal, he had all his money in CD's. He was getting a 5% rate of return and was very satisfied with what he believed was a safe, conservative strategy.

Unfortunately, Doug was not keeping all 5%. The CD's were not sheltered or tax-exempt, so he was losing about 25% to federal and state income taxes, bringing the return down to 3.75%. Taking the 4% inflation rate into consideration, we can determine that he is actually losing purchasing power each year. If he were to do this year after year, he would lose a lot of money because it would cost him more to buy the same services or goods.

Don't confuse *stable* with *safe*. CD's and other fixed-income instruments are stable, but after we account for taxes and inflation, they are not always safe. Too often people look at pre-tax returns on fixed investments and fail to consider this type of insidious risk. Unfortunately, we cannot escape risk; it's not something you can decide to live without. You just have to decide which risk(s) you are willing to take and have the capacity to weather. While I don't believe risk tolerance can be determined with a questionnaire[18], risk capacity can be measured.

It's also important to recognize the risks inherent in different investment *structures*. Risk can be sneaky and hide in places you'd never expect. Annuities are a perfect example. Many people glaze over when the subject comes up, but the idea is fairly simple: In concept, a fixed annuity[xiv] is similar to a (tax deferred) CD. Fixed Annuities are long-term insurance contracts and there is typically a surrender charge imposed during the first 5 to 7 years that you own the annuity contract. Variable annuities[xv] can also have surrender charges and offer tax deferred subaccounts similar to mutual funds. Withdrawals prior to age 59—½ may result in a 10% IRS tax penalty, in addition to any ordinary income tax on the gains if it is held outside of a retirement account (pre-tax retirement accounts are subject to tax on 100% of the distributions). Any guarantees of the annuity are backed by the financial strength of the underlying insurance company. These vehicles are touted as very safe. If you buy them expecting a guaranteed income, you can decide how much you'll need by a certain date, turn on the annuity, and sleep soundly, knowing you'll receive your monthly payment as promised. What could be risky about that?

---

18 Risk Tolerance questionnaires are often used by advisors to gauge an investor's reaction to potential future situations. They are often required by compliance managers and regulators. In my opinion, these questionnaires do a poor job of predicting responses to market volatility--both down and up. Behavioral finance recognizes that we are not mathematical animals; we are emotional beings. Answering 10 or 20 questions on a piece of paper when nothing is at stake can lead to misleading conclusions. This is why I believe measuring risk capacity is far more relevant.

One problem is that fixed annuities are not great inflation hedges, and they are not as liquid as other alternatives. Once you've turned on the tap to convert your investment contract into a payment plan, you've lost access to your principal, *and there is no turning back.* The traditional annuity guarantees a specific payout each month; in fact, traditional pension plans (which are becoming as extinct as dinosaurs) are often funded by annuities. However, since that payment amount is based on today's interest rates, it's unlikely that it's going to be enough income ten years from now.

Variable annuities can be an effective financial vehicle to manage inflation risk depending on how the subaccounts are invested. Riders on the annuity can also provide guaranteed income even if the subaccounts have lost money. These "living benefits" can be complicated and very expensive. They need to be managed to optimize the benefits so it's not a waste of money.

For the record, I'm not against annuities per se. If you are in a high tax bracket, annuities can be effective and appropriate in certain situations, but only for a portion of the portfolio and if nothing else works. For example, I've had some clients who were just on the edge of financial demise but could not tolerate the fluctuations that come from having money in the stock market. If, during periods of volatility, someone wants to sell everything and move their investments to cash and even bonds—and those projected rates of return almost guarantee running out of money—*then getting a net return that was chewed to death by fees might have to be acceptable.* It's like a mutual fund portfolio with a net underneath, but it's important to know that the guarantees are only as good as the insurance company providing them. Stick with highly rated carriers who have tons of reserves to back up their promise. The rate of return on the investments will probably be about 3% lower than the same funds outside of the annuity wrapper, but if things don't work out, you can turn on a tap to create a stream of income similar to a pension.

Here's where the brain hack comes in: even with their higher (often hidden) fees and complicated features, nervous investors might be more inclined to invest in riskier growth-oriented assets knowing that they have an annuity that will cover their expenses. This approach can be an effective way of bridging the gap between investment return and living expenses, creating an extra layer of safety. It can also make the money last a little bit longer than having everything in a conservative allocation that may not provide the needed returns. Just keep in mind that the net return (after fees and expenses) is what matters.

A Potentially Fatal Risk: A Case Study

Inflation is an insidious risk that affects everyone, but in different ways. It's also hard to quantify on a personal level. For example, services tend to inflate faster than goods. Therefore, as people age, they will often feel inflation more than the younger generation, because they have most of the goods they need to survive but they may need more help around the house or with their healthcare. Earlier we used an example of someone needing $60,000 per year with inflation at 3%. In just 5 years, that same person needs $69,556 to buy what she did just a few years earlier, and $80,365 in just 10 years.

Consider a fifty-year-old widow named Susan. She has a $500,000 portfolio earning 7% annually. Let's assume she needs $25,000 to live on each year and inflation is 6%. Bear with me on this—even though inflation spiked to 9.1% in the post-COVID-19 economy of 2022 and averaged closer to 3%, we're going to use 6%. I know inflation hasn't averaged 6% for many years, but none of us knows the future, *and this risk can be very sticky.* Let's remember that inflation measures price increases, so if inflation is low—for example, 2%—that means that prices increased overall by 2% from the year before—*they did not go back down to previous levels.* (Keep that in mind when you hear the inflation rate is "going down".)

By comparison, stock and bond markets can also be categorized as risky because values fluctuate and are often volatile. What makes market risk sticky is if you need or choose to sell the stocks or bond and recognize those lower values, *creating an actual permanent loss.* Inflation, on the other hand, **just is**.

Susan's Inflation Risk

Portfolio:	$500,000
7% Annual Return:	$35,000
Living Expenses (5%):	$25,000
Excess Return:	$10,000

Looking Good!

However, 6% inflation rate will cut purchasing power in half every 12 years

Purchasing Power

Age	Principal	Return
50	$500,000	$35,000
62	$250,000	$17,500
74	$125,000	$8,750
86	$62,500	$4,375

Back to Susan. Initially, her 7% return is beating that 6% inflation rate. She has $35,000 coming in and only needs $25,000 to live, so she's feeling very secure or, as my kids would say, "She's living *large.*"

If we look into the future, however, we see that *she is living with a false sense of security.*

The Rule of 72 can be utilized to determine how many years it takes to double your money at a specific rate of return. It can also be used to determine how long it will take to reduce the purchasing power of your money by half.

To see the impact of inflation on Susan's capital, we take seventy-two and divide it by the 6% inflation rate. In this example, her income and principal will lose half their purchasing power every twelve years. By age sixty-two, Susan will be spending her principal as if it were $250,000, while the income it generates is worth only $17,500. You can see in the Inflation Risk chart above that if she lives to eighty-six, her principal in today's dollars is only worth $62,500 and the purchasing power of the income will be $4,375 today.

That's the tragedy of inflation. People run out of money.

Why? Because chances are that Susan won't just keep collecting the 7% yield; *she won't be able to live on just that.* I typically get calls from clients around year eight, and the conversation goes like this: "Patti, I'm worried. I feel like my investments aren't generating enough income, and I'm beginning to dip into principal." *This woman has every right to be worried*; she'll be out of money soon after she hits seventy.

Inflation is like hypertension. You can't feel it, but over time it can kill you.

Think about your portfolio as if it's an apple tree. While you're working, you're feeding it, exposing it to sunlight and even storms so it can be more resilient and grow over time. As it gets bigger, it sprouts more branches, and the new branches get stronger because they're sheltered by the others. That's the benefit of asset allocation, a topic we'll discuss in the next chapter. The larger tree with more branches also bears more fruit.

When you retire, you start living off the fruit. But inflation means the tree has to keep growing taller because you'll need more fruit in the future; otherwise, you'll have to start taking down the branches, like the woman who had to dip into her principal. Fewer branches will leave her with less fruit, and soon she'll be left with just the trunk.

You can prevent that by taking inflation into account when you set up your investment targets. Let's go back to Susan: In this case, we know that she needs 5% of the portfolio for living expenses ($25,000 divided by $500,000 is 5%), and we know that inflation is 6%. That means Susan needs to have an 11% target rate of return to reduce the possibility of running out of money one day. If we can reach that target, she will continue to receive her 5% income while we reinvest 6% into the principal so the base increases with inflation. When we do that, her income automatically grows by that same 6% each year and Susan will never have to dip into her principal.

Okay, now you can all get up off the floor. In today's economic environment, we don't need to achieve an 11% return because *inflation has not averaged 6% for decades.* Perhaps now you can understand why the Federal Reserve's target for inflation is 2%. Replacing the 6% number with the 2% rate means we have a new total rate of return target of 7%. That might seem a little high but can be doable over time. In this case, *it has to be.*

"Riskless" Investments

When it comes to investing, risk is going to be lurking in the shadows everywhere you go. Earlier, I referred to a CD as a guarantee, but there is no such thing as a riskless investment. That's why most people who are retired and living on their capital still need a portion of it diversified into equities.

Each day, news outlets report on what happened in the market that day, typically hyping up reasons why it is just bound to go down. But in addition to market risk there is also inflation risk, credit risk, opportunity costs, reinvestment risk, and currency risk, to name a few others. On the business side, unforeseeable events can occur that affect one company but may not impact others in the same sector. To take this further, concentration in one or two sectors leads to regulatory and political risks, as the drug and biotech companies have had to learn over time. Finally, if you own (supposedly) safe bonds, what about the risk of defaults, or the risk of wanting to sell a bond that no one wants to buy? In various types of investments that's called liquidity risk, and typically the seller must keep cutting the price to unload it. Liquidity risk is in many types of investments; just ask people who owned property in Florida during the 2008 financial crisis.

You can't avoid risk, but you can decide exactly which risks you are willing (and need) to accept.

The Most Important Tool We Have: Time

You have learned that the timing of your financial needs will play a major role in your portfolio. Cash-flow timing risk has a large influence on portfolio performance.

It is generally understood that the higher the return, the higher the risk, but what many don't realize is that risk is a function of time. *Investors need to take on a lot more risk to get a 6% return over twelve months than if they are looking for a 6% average return over ten years*[19]. The longer the time frame, the less risk is involved achieving the

---

19   Unless stated otherwise, when "average" returns are discussed in this book, I am using time weighted geometric (compounded) returns.

returns needed to make the plan work. That's why using the Three Pools of Money system is so powerful. The first pool gives you the time you need to ride out normal volatility in the markets, with a buffer in Pool 2. The key is to keep monitoring the Three Pools as you begin taking distributions—this is not a set-it-and-forget-it system.

Remember that working with the Pools of Money approach before you need to start living off your portfolio doesn't mean you never rebalance or touch the portfolio; that's a recipe for a different kind of disaster. It's important to monitor how your investments are doing and tweak when necessary.

There is one more very important benefit to this methodology: It's called sleep. Lack of sleep can contribute to emotional reactions, fear and impulsive mistakes that can turn out to be very expensive. Too many Americans are underinvested because of the trauma caused by the tech bubble, the financial crisis, and more recently COVID-19. Unfortunately, they are taking an even bigger risk. Even though interest rates have risen, these people are almost guaranteed to be underfunded when it comes time to retire, stay retired, and provide for their own healthcare.

It's really about execution. If you systematize your investments into three pools of capital, you can let your money grow when the market is on a tear, allowing you to live the life you planned for—even when the market isn't growing at all. Like many concepts, it's practical and simple but not easy. If you can't set it up yourself, find someone who will do it for you.

Keep It Rational: Back to the Obvious Risks

Five biggest market declines and subsequent five-year periods (1929-2023)							
Periods of Decline	Decline	S&P 500 Index 12-month returns (%)					Average Annual total return for the 5-year period
		1st Year after low	2nd Year	3rd Year	4th Year	5th Year	
9/7/29-6/1/32	-89.2	137.6	0.5	6.4	56.7	46.5	35.9
3/6/37-4/28/42	-60.0	64.3	9.0	31.1	32.2	-19.9	20.0
1/11/73-10/3/74	-48.2	44.4	26.0	-2.9	11.8	12.8	17.4
3/24/00-19/9/02	-49.1	36.2	9.9	8.5	15.1	18.1	17.2
10/9/07-3/9/09	-56.8	72.3	18.1	6.1	15.7	23.6	25.3
Average		70.7	12.7	9.8	26.3	10.2	23.1

Indices are unmanaged and investors cannot invest directly in an index (Capital Group, Guide to Stock Market Recoveries)[20]

Since the Great Depression, we've had five very bad bear markets, with losses of anywhere from 50% to 86%. It's human nature to want to sell when everyone else is selling—no one wants to be left

---

[20] Market downturns are based on the five largest declines in the S&P 500's value (excluding dividends and/or distributions with 50% recovery after each decline). The return for each of the five years after a low if a 12-month return based on the date of the low. For example, the first year after the most recent decline displayed is the 12-month period from 3/9/09 to 3/9/10. The percentage decline is based on the index value of the unmanaged S&P 500, excluding dividends and/or distributions.

behind—but even these awful declines were temporary, and markets did recover. If you can remember that annual returns five years after the six worst bear markets (including the Great Depression!) averaged 23% you will be less likely to sell good assets when you don't need to. If you follow the Pools of Money process, you'll have plenty of dry powder and you should *never* need to. Don't make the terminal mistake of not having a system in place, panicking, and missing out on the recoveries.

But let's just assume you can't take it anymore and you decide to get out of the market when it's going down. Eventually you'll realize, as most people do, that there's going to come a time when you'll need to get back in. The absolute best time to add securities back to your portfolio *is when things are even worse* than when you sold!

Bottom line: If your financial future is resting on anything above a 2% or 3% return, some of your portfolio needs to be in a diversified portfolio of stocks, preferably in stock mutual funds or ETFs, knowing that at any time, you could face market losses of 20%, 30% or more.

Chris Davis of Davis Investments quotes his equally famous father Shelby Davis as saying, "You make most of your money in a bear market; you just don't know it at the time." In other words, think of it as you would a sale; most of us just love getting a deal.

How does that work with your money? Whenever possible, the key is to rebalance the portfolio *into*—and in spite of—the bear market. You take that buffer money in Pool 1 and Pool 2 that you aren't going to need right now and invest when everyone else is selling. This is one of those times when you really have to stop overthinking. *Yes*, while it's happening, things *are* bad, *and they could get worse.* The latest pundit is probably predicting the next apocalyptic depression, and yes, unemployment is going to soar. Rebalance anyway. You may be early; you may be late. Either way, you will be right.

Unfortunately, people often sell in bear markets, with perfectly rational reasons for doing so. *It's the rare investor who is willing to jump back into the stock market when things are even worse than they were when the investor sold.* During the financial crisis, three of our smart well-informed friends sold some or all of their equities in 2008 when the Dow dropped to 8,000. Honestly, that looked brilliant when it dropped to 6,500 in March 2009. The problem is that they didn't even think about getting back in until the Dow hit 10,000 in 2010, and two of them didn't actually pull the trigger until after it hit 12,000.

The thing to remember is that markets are completely unpredictable over short periods of time. They will get bumpy, but that's not the time to change your investment strategy. If you are going to invest in any market, it is important to accept the fact that there will to be times when your statements show losses. You are going to lose principal (on paper), or at least end a period lower than where you started and feel like prior returns just evaporated into thin air. There is a saying that the market goes up like an escalator but drops like an elevator. And when it's dropping, *it feels like the cables snapped* without warning. At first you wonder what's happening, then it accelerates, and as it's plummeting, it's natural for panic to set in. But selling during a bear market is about as logical as trying to jump just before the elevator hits the ground, thinking you won't get hurt!

On average, from 1900 to 2020 the market lost 5% about three times a year. The average length of those declines was forty-seven days. The market lost 10% about once a year, 15% about every two years, and 20% on average every five to seven years. Typical bear markets—losses of 20% to 40%—have lasted about 11 months and have taken 14 months to break even (J.P. Morgan Asset Management, *Guide to the*

Markets). Mega meltdowns of over 40% lasted just short of two years, and full recovery took 58 months (Carlson, *9 Facts to Know*). Keep in mind that if you rebalanced in the midst of the chaos on the way back to breaking even, you would benefit from a climbing market. That's why rebalancing in a bear market can turbocharge your portfolio, helping you to recover much faster.

All this means that when you invest in the market, whether it is in a mutual fund, an ETF or even your favorite stock—do so understanding you are probably going to lose money during the year. But you don't need to do anything about it because you know that's what has happened historically. Eventually, the market recovered. The problem is that <u>no one</u> can guarantee *it will* or give you any idea *when it will*. If you're not watching it every day, you probably won't even know a decline happened and you won't feel the need to jump. Jumping doesn't work in elevators, and it is a terrible long-term approach to the health of your portfolio.

A Real and Recent Case Study: Why You Should Always be Ready

Chances are you've heard the phrase "Think long-term" many times; it almost sounds trite, <u>if not a little bit patronizing</u>. *Here's why*: most people don't live in the long term. You live in the here and now, and you're often exposed to scary headlines, screaming newscasters, and clickbait.

I get it. But they don't know what's going to happen or even how <u>you</u> might be affected, *if at all*. Time is the most important portfolio management tool you have.

Let's look at recent history. At the end of 2018, economic indicators were pointing to a looming recession. It seemed like we were hearing about a phenomenon called an "inverted yield curve" every hour of the day. This curve occurs when long-term interest rates on treasuries fall below rates with shorter maturities. Think of it this way: if you go to the bank to purchase a CD, it is reasonable to expect that one maturing ten years from now will pay a higher interest rate than one maturing in three or six months. When the opposite occurs, the curve is said to "invert." In theory, an inverted yield curve is a statistic that has a striking record of predicting every recession since 1950[21].

In a situation like this, if you had a financial plan in place, you didn't panic because you had a system for managing and rebalancing your portfolio in spite of the chaos, as well as monitoring the Three Pools of Money. You had a sense of what you were going to need, and you had that money earmarked to cover your cash flow and any income taxes you had to pay. You may not have changed a single thing, but you became a little more aware of the assets in Pool 1 and Pool 2 that could ensure you were ready for the next bear market.

In 2019, the Federal Reserve stopped increasing interest rates and eventually lowered them. The market pivoted quickly, and the S&P 500 returned 28%. Remember: the stock market is just one of the ten leading indicators[22]; it tends to go up or down about nine months prior to a perceived economic event, *but it isn't always right about* the future of the economy. Sure enough, at the start of 2020, the economy miraculously turned around.

---

21   There are plenty of caveats to that theory, including the fact that we are talking about a *very* limited data set: *less than 20 recessions have actually occurred in those 70 years.* Also, I have a really hard time looking back and crediting to the inverted yield curve in 2018 for predicting the recession in 2020 when the catalyst was actually a virus originating halfway around the world. Besides, those who sold equities based on its predictive value completely missed out on two amazing years of stock market returns. Isn't that what really matters?

22   The U.S. Conference Board publishes a leading index to measure factors that could help determine what is going to happen in the future. Keep in mind, it isn't always right.

"Ah… But wait, Patti, look at what happened in 2020!" you say. Yes, in April you might have been wishing you had sold in 2018, but if you didn't, you were rewarded for your patience and long-term perspective. *And by the way, it would have been too late to sell anyway.* By the end of 2020, despite the pandemic lockdown, the S&P 500 achieved an 18.37% return.

The Pools of Money system that worked before can work again, and while we now know the outcome of the 2018 scare, the only thing you needed to focus on while it was happening was having six years of cash flow in Pool 1 and Pool 2. It wasn't necessary to change asset allocations or sell equities in 2018. With a total return on the S&P 500 of 28% in 2019, selling would have reduced returns—and the value of your portfolio—significantly. Yes, we did have a recession due to the pandemic and the economic lockdowns in 2020, *but that had absolutely nothing to do with the inverted yield curve,* and by the end of that year the S&P 500 still returned 18.37%! The Three Pools of Money system ensured that those who employed it and relied on distributions from their portfolio had money available for the next six years, no matter what the markets were about to do.

CHAPTER 4

Leveraging Tactics for a Measure of Safety

Start where you are; the rest is history. Everything has a beginning. With investments, that beginning starts with saving money in the first place. Initially, the increases are so modest that you wonder why you're even trying, but growth becomes exponential if you just stick with it. The "Penny Saved" chart below illustrates how just one penny, doubled every day for thirty days, results in a savings of more than $5 million by the end of the month[xvi].

THE POWER OF COMPOUNDING

DOUBLE ONE PENNY EACH DAY FOR 30 DAYS AND SEE IT GROW TO OVER $5 MILLION

DAY 1	$0.01
DAY 2	$0.02
DAY 3	$0.04
DAY 4	$0.08
DAY 5	$0.16
DAY 6	$0.32
DAY 7	$0.64
DAY 8	$1.28
DAY 9	$2.56
DAY 10	$5.12
DAY 11	$10.24
DAY 12	$20.48
DAY 13	$40.96
DAY 14	$81.92
DAY 15	$163.84
DAY 16	$327.68
DAY 17	$655.36
DAY 18	$1,310.72
DAY 19	$2,621.44
DAY 20	$5.242.88
DAY 21	$10,485.76
DAY 22	$20,971.52
DAY 23	$41,943.04
DAY 24	$83,866.08
DAY 25	$167,772.16
DAY 26	$335,544.32
DAY 27	$671,088.64
DAY 28	$1,342,177.28
DAY 29	$2,684,354.56
DAY 30	$5,368,709.12

This is, of course, an extreme example—no one is going to get a daily 100% rate of return on their investments—but compounding really does grow wealth over time. The earlier you start, the easier it is to reach your goal because at some point your money starts doing the saving for you. You'll notice that the compounding starts off slowly, but then on about Day 25, *the value escalates rapidly and begins to look like that hockey stick shown previously.* Time is like that upright portion of the hockey stick, and the money is doing the saving for you. The biggest obstacle here is impatience. *You have to stay in it for the first 25 days to get the leverage of the last five.*

There are two approaches to finding the money to save. The first is to develop an acute awareness of your daily, weekly, and monthly expenses. Once those are defined (note that I am not using that dreaded word "budget"), you can determine a realistic amount to set aside. People are notorious for overestimating income and underestimating spending, so this knowledge can provide a solid foundation to build upon. By using it to guide savings and investment choices, you can make more focused and logical decisions.

The second approach is simpler, though it might allow leakage and waste. Here you define what the end goal is, figure out what you need to save to achieve that goal realistically, and spend whatever is left. You are basically earmarking the money for the objective you're putting it toward. The earlier example of how Ed and I saved to send our four children to college was what worked for us. It still takes discipline to save, and it's better if those earmarks are completely automated. This approach can be especially powerful for busy households like the Brennan family.

Beware of Benchmarks

Your portfolio needs to align with your values, goals, and resources—*not those of the guy at the desk next to you* or compared to some arbitrary benchmark. The S&P 500 *doesn't care* whether you want to put your kids through college, buy the dream home, or fund an extraordinary vacation. It also doesn't care if you run out of money. *The journalist* writing that article on investments that you read this morning doesn't care either[23]. When you have a plan, you can establish the returns you need, as well as the level of risk you are willing to—and can—take.

Sitting on Cash

What should you do if you come into a large sum of money and don't know what to do with it? Maybe you've received an inheritance or sold a business or taken a lump-sum pension payout. It's human nature to look at the current economic environment and think that it's a terrible time to invest. When markets are up, your inner voice tells you that it might be time for a downturn, and in the midst of a crisis, that same voice says, "Cash is king." In both scenarios, wouldn't it make sense to hold on to the cash and invest it slowly—for example, monthly over a period of 12 or 18 months? This approach is a systematic implementation strategy called dollar cost averaging (or DCA) and is one way to avoid investing all your cash either at a peak market value or when things are uncertain.

According to research done by Vanguard, on average, money invested immediately as a lump sum outperformed the dollar cost averaging approach (Vanguard, *Lump-sum Investing versus Cost Averaging*). Depending on the asset allocation, the immediate investment outperformed systematic strategies between 65% and 68% of the time. Even more striking, on a yearly basis, immediate investment outperformed systematic investment by about 2.4% per year.

I know what you're thinking. "That's easy for you to say, Patti, it's not your money! I don't think I could invest it all at one time and sleep at night."

---

23   This is *not* a knock against journalists. With word count pressure and drop-dead deadlines, their hands are tied. As I write this to you, even having the freedom of enough pages to fill an entire book can be challenging!

And I understand that. Distributing the investment a little over time can feel much safer, even if it may not be. Many investors are willing to give up a little bit in potential earnings in return for a good night's sleep. In that case, I'd still recommend that you try to invest the capital within a year, and even that depends on where the money is parked. When interest rates are at generational lows, it just makes sense to get cash into something with some return potential. If they are higher, a longer period might be more comforting.

Another Case Study: Why Asset Allocation Is Usually a Better Approach

Here is a story of couple Todd and Mary. They each have $100,000 to invest.

Todd heard that over the long term you couldn't go wrong if you stuck with the stock market, so he decided to put the entire $100,000 into a blue chip stock—that is stock in a large well-established company that has operated for many years and has an excellent reputation (this designation has no bearing on the performance of its stock price).

Mary, on the other hand, didn't know a lot about investing, so she spread her money around. She ended up investing her $100,000 equally across five different asset classes: Commodities, "a hot stock," municipal bonds, the S&P 500 index and a new technology company.

So, what were the results?

Todd's Investment:			
Initial Investment	(Hypothetical Asset)	Return	Value in 20 Years
$100,000	Blue Chip Stock	8%	$466,095
		Total:	**$466,095**
Mary's Investment:			
Initial Investment	(Hypothetical Investment)	Return	Value in 20 Years
$20,000	Oil & Gas	(-100%)	$0 (Total Loss)
$20,000	"A Hot Stock"	0%	$20,000
$20,000	Muni Bonds	5%	$53,066
$20,000	S&P 500 Index	10%	$134,550
$20,000	A "Tech Bet"	15%	$327,331
		Total:	**$534,947**

Todd did well and earned 8% compounded over twenty years, turning his $100,000 investment into $466,095. Mary's first investment pick was not what she hoped for—the well was dry, and she lost *all* of her money in that investment. The second one, "a hot stock," ended up not being hot, but she did get her principal back. The third investment, in municipal bonds, fared just so-so, but she did get income from it. The S&P 500 Index fund did well, but it was the tech bet that was the real winner. So, despite three out of five of her investments doing poorly by comparison to Todd's investment, Mary ended up with more money.

How did that happen? We've all heard about this thing called asset allocation, <u>but what is the underlying principle that makes it so effective?</u> Take a look at Mary's portfolio. What is the maximum amount of money she could have lost in any single investment? It's $20,000, right? When asked, most people get that part right: don't put all your eggs in one basket.

But that's only *part* of the answer. The benefit is revealed when we ask the next question: What's the maximum amount of money they could have earned? It's unlimited. When designing a portfolio, you want to make sure you limit your downside *but not your upside.*

In the previous chapter, we talked about how a loss impacts a portfolio more than a gain. It's virtually impossible to pick the winners consistently. As in a baseball game, even a star hitter may go through an extended period of striking out. It's up to the other players to step up with great defense and a few hits of their own. *Home runs are exciting, but the key to winning a baseball game is getting more people on base.* You do that with walks, singles, and doubles. It's the same with investing.

Todd and Mary's comparison is just a hypothetical example: I've randomly selected the types of investments and returns to illustrate a powerful point. While my numbers may not actually reflect those types of investments during any particular twenty-year period, the principles behind Mary's success are the basis for a portfolio approach that can fuel the financial plan[24].

Are Diversification and Asset Allocation the Same Thing?

You've probably heard a lot about the importance of the principle of diversification. You can be diversified holding twenty stocks, or even one mutual fund or ETF, but diversification and asset allocation are not the same. If those diversified assets are all highly correlated, that means they respond very similarly to the same economic events. In other words, those investments are likely dangerously concentrated, so when one goes down, they all do. In a well-balanced portfolio, you want asset classes that are negatively correlated and do different things under the same set of circumstances. When it comes to compound-

---

24   Remember: Portfolio management is just one of many tools in a *real* financial plan.

ing and real wealth accumulation, *it's probably the only time when something negative is actually positive.*

Asset allocation is the *how* that fuels a diversified portfolio with purpose and intention.

A well-allocated portfolio takes diversification to the next level, kind of like a coach does when he picks players for his baseball team. Everyone knows that pitchers are not always great hitters, but being at bat isn't the role they play on the team. The coach understands the principle of asset allocation. You can't win a game without players who can hit a fastball, but you also need great pitching. You need both to win consistently.

That same coach also knows that players go through slumps. The roster of a professional team typically has five starting pitchers and seven relief pitchers, including a couple of closers. The coach has "diversified" his "asset class" of pitchers.

Can Soccer Teach Us Something About Portfolio Management?

A market outcome is simply the result of millions of trades representing the opinions of the people making them. Unless we can read minds, it is impossible to know all the mental gyrations that go into creating these opinions. Decisions are often made in nanoseconds, or by someone's very complicated algorithm.

What's that got to do with soccer? Bear with me.

In soccer, there is typically a player designated to take penalty shootouts and sudden death kicks. For human beings, when there is a lot at stake, there is an *inevitable urge to do something.* As they prepare for the game, the kicker and his coach will have analyzed the stats from prior games, looking for the number of times the goalie dives left versus dives right. Meanwhile, the opposing goalie has studied similar films, watching for the lean of the body and angle of the dominant leg as the kicker approaches the ball.

The outcomes are actually quite interesting: almost a 50/50 split in terms of the kicker choosing to target the left or right side of the goalie. As fate would have it, sometimes the kicker's team will score when his guess happens to be accurate. Occasionally, the goalie too will guess correctly resulting in a blocked shot. Sometimes, however, as a result of focusing the target too narrowly, the kicker actually increases the margin for error and misses the goal altogether.

Sometimes the goalie dives left, sometimes, right.

That's not really the point of the story. These are *professional* athletes. If the kickers were in tune with this thing called "human nature," they'd know that trying to read the goalie's mind is futile. Research has indicated that when shooters simply kicked high and, in the middle, a goal was scored over 90% of the time. An astute kicker understands that *whether the goalie dives to the left or to the right is irrelevant because either way, the center of the goal is likely to be vacant.*

So, let's not overthink these things, or pretend to know how to read the mind of the market. Just "kick it high and in the middle," so you can win the game. The key comes down to how you weight the different asset classes. You want a mix that gives you the highest probability of achieving the return you need to meet the objectives that are most important to you. *Think of asset allocation as the equivalent of kicking it high and in the middle.*

The Many Problems with Relying on Past Performance

Herd mentality is often counterintuitive. Fund flows published monthly on sites like YCharts.com help to demonstrate that investors have a remarkable ability to sell low and buy high, capturing losses and missing out on recoveries and further gains.

When choosing funds, most investors base their decisions on a fund's past performance. They look at how it has performed recently and assume it will continue to perform at that level going forward. In some areas, that makes a lot of sense. For example, a top university will likely remain a top university, a good neighborhood will continue to be a good neighborhood, and our favorite chef will rarely disappoint. We rely on past experiences to forecast the future in other areas of life, so why not for financial investments? Because it's actually one of the worst ways to pick an investment, a methodology that often leads to disappointment.

There's a reason your windshield is much larger than your rearview mirror. What you just passed is irrelevant going forward; you want to keep your eyes on what's ahead of you. The same goes for your portfolio.

It's rare to find a fund manager who is consistently in the top quartile year after year. Quartiles measure performance against peers. Persistency of performance relative to peers in the same category is what is relevant here; otherwise, a high score could just be a sugar high. What was it that made that manager or fund outperform over a period of time? What is the likelihood that the next ten years are going to be like the last ten years?

As you see in the following chart, research has shown that although fund managers who are in the bottom quartile rarely rise above that level—meaning it's best to avoid those funds—managers in the top quartile are more likely to fall into the second or third than they are to remain on top (Ptak, *Setting the Record Straight*).

Over a ten-year period, 83% of active funds in the United States didn't even match their chosen benchmarks, much less beat them. In fact, 40% did so poorly that they were dissolved before the decade was over. Another statistic to note: 64% of funds drifted away from their originally declared style of investing, which could have a negative impact on an investor's portfolio if that particular fund were chosen to fill a particular risk/return (Ellis, *The End of Active Investing?*).

Starting Overall Rating	Morningstar Rating of Next 10 Years of Performance					Merged	Liquidated
	1	2	3	4	5		
1	8%	9%	9%	3%	2%	48%	21%
2	7%	14%	14%	7%	2%	41%	16%
3	6%	14%	22%	11%	3%	30%	14%
4	6%	14%	25%	17%	6%	21%	11%
5	8%	13%	22%	21%	14%	13%	9%

(Ptak, Setting the Record Straight)

Yes, it's counterintuitive, but all this means that if you choose only top quartile funds because you think they are most likely to beat a particular benchmark, you are more likely to be disappointed than if you were to choose a second or even third quartile fund that has held that spot year after year, as long as that fund meets your needs.

Choosing Investments and Capture Ratios

If past performance is such a poor guide, how do you filter through all the choices? When looking at the performance of any investment, a better approach is to measure outcomes called capture ratio. This tells you how much of a market's possible upside a stock or fund was able to realize, as well as how much of its downside it was able to avoid. As always, it's only a guide, not a guarantee that these attributes or performance will continue. Monitoring is key.

And by the way, if you don't want to bother trying to find those gifted superstar stocks or managers—and yes, there are more out there than you might think—you can simply choose a low-cost index fund. Index funds can serve as a proxy for the market in which you want exposure. There is no analysis of the underlying companies or a manager buying and selling stocks; an index fund is built on the premise that no one can cherry-pick winners consistently, so it buys all of them. And in the end, the actual mutual or index funds don't matter nearly as much as the asset allocation of the total portfolio.

Basics on Bonds: Do They Have a Place[xvii]?

Let's reframe the discussion around fixed income investments like bonds. Even though interest rates have risen, many investors looked at the recent historically low bond rates and wondered why they should even bother with these "losers." Here's why: Investing in bonds should not be viewed solely as a source of return. Instead, they are diversifiers in the portfolio and a means to smooth out stock market risk.

Historically, and depending on the type of fixed income investment, they can hold their value, and their prices can rise as stocks go down. Think of these assets as you would insurance; you almost don't want to collect, but when stocks go down, you'll often find yourself grateful that you included them in your portfolio.

Bonds have provided a measure of capital preservation in periods of market turbulence

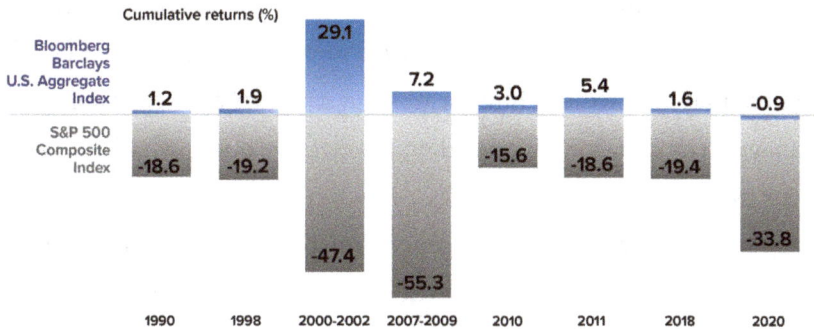

xviii

Let's clarify what might be a basic definition for some of you reading this book. What's the difference between a bond and a stock? Here it is: bonds represent debt, stocks represent ownership. If I have a $100,000 thirty-year corporate bond backed by IBM paying 3%, I have loaned that company $100,000. In return, they are going to pay me $1,500 semiannually ($3,000 per year) for thirty years. At the end of the term, IBM will give me my $100,000 back[25].

According to Vanguard, 70% of a bond's total annual return comes from its income component, with only 30% coming from its price (Aliaga-Diaz, *Here's Why Bonds Still Belong in Your Portfolio*).

---

25 Hopefully. Like any loan, that will depend on any number of factors, including whether they are in a position to pay you back.

The consistent interest income in a diversified portfolio of loans is the real reason to invest in bonds. Even though bonds represent debt, keep in mind that blue chip companies and even governments can default on their loans. Typically, though things have to be really dire before they do so. Corporate boards know that their stock will plummet, and their ability to raise cash in the future may be a more expensive proposition if they default. Municipalities have suffered greatly for this misstep. In other words, instead of a 3% or 4% interest rate, the market will require 8% to 10% to warrant the risk that bond holders may not see the interest or even a return of their money. If management decisions forced them to default once, what's to stop them from doing it again?

There are two major influences on bond prices. The first is default risk, which occurs when the entity stops making the interest payments or is unable to give you your money back at maturity. Companies (*and* governments) can go into bankruptcy, insurance entities can go into receivership, and municipalities can break their contractual promise to pay as well. Default risk can be mitigated through diversification and active management[xix] of a bond portfolio, which can reduce the chance of widespread defaults by researching the borrowing entity's creditworthiness.

While that exposure is always there, investors tend to get really hung up on the changing prices of bonds they hold in their portfolios. Yes, rising interest rates typically cause the prices of existing bonds to fall. *But did you ever wonder why?*

It really comes down to choice, which frankly is what defines the concept of the term "market" itself. Why choose to invest in one business (through its stock) or another? It ultimately amounts to the earnings potential of that business in the future, and to *the opinions* of investors who are buying and selling the stock. The person who is selling the stock may need some money and may feel that the price has gotten ahead of itself. The buyer, on the other hand, thinks the best is yet to come. Remember: what happened yesterday or over the past twelve months is done. *Are the factors that have led to that past performance still there?*

Bond prices fluctuate like stock prices do, but the range tends to be tighter. For example, let's assume I've held a particular AAA $100,000 bond for five years and for whatever reason I need to sell it. Lo and behold, it just so happens that you want to buy a bond issued by IBM. Let's also assume that IBM is issuing new bonds and interest rates have risen to 5%. You have two choices: you can buy a brand-new thirty-year bond issued by IBM paying 5%, or you can buy my bond paying 3%. Like any smart investor, you'd prefer the 5% to the 3%, right? But what if I *have* to liquidate because I really need the money? What do I have to do to *entice* you to buy my bond instead of the new issue? What if I offered it to you at a discount—you can pay me $90,000 today, and when it matures, you'll get $100,000 back. Not enticing enough? What if you gave me $85,000?

Bond maturity simply tells you the number of years before the principal payment is due. *Duration* of a bond (or fixed income portfolio) measures the sensitivity of a bond to changes in interest rates. While duration is also quoted in years, it is different from maturity. In general, for every 1% increase in interest rates, the bond price will fall by its duration. If you have a bond that has a duration of five years and interest rates go up 1%, the price goes down by 5%. But what people forget is that the bond is still earning interest, so if it's earning 3%, you have to add that back into the return to get the total return. Instead of a 5% loss, it's really a 2% loss. However, unless you're planning on selling the bond today, that's just a paper loss. You're still receiving the interest payments, and you'll still get your principal back when the bond matures. You will only lose that return if you sell prematurely or the issuer doesn't pay the loan back. And if the reason you bought that bond in the first place hasn't changed, why would you sell it?

Long-term total returns on bonds tend to equal the interest rate the issuer promised to pay when they borrowed the money (often referred to as the coupon). We are coming out of a period of unprecedented low interest rates that *didn't* last for just a year or two. If the interest rate you're getting on your bond is 2%, that's probably a reasonable assumption for total return going forward. But this assumption is based on *that* bond; what about new bonds? Will historical averages hold in today's world, as we are coming out of 2% interest rates and new bonds are paying 4%-5%? It is reasonable to tone down expectations, for example, if you have a portfolio or bond funds that include government, corporate, and even high-yield bonds. While long term bond returns may have been in the range 5% or higher, an assumption of 3%-4% overall long-term return is probably more realistic. That is going to skew a lot of rules of thumb when we're projecting future returns on a balanced portfolio, and it can significantly impact retirement planning.

Just as a stock portfolio is managed, fixed-income portfolios can be aligned to focus on issues whether rates are low or we need them to be more resilient in a rising interest rate environment. Remember that you may want the dry powder a bond portfolio can provide, as well as the income it can generate. When an economy rebounds faster than anyone anticipates (and interest rates rise to combat the inflation that often occurs as a result), you also don't want to invest *all* of your fixed income in investments that fundamentally could lose value during that period of time. Remember too that no one knows what's going to happen in the future: we just want to be prepared for the unknowable. For example, short-term, convertible, floating-rate, and high-yield bonds tend to stay flat or go down when there are threats to the economy. They can be more resilient when interest rates go up. They are not guaranteed, and you certainly don't want your bond portfolio to be totally made up of these bond classes. Adding satellites to a core portfolio often makes sense. Don't go out and sell bonds already in your portfolio before maturity, but as some of your current bonds mature, it may be a good idea to diversify your fixed income into different types of debt for different economic outcomes.

How Economic Sentiment Drives Interest Rates

In 2018 and 2019, everyone was focused on the Federal Reserve's decision to increase interest rates. The Fed only controls very short-term rates; the bond market drives the rate of longer-term maturities.

Okay, what does that really *mean*?

What many people don't realize is that the U.S. bond market is more than twice the size of the U.S. equities market, with more than $42 trillion dollars outstanding compared to the stock market's less than $20 trillion. Most bonds are *not* held to maturity. According to the Securities Industry and Financial Markets Association (SIFMA), $700 billion in bonds trade daily. That's more than three times the $200 billion dollars' worth of stocks that change hands every day (SIFMA, *Fixed Income Outstanding*).

Typically, at issue, bond yields rise in a predictable manner based on their maturity, with three-month Treasuries paying the least and thirty-year Treasuries paying the most. It's like going to the bank to get a CD. You'll get a higher interest rate if you're willing to commit for a longer period. But when bonds are traded, the yield is simply the payout (the interest payments) divided by the price you paid, *not* the maturity value. If demand caused you to pay more for the bond (a "premium") but the payments stayed the same, your yield to maturity (YTM) went down.

For example, when investors begin to believe that the economy is headed toward recession, they will start moving their capital out of riskier investment classes and putting it into the relative safety of long-term fixed-income products. This means *demand*—the competition for a finite number of bonds—causes prices to go up. *Traders fall all over each other to buy* the bonds, bidding up the price, while payouts remain the same. This drives *down* the yield (YTM) of bonds.

If you are looking for a safe haven during a recession, bonds can have a place of honor in a portfolio with several asset classes. Diversification is probably the easiest way to manage risk in portfolio management, and this includes your fixed income portfolio. You can diversify by investing in various maturities, credit worthiness, governments, municipals or even in corporate bonds. If you are worried about interest rates increasing in the future, even short-term bonds (those with maturities of less than five years) earned constant positive returns during the past three tightening cycles. In addition, bondholders who held on to their bonds through those rate hike cycles no matter what the maturity, were rewarded with better returns than those realized by investors who sold their holdings early because they were worried that interest rates were going up. The losses were compounded by two factors: not only did those sellers lose the income the bonds had been generating, but they had to sell the bonds at a discount because the interest rates were lower than those on bonds currently being offered.

Don't make the mistake of forgetting the role bonds are supposed to play. They are your relief pitchers, ready to step in if and when you need them.

Other Asset Classes and Alternatives such as Real Estate, Crypto, and Commodities

Typically, when talking about asset allocation, most advisors focus on the three main asset classes: cash (guaranteed, safe investments), fixed income, and equities. Yet within these broad classes are subcategories, for example, U.S. stocks paying large dividends, or stocks in small or international companies or in the emerging markets. In addition, there is a laundry list of "alternative" investments, including real estate, commodities, hedge funds, private equity, and—dare I forget—bitcoin and other cryptocurrencies[xx].

While I would love to publish a pretty little pie chart with an ideal asset allocation featuring many of the asset classes above, with names of amazing mutual funds and ETFs/stocks, I believe that would be a disservice to you. How to allocate your investments will depend on a whole host of factors and your financial plan. You probably own some good investments, so don't let anyone sell all of your portfolio and stick you into a model with their preferred funds or investments. For one thing, the tax implications need to be understood first, and this has to be coordinated with your other priorities.

You Aren't a Pie Chart

You worked hard for your money, and you want to preserve what you worked hard for. Keeping what you have is just as important as growing your net worth over time. Building wealth is fun. You can track progress and be motivated by the outcomes. Preserving wealth isn't as exciting, but it too has its own set of motivators. It's a little like the carrot and stick; growing assets is the carrot, while working to avoid loss is the stick. The Pools of Money system is the first step in preserving your assets, but there are other threats to your money, such as taxes and insurable losses, which can be permanent.

CHAPTER 5

Taxes: Pain Is Inevitable, Suffering Is Optional

We could refer to taxes as a chronic disease, something we want to avoid altogether, but during the COVID-19 pandemic, we all witnessed the impact of having the government come in and provide relief in the midst of a crisis no one asked for. That was possible because we happen to live in the wealthiest nation in the world, and because our leaders—of both parties on the local, state, and federal levels—and in the Federal Reserve—were willing to spend the money to keep our economic machine running. During a crisis, the goal of government is to reduce the pain that individuals and businesses suffer until the economy can get back on its feet.

THE IMPACT OF TAXES ON COMPOUNDING

	GROSS OF TAXES	NET OF TAXES
DAY 1	$0.01	$0.01
DAY 2	$0.02	$0.02
DAY 3	$0.04	$0.03
DAY 4	$0.08	$0.05
DAY 5	$0.16	$0.08
DAY 6	$0.32	$0.14
DAY 7	$0.64	$0.24
DAY 8	$1.28	$0.41
DAY 9	$2.56	$0.70
DAY 10	$5.12	$1.19
DAY 11	$10.24	$2.02
DAY 12	$20.48	$3.43
DAY 13	$40.96	$5.83
DAY 14	$81.92	$9.90
DAY 15	$163.84	$16.84
DAY 16	$327.68	$28.62
DAY 17	$655.36	$48.66
DAY 18	$1,310.72	$82.72
DAY 19	$2,621.44	$140.63
DAY 20	$5.242.88	$239.07
DAY 21	$10,485.76	$406.42
DAY 22	$20,971.52	$690.92
DAY 23	$41,943.04	$1,174.56
DAY 24	$83,866.08	$1,996.76
DAY 25	$167,772.16	$3,394.49
DAY 26	$335,544.32	$5,770.63
DAY 27	$671,088.64	$9,810.07
DAY 28	$1,342,177.28	$16,677.11
DAY 29	$2,684,354.56	$28,351.09
DAY 30	$5,368,709.12	$48,196.86

PENNY IS DOUBLED EVERY DAY FOR 30 DAYS
30% TAX RATE IS APPLLIED TO PROFIT
EACH DAY

During World War II we faced another kind of enemy. Deficit spending and an increase in government debt was necessary then, and many governments worldwide felt it was necessary in 2020 as well. We aren't going to debate how the money was spent or the merits of additional stimulus, we're just going to be realistic about what might happen on the other side of the spending: taxes may go up. Let's try to make sure that the impact on you isn't more debilitating than it needs to be.

Like it or not, if we agree that taxes are a necessary contribution to society—whether for crisis intervention, schools, roads, a safe power grid or to defend our nation—is it possible to control what you pay? I think the answer is yes, and your financial life will be more productive if you do try to control what you pay the government, *which will make you less dependent on that same government.* Don't make Uncle Sam the majority partner in your financial life.

In the previous chapters, we showed how a penny doubled every day for thirty days would end up being worth $5.3 million. Compare the chart above[xxi], which shows the same compounding, but with taxes taken out each day.

Quite a difference, right? Total without taxes = $5.37 million; total with taxes = $48,200.

Obviously, this chart does not show a real situation—no one doubles their money every day for thirty days, and taxes aren't assessed on a daily basis—but the shock value provides a very powerful argument for why investors need to pay attention to tax-efficient strategies when setting up a portfolio or even an estate plan.

Taxes impact the bottom line because they prevent income from being invested or remove principal that could otherwise be retained to grow for the future. In both cases, you have less money to compound, which has the same impact as a loss and takes a greater return to make up. The best way to avoid this scenario is to manage tax efficiency.

You also don't want to commit the mistake of making taxes the primary driver of decisions. It's as if you don't want to play the lottery because you'd have to pay taxes on the winnings. There are many valid reasons not to play the lottery, but paying taxes on the winnings isn't one of them. Similarly, let's say you have a friend who doesn't want to continue working after age sixty-six—though she loves what she does and could use the income—because she would have to pay taxes on more of her Social Security income. You'll learn more about Social Security later in this chapter, but please remember that while the impulse to manage tax liability is good, don't let it take you down an unproductive path.

Retirement Plans: A Great Incentive

So far, we have focused on how to accumulate wealth. Now we will concentrate more on how to hold on to as much of your income and capital as possible so that it remains on your balance sheet to compound and grow. That's sustainable wealth.

To encourage Americans to save for their retirement, several tax-efficient retirement plans are available: traditional IRAs, Roth IRAs, 401(k)s, Roth 401(k)s, Thrift Savings Plans, 403(b) plans, 457 plans, as well as a few rarely used iterations. If you are self-employed or a business owner, you can do an SEP (Simplified Employee Pension Plan), a SIMPLE (Savings Incentive Match Plan for Employees) or—my personal favorite for entrepreneurs just getting started or staying small—a Solo 401(k).

This is a long list of options, but most people saving for retirement will only be choosing among a traditional IRA or Roth IRA and 401(k) or Roth 401(k) plans. The other plans are available to specific groups—teachers, hospital workers, government employees, military personnel, or those who are in business for themselves. People who teach or work for a hospital or the government have access to a 403(b), while most corporations offer a 401(k). When you reduce the choices to those that might apply to you, the job of deciding which one to use, or which combination to use, doesn't seem so daunting.

The options you're given by any employer have the same basic benefit: they allow investments held inside the structure to grow for decades tax-deferred or tax-free (a Roth option). The real choice comes down to whether you want to use before-tax or after-tax funding, and how flexible you need the distribution schedule to be.

Before-tax or After-tax: Regular or Roth?

Everyone wants to avoid taxes, so the gut instinct in funding a retirement plan is almost always to go with the before-tax option, but this might not be the best choice for the future you.

The best choice really boils down to one question: When will you be in a higher tax bracket? If you expect to be in a higher tax bracket when you retire than you're in now, it makes sense to populate your retirement fund with after-tax money—the Roth option. In other words, pay the taxes now when you're in a lower bracket, and take your distributions tax-free later on. If you expect to be in a lower bracket when you stop working, it makes sense to hold off paying the taxes until retirement. There's a little more to this if you're approaching your retirement years, but it's a good start.

In the example below, we have two investors, Kim and Blake. To keep things simple, let's disregard state, local, and payroll taxes, assuming a flat 20% tax instead of the marginal tax system we have in the U.S.. Kim decides to put her retirement savings into a Roth 401(k), while Blake is using his company's pre-tax option. Both Kim and Blake have $10,000 to invest. Kim, however, is using after-tax dollars, so she first needs to pay $2,000 in taxes (20%) up front and only gets to invest the net amount, or $8,000. Blake is using before-tax dollars, so the entire $10,000 ends up in the 401(k) plan. Now they both leave the contribution alone. At a 7% return, that investment will almost double every ten years. Forty years after the initial investments, both are ready to take distributions.

Pre-Tax 401(k) vs. Roth 401(k)		
	Kim's Roth	Blake's 401(k)
Earmarked Funds:	$10,000	$10,000
(Less) 20% Tax:	($2,000)	-
Contribution:	$8,000	$10,000
Return:	7%	7%
In 10 years:	$15,737	19,671
In 20 years:	$30,957	$38,696
In 30 years:	$60,898	$76,122
In 40 years:	$119,796	$149,744
20% Tax Rate	-	($29,948)
Actual Net Fund Value:	$119,796	$119,796

Blake is feeling pretty good about his choice to use the 401(k) plan. He has $149,744 compared to Kim's $119,796. However, Blake will need to pay tax on his distributions, while Kim will be able to take her payouts tax-free. If Blake is in the 20% tax bracket, his 401(k) account will only be worth $119,796 after he pays taxes on it—the same as Kim's account!

So why would anyone choose one plan over another? Remember those scenarios and projections we discussed in Chapter 2, about tailwinds and Key Force Multipliers? This is where knowing your numbers comes into play. If Kim was a young rising star in her company and was in a very low tax bracket when she made her original contribution—say 12% rather than 20%—she would have come out ahead in these calculations. For example, her net after tax contribution in the 12% tax bracket would have been $8,800 versus the $8,000 shown in the chart. Just about doubling every 10 years would have given her $131,775 instead of $119,676, making that a much better decision over the long run. On the other hand, if Blake was in a high tax bracket at the beginning and a low one when he began to take distributions, he would have come out ahead.

Changes in the tax law itself can have an obvious impact, but we can't know with any degree of certainty how the rules of the game will change. And keep in mind that *when* returns are earned can also affect the accumulation and preservation of wealth. It is hard to predict the impact of taxes on those higher or lower values, and you don't want to wing it. That's where software can help you get a sense of these dueling challenges (see Key Force Multiplier 1).

Unintended Consequences: Taxes on Social Security and Higher Medicare Premiums

There is more to tax strategies than just saving money on taxes today. For example, your chosen retirement plans will impact the cost of Medicare and how much of your Social Security income will be taxable. Running those projections under various scenarios can help you understand the domino effect on other areas of your life, such as your cash flow and ability to invest to get a full match from your employer. Also, if your contributions are all pre-tax, you have deferred and deferred and deferred, so when you have to start using that taxable income, the premiums you might have to pay for Medicare will be higher than if you got the taxes over with when you were younger, and more of your Social Security will be taxed as well.

The calculation to determine how much of your Social Security is taxable is called Modified Adjusted Gross Income, or MAGI. It's your adjusted gross income plus your nontaxable interest plus one half of your Social Security benefits.

Social Security Retirement Income Taxation (2022)		
Tax Filing Status	Provisional Income*	Taxable Portion of Social Security
Individual	Less than $25,000...	None
	$25,000-$34,000...	Up to 50% of benefits
	More than $34,000...	Up to 85% of benefits
Joint	Less than $32,000...	None
	$32,000-$44,000...	Up to 50% of benefits
	More than $44,000...	Up to 85% of benefits

*Provisional Income includes your adjusted gross income plus tax free interest income and 50% of your Social Security benefits.

(Social Security Administration, Income Taxes and Your Social Security Benefit)

When age 65 rolls around—*usually way too soon*—high earners are often surprised by the per person cost of just Medicare Part B, and the impact of higher income:

Medicare Penalty Premiums—Income Related Monthly Adjustment Amount (or "IRMAA"):

Medicare 2022 Part B Premiums by Income			
If you filing status and years income in 2020 was:			Total Monthly Premium Amount
File Individual Tax Return	File Joint Tax Return	File Married & Separate Tax Return	
$91k or less	$182,000 or less	$91,000 or less	$170.10
Above $91,000 Up to $114,000	Above $182,000 Up to $228,000	N/A	$238.10
Above $114,000 Up to $142,000	Above $228,000 Up to $284,000	N/A	$340.20
Above $142,000 Up to $170,000	Above $284,000 Up to $340,000	N/A	$442.30
Above $170,000 Less than $500,000	Above $340,000 Less than $750,000	Above $91,000 and less than $409,000	$544.39
$500,000 or above	$500,000 or above	$409,000 and above	$578.30

(Medicare, Costs)

We'll get into more detail about both of these programs—Social Security and Medicare, including important considerations before making decisions—a little later. When you consider the long-term systemic impact of your decisions, you'll see that financial planning is rarely as straightforward as numbers on a chart would make it appear.

Fortunately, for most people, deciding on which tax-deferred plan to use isn't an either/or situation. You may have a 401(k) at work, plus a private individual IRA or a Roth account. Under the new SECURE Acts (1 and 2), even workers over the age of 70 can make IRA contributions.

Backdoor Roth and Conversions

First, allow me to explain what a Roth conversion is. If you have money in a pre-tax IRA or retirement plan, this means that you received a tax deduction when you made the contribution, or you didn't report that portion of your W2 income on your federal taxes. All earnings on the account weren't taxed each year, but eventually, you or your heirs will have to pay the piper.

A partial or full Roth conversion is often appropriate if your tax bracket is low in retirement, or you want to "prepay" the tax for your heirs to avoid the double taxation that can occur at death. Under current law, there is no income limitation to convert pretax retirement accounts to Roth retirement accounts, you just have to pay the income taxes at your rate when you do so. For example, if you have $10,000 in a pre-tax IRA, you can transfer the balance—ideally paying the income tax amount due from other savings—into a Roth IRA to grow tax-free from that point on. If you are under 59 ½ there is no 10% penalty—Uncle Sam is very happy to collect the tax sooner versus later[26]. Once in the Roth account, earnings grow tax free, and you would not be subject to required minimum distributions. A Roth account is probably the best kind of account an heir could inherit, because that tax free benefit extends to them for 10 years after an owner's death.

So, what's this "backdoor" Roth all about? For anyone at any age whose income is too high to qualify for a tax-deductible or Roth IRA because they have access to a retirement plan at work, consider a "backdoor" Roth IRA. You can still make a contribution of up to $6,000 (which increases each year) if you are under age fifty, or $7,000

---

26   He could probably use a *Financial Planner*, but I digress.

with the catchup contribution[27]. With the backdoor approach, the contribution is not deductible, but the earnings grow tax deferred.

Even better, *there is no income limitation when it comes to implementing a Roth conversion.* In the "backdoor" strategy, you choose to convert an after-tax IRA into a Roth IRA and pay tax on the money that was earned on the account (but deferred in the after-tax IRA) until that time.

Perhaps an example will help: Let's assume you make an after-tax contribution of $6,000 to the IRA, earn 5% on the investment ($300) and convert it to a Roth IRA the following year. You'll ideally pay the taxes on the $300 from other funds, not from the account itself. Now you have $6,300 growing tax-free for the rest of your life, and you aren't required to take minimum distributions on Roth accounts.

A word of caution on Roth conversions: Watch out for the pro-rata rule. If you have several IRAs (including Simple and SEP IRAs), you have to aggregate them to determine the taxable amount of the conversion, even if you were only converting the after tax account. In other words you are adding (including simple and SEP IRAS). Not understanding this could lead to a nasty surprise the following April when you have to pay your taxes.

No matter what other plans you choose to use for retirement, maxing out your contribution to a 401(k) plan each year is a great default decision. Further, if your employer matches all or part of your contribution, you're ahead of the game right from the beginning. If it's a dollar-for-dollar match, you're getting a 100% return on your investment up to the percentage they match from day one. You will never beat that! Keep in mind that the company match may be subject

---

27 The catch-up contribution is there for anyone who woke up at age 50 realizing they are way behind on their retirement savings, or those with excess cash flow they'd like to shelter.

to a vesting schedule, so make sure you understand what the schedule is before you take that next job offer.

Always remember that the devil is in the distributions. Earlier I said that retirement planning is almost more important after you stop working. How and when you take distributions can have as great an impact on how much income is lost to taxes as whether you funded the vehicle with before- or after-tax dollars. These are two areas you have a great deal of control over, and both can dramatically change your outcome.

What to Do with 401(k)s and Pensions

For many employees, the days of staying with one company for an entire career are long gone. According to the Bureau of Labor Statistics, the average person changes employers twelve times in their career (U.S. Department of Labor, *Number of Jobs Held in a Lifetime*). So what's the best thing to do with those abandoned 401(k) plans? Typically, there are four choices: cash out the plan, keep it where it is, transfer it into a new employer's 401(k), or roll it over to an IRA.

Cashing out is rarely the best choice. You will have to pay taxes on the entire amount, plus a 10% penalty if you are under age 59 ½. That means you will lose approximately 30% (or more) of the account in one fell swoop. Why allow taxes to impact your retirement this way? Even if someone has large credit card balance at high interest rates and little hope to pay them off in a reasonable time with other income sources, I don't advocate the cash out. Why? Significant credit card debt suggests forced savings are the best way to create the possibility of an independent future. It's an irrevocable decision, and there are much better options.

For example, many Americans are working side gigs as sole proprietors. If this is your situation, your income from these efforts is not reported to the IRS on a W2 (as an employee); you are an independent contractor receiving Form 1099 at the end of the year (Internal Revenue Service, *Seniors & Retirees*). Examples include everything from service workers in many fields, consulting, or even babysitting!

Instead of cashing out the 401(k), this person might consider rolling the 401(k) into a "Solo 401(k)" maintaining the tax benefits. Once in the new retirement plan, you can take a loan from the new retirement plan to pay off high interest debt such as credit card balances. No taxes, no 10% penalty, and federal law gives you 5 years to pay it off. This option can buy you some time, even if you do end up cashing it out later.

Keeping the account where it is can be a good choice if you're happy with the investment options being offered and you're comfortable with the level of management fees. If your old employer 401(k) has high administration fees or has a very limited pool of investment funds to choose from, transferring the account or rolling it over can make more sense. If you're with a new employer, many plans give you the option of transferring other 401(k) accounts into the new 401(k). However, make sure you're happy with the new investment alternatives and fees, because it might be hard to get your money back out. If you've had several employers, and thus several accounts, rolling them all into one IRA can be easier to manage, both from a paperwork and portfolio management standpoint. Remember to look under the hood when considering all your options. IRAs can—and often do—have fees as well.

But if you're 55 or older when a downsize occurs, think long and hard before rolling your 401(k) into an IRA. While I hope you never have to tap into a 401(k) during the transition between jobs, there is no penalty if you're in this age category and you do. Once you roll it into an IRA, you have to wait until age 59 ½ to be able to take a withdrawal without a 10% penalty.

If the downsizing scenario at or after age 55 doesn't happen to apply to you, or if you have (ideally) plenty of other rainy-day funds in non-retirement accounts, there may be a compelling reason to consider rolling one or more 401(k) plans into a single IRA. Ironically, it's often the last thing anyone thinks about—but having your retirement accounts consolidated provides a lot more control when it comes time to begin taking distributions. You don't want to be a victim of circumstances, and this is one area where that will often happen. When you arrive at age 73[28] you are required to take a certain amount out each year. This is called a Required Minimum Distribution (RMD). If you haven't consolidated by this time, the amount you must take has to come *from each* 401(k)—or if you worked for a non-profit, 403(b)—separately; you can't take more from one and have it count toward the other. In other words, if you have three 401(k)s, you have to apply the formula and take the proper amount based on that account only and take it out of that same 401(k). Otherwise, it doesn't count toward the RMD, and you can get hit with a 25% penalty on the required amount.

It gets worse. Most 401(k) plans allow scheduled withdrawals, but some require that the funds be liquidated at one time, while others do it on a prorated basis. *This is not optimizing the withdrawal process.* If it's automated (which may seem easier), the administrator is going to make the sales irrespective of what's going on in the market or the rest of your portfolio. (So much for not selling low.) Assuming you have a diverse group of investments in the plan, you may want to choose specific funds from which to withdraw. Or you may not want

---

28   Under a new law passed in December of 2022, the age in which you must begin taking RMDs has increased from 72 to 73 in 2023, and 75 in 2033. In other words, some younger readers will be able to wait until age 75 before having to take distributions and pay taxes on the required amount (RMD).

to wait for a scheduled withdrawal to occur in a particular month or day, but instead take advantage of an unusual spike in the market. Being able to withdraw from certain investments based on what's happening at the time can improve your outcome. *Don't become a victim of circumstances.*

The nurse in me feels compelled to tell you that studies show that as people age and cognitive decline occurs, this can turn out to be a real mess. (*Actually, handling RMDs can be a real mess with* **or without** *cognitive decline!*) RMDs can be complicated—especially if they involve multiple accounts—and are nothing to fool around with. *That 25% penalty is the fiscal equivalent of capital punishment by confiscation.*

Finally, another compelling reason to roll over an old 401(k) plan may have nothing to do with investments and everything to do with what you want for your family. Consider the following:

Janet is an only child. Her father has $1,000,000 in a 401(k). When he passes away, federal law states that his employer must allow his spouse to keep the 401(k) there. If Janet's mom likes the investments and the management, she can leave the money right where it is. But upon her death, most plans will require Janet to take control of the assets and pay taxes on the entire $1,000,000 all at once or, if she meets certain deadlines, within five years. She has no choice. So instead of having $1,000,000 in a retirement plan, let's assume federal and state tax rates totaling 40%, she ends up with roughly $600,000. In addition, it is likely that this payout will push her into a higher tax bracket, which will also increase the amount of taxes she pays on her other income. Imagine that she was in the 22% tax bracket; because of her inheritance, she is now in a 37% tax bracket (or 39.6% if the sunset provision kicks in. More on that later). Five years is a bit more forgiving; Ten is even better[29].

Let's assume Janet invests her $600,000 in a portfolio targeting 7%. However, because that account is not tax-deferred or advantaged, she needs to pay taxes on a portion of the returns, which probably brings the real return down to less than 6%. Compare that to $1,000,000 earning 7% in a retirement account, and you can see how much asset growth she's losing each year. *It doesn't sound like much, but over time, the gap just gets wider and wider.*

Fortunately, it doesn't have to be this way. Janet could have changed the outcome by rolling the money into an inherited IRA, which allows her to stretch out tax payments over the ten-year life of the IRA. As of 2022, inherited IRAs must be liquidated within ten years. The formula for taking required minimum distributions depends on the age of the owner when they died. The rules for distributions are very complicated and—frankly—murky even as I write this. One thing is clear: An inherited IRA should be held in a separate account titled, for example, "Inherited IRA FBO Janet Smith." FBO means "for benefit of," and this account should never, ever be comingled with Janet's other IRA that she funded either annually or from her own 401(k) rollover. Unlike Required Minimum Distributions, which must begin at age 75, Janet must have 100% of the account distributed within 10 years. Depending on the facts in her situation, she might be able to withdrawal a tenth per year, or stagger the distribution out using the minimum distribution tables. All that matters is that it is out of the tax shelter by year 11.

While there may be a benefit for Janet if she could increase the time the assets would be tax deferred, a better outcome might be leveling out the taxable income by taking out a smaller percentage of

---

29   If it's rolled into an inherited IRA.

the balance each year, with the goal of reducing the bracket and total tax she'll have to pay over the term. Or if she's approaching retirement, maybe she does the minimum required for the first five years, then uses the inherited IRA as her retirement income for the next five years. She might even be able to delay taking Social Security, so that income gets a guaranteed increase of 8% per year until age 70.

If Janet is under 59½, doesn't an inherited IRA tie up the money until she retires? Not in this case. The beneficiary of an inherited IRA can take the money out for any reason without the 10% penalty. In fact, Uncle Sam would love that since the government is getting the money sooner. Janet could use whatever she needed for school, a house, a car, or to start a business. Whatever isn't used can stay in the inherited IRA to grow on a tax-deferred basis.

The point here is that you are giving your family the opportunity to optimize their own retirement planning by letting them choose when it's best for them to pay the tax on the retirement account based on their personal situation at the time. Chances are you worked hard to build your retirement account over your working lifetime. For many families, this legacy can be significant.

Lump-sum Pension or Monthly Check?

For those lucky enough to be covered by a pension, there will come a time when you need to decide how to receive this retirement plan. Most companies now give retirees the option to take the pension in one lump sum or elect to follow the traditional monthly payment model. There is not one right answer. As with everything financial, each decision involves trade-offs. The moving parts in this particular decision include your age and health (and that of your spouse if you're married), your years of service, your income, applicable interest rates, your tax situation, and your other resources—to name just a few!

Most people are familiar with the concept of a monthly pension payment, which is basically an annuity. An immediate annuity is simply the purchase of a guaranteed stream of income, this time funded by your employer. These payments will arrive in your mailbox (or, more likely, be deposited in your bank account) every month like clockwork. It won't matter if the market is up or down. It won't matter if you set a world record in life expectancy. You will receive the same amount every month for as long as you live. It's hard to put a price on certainty.

Also, monthly payments remove responsibility for managing the underlying account. They are guaranteed, assuming your prior employer stays in business for the rest of your life. Your pension payments will be safe if the company merges with another, and if there is a bankruptcy, the Pension Benefit Guaranty Corporation (PBGC) guarantees at least a portion of your pension payment.

The downside of a monthly pension is that you are locked into a set monthly payment. If you need more cash flow in any particular month, you will have to look elsewhere. In addition, pensions don't increase with inflation, while costs surely will. Finally, if you die within a few years of retiring, your family may receive much less than if you had taken a lump-sum distribution. The health factor is often overlooked but is tremendously important.

My dad was sixty-one when he retired, but he had already had open-heart surgery, while my mom came from a family with long life expectancies. The company he worked for at the time only offered annuity options with no lump-sum alternative. Looking at his health and the resources that would be available to my mother if he passed, we decided the best course of action was for him to take the 100% joint and survivor option, meaning that he and my mom would receive less per month while he was alive but that she would continue receiving that same amount after he was gone. My father only lived another five years, *and that decision made all the difference in my mom's life*[30].

Now, let's change the facts of the case. If Mom and Dad had $1,000,000 in a 401(k) in addition to his pension, would we have chosen the 100% joint and survivor option? *Probably not.* Since we didn't know how long he was going to live, it might have made more sense for Mom and Dad to have more income while he was alive, with the 401(k) continuing to grow during those five years. Then, when the pension payments were reduced by 50% after his death, Mom could have turned to the 401(k) for additional income. If she'd been the one in poor health and Dad was the one from a family with long life expectancies, we might have chosen another option.

Keep in mind that a pension election is an irrevocable decision, *and you aren't going to truly know the "right" answer until well after the fact, probably in your late seventies or eighties.* if you have a pension, run projections and look at best-case and worst-case scenarios to make an educated choice. This really isn't the time to guess, because once the decision is made, you can't go back, so make sure you know as many facts as possible before pulling the trigger.

Instead of taking the monthly annuity, you might be leaning toward selecting the lump-sum option. You might like having more control and not being tied to the mother ship anymore. But this is not for everyone. Each company has its own pension formula and it is important to do an analysis to determine "breakeven years" and "hurdle rates." The breakeven year is determined by calculating how many years of payments would equal the original lump sum, while the hurdle rate is the rate of return a lump-sum investment would

---

30 And it wasn't his heart that gave out in the end. He died from cancer; something we didn't know he had at the time.

have to earn to equal the sum of the monthly payments over your projected lifetime. While life expectancies for a 65-year-old male is age 83, and age 85 for a woman, we also do these calculations to at least age 95, and in some cases even longer. Pension formulas rely heavily on interest rates and when they ran very low for quite some time, the hurdle rate was often surprisingly low. When rates are higher, choosing the monthly pension can look like the better choice. The big unknown is how long you are going to live.

If a lump-sum rollover is the option you choose, the key is to do a direct (trustee-to-trustee) transfer into an IRA, or if permitted into your 401(k) to allow for continued tax deferral. What this means is that the check mailed to you would be payable to the new custodian of your IRA or retirement account. Rather than having taxable monthly payments sent to you for the rest of your life, this gives you flexibility in your planning. For example, you can choose to wait before taking distributions from the rollover, living on after-tax investments instead, which will probably affect how much you have to pay for Medicare, as well as the amount of tax you pay on Social Security. You also might spend more in one month and less in another, paying taxes only on the amount of your withdrawal. Keep in mind that the IRA will be subject to Required Minimum Distributions at age 73 (or up to age 75), but you can do some really neat tax planning up until that time. Since you now control the principal, as well as the growth of it during your lifetime, you know your family will still get the balance of that money even if you die prematurely. Depending on the pension option you choose, this might not be the case with a monthly annuity.

Even aside from hurdle rates and breakeven years, a lump-sum distribution also has its downsides. Some people find that they spend too much in the beginning and have too little later in life. Others may be confused about the tax implications or do a poor job of managing the portfolio. The best ways to invest during your working years are very different from these in the drawdown years of your retirement. Sequence of return risk as discussed in Chapter 4, can be fatal for those who don't understand it. Inflation fluctuates, too.

With a little planning, however, you can have the best of both worlds. The trick is to put the lump-sum payment into a pre-established IRA or 401(k)s thus deferring taxes. Once the lump sum payment is housed in the IRA, you can make withdrawals at intervals as needed (or required) and spread out the tax burden. You can even use some or all of the distribution to purchase your own income annuity, which would give you the type of stable cash flow provided by the standard pension model.

Once you have real numbers, you might look at the scenario, know that the lump sum might make more sense on paper, and still opt for the monthly annuity simply because you'll sleep better at night. *This is important too.*

But here's the key: the pension decision shouldn't be made based on a stand-alone analysis. Projecting out your cash flow needs, your tax situation, and the availability of other resources is really important. Running "what if" scenarios with higher spending, lower returns, bear markets, and unexpected emergencies can give you potential longer-term implications of one decision versus another. *It sounds like a lot of work, but remember,* you only get to do this once. As always, you want to see how each option fits into the bigger picture—the one on the top of the puzzle box.

Portfolio Management to Save Taxes

People are drawn to tax-free municipal bonds like toddlers are drawn to puddles. They see "tax-free" and immediately jump on board. The tax-free quality is a true benefit if you're placing these bonds in a non-retirement account, but if you put them in a tax-deferred or tax-advantaged retirement account, you're often cheating yourself out of a higher yield without any offsetting benefit[31]. The mistake people often make is to think they need to balance[32] each account within an overall portfolio. If a 50/50 asset allocation is the target, they will have 50% stocks and 50% in each of their 401(k) and their Roth IRA plans, as well as their everyday investment portfolio. A better way to look at your investments is to consider them all one big portfolio. If you want a 50/50 split of stocks and bonds, you can put nearly all of the stocks in the tax-deferred plans, and nearly all of the bonds in the taxable plans. That allows you to enjoy the higher returns from stocks while deferring taxes, as well as to take advantage of the tax-free status of municipal bonds.

Timing Your Taxes

If you're going to time *anything*, this is a great area for it. A person's tax bracket often goes way down during the time between when they retire and when they begin taking required distributions, especially if they are deferring Social Security and just living on the money they have in the bank. That is a terrific opportunity to sell highly appreciated investments. For example, in 2022 if we can keep a couple in a 12% tax bracket or lower, they will pay no taxes on capital gains up to about $83,550 of taxable income.

From a portfolio management standpoint, let's say you've retired and are looking at rebalancing your portfolio. Maybe you're overweight

---

31   With one exception: municipal bonds that pay taxable income can be placed in a retirement account.

32   A hypothetical portfolio might consist of half of the assets allocated to equity investments and the other half to fixed income investments (i.e., "50/50").

in company stock, and you want to sell some of it. Depending upon your outlook for the stock (the expected future return is usually more important than the tax implications, but very difficult to predict), you might want to systematically sell (dollar cost average) out of the stock over a period of years when you're in a 12% tax bracket. *This approach can avoid the capital gains tax on the appreciation altogether.*

Let's take this one step further. Keep in mind that once you qualify for benefits, you can start receiving Social Security in any month of any year. The benefit is simply recalculated accordingly. It might make sense to hold off taking Social Security if you know you want to sell those investments and pay no tax on the gain. Even if you like the investment, go ahead and sell it, then buy it right back. The wash sale rule explained in the next few pages does *not* apply to gains.

An example might help. Let's assume that an investment you own has a cost basis of $20,000 and is now worth $50,000. Calculations show that you would be in the 12% tax bracket and pay *no* tax on the sale. The next day, you buy the exact same investment back, and it grows to $70,000 over the next few years. At this point, you're in a 32% tax bracket, so you'd be paying a or 20% tax on capital gains, or maybe even 23.8% including the Medicare tax. You are getting nervous and thinking it's time to get out of the stock for good. Your new cost basis is $50,000, the amount you invested when you purchased it back the next day years before. *Even if you aren't in the 12% tax bracket anymore and you have to pay a capital gains tax, you're paying it on the $20,000, not the entire $50,000 profit gained from this great investment.* That's why there is more to tax planning than just the bracket you are in today.

The years between your retirement date and age 73, when RMDs must begin, are also good years to consider Roth conversions. If you have set up your plan to be in a low tax bracket in these years, you will pay taxes on the conversion, but for example, you could be in the low 12% rate instead of a 25% (or higher) rate you might be paying in just five to ten years when you are forced to take distributions and pay taxes. This is yet another reason why financial planning with integrated tax projections is important; they can help you make better decisions based on tax laws in place and the information you have today. That Roth IRA grows tax-free for the rest of your life, no matter how long you live. You don't have to do an RMD on it, so it just compounds over time, creating one of the best legacies you can leave.

Tax-loss Harvesting

Tax-loss harvesting[xxii] is an important concept that can make lemonade out of lemons. They don't even have to be real lemons, just perceived or temporary, lemons. The basic concept here is that the IRS allows you to reduce taxes by offsetting gains with losses and only paying tax on the balance. If you want to sell stock and it turns out you've had a loss over time, it makes sense to sell some of your winners too. That way you capture the gain on the stock or fund that did well, without losing any of it to Uncle Sam.

Investment A $50,000 Taxable gain
Investment B - $50,000 Tax loss
Taxes due $0

But what if you don't have a gain to offset the tax loss?

While I am a real advocate for diversification, mutual funds can create an unwanted capital gains tax each year, but you can offset it if you understand how tax-loss harvesting works.

Here's an example. Five years ago, Ashley invested $100,000 into a mutual fund. She has received $10,000 each year in dividends and capital gains, which she reinvested in the fund.

At the end of five years, the account stands at $120,000, and Ashley wants—or perhaps needs—to sell. When it comes time to complete her tax form, Ashley enters $100,000 on the cost basis line and $120,000 for the proceeds and comes up with $20,000 she needs to pay taxes on. Seems pretty straightforward, right? *Wrong!* This is a common mistake people make on their tax returns: they determine their cost basis incorrectly.

Ashley actually *did* make $20,000 on her initial investment, but that's *not* how it should be reported on her tax return. Her cost basis is her initial investment, *plus each of the reinvested amounts*, since she reported the dividends and capital gains as income each year. Sure, the increase in the number of shares from the reinvestments of $10,000 per year, but in this case, just when Ashley needed to sell it, the price per share of the investment declined. Therefore, her *real* cost basis is $150,000, which translates to a *$30,000 loss for tax purposes*.

Now, what is she going to do with that loss? While you can offset an unlimited amount of capital gains, the most you can deduct against ordinary income (wages, Social Security, pension income) is $3,000. If this was happening in 2008, all she would really have is a $3,000 tax deduction against her income because there were no capital gains on any of her other investments. This is a safe assumption because the entire market was down. But she doesn't lose the balance of this benefit; it's like she has a bank account with an unused $27,000 tax deduction that is carried forward each year until it is all used up.

By 2009, the stock market had rebounded. If Ashley sells a different stock at a $10,000 profit, she can use that $27,000 loss from the previous year to offset her gain. She won't pay any taxes on that gain, which will save her between $1,500 and $2,300 in taxes, depending on her bracket. In addition, she can take another $3,000 deduction against ordinary income. *Even better, she still has the remaining $14,000 loss to carry forward to the next year.*

Depending on her marginal tax bracket, Uncle Sam gave her about $6,500 back in the form of tax savings.

Ashley's example shows the math, but who wants a tax deduction if it means you've lost money? We don't want to upset the integrity of the portfolio, and we certainly don't want to sell low. *In reality, Ashley did not need the money, but she still wanted this tax benefit.* The only thing she needed to do was make a phone call to her fund company or advisor and move the $120,000 from one fund to another. That is typically a free same-day exchange, and ideally, she'll be moving to a similar type of investment: Blue Chip Fund A to Blue Chip Fund B. Ashley remained fully invested, maintaining the same asset allocation, but now she had a $30,000 tax deduction that she otherwise wouldn't have had. That's "harvesting" a tax benefit.

You can also do this with stock, but you have to be careful. If you really like the investment you're holding, you'll need to remain out of the stock for thirty days in all accounts before repurchasing. This is called the *wash-sale rule* and you need to be aware of it to be able to reap this benefit. If you buy the same investment back within the thirty days, you lose the tax deduction altogether. (Remember, this wash-sale rule doesn't apply to gains.) Let's assume you really think the company you're invested in could do well in the future but you want the tax benefit until the rest of the world realizes how smart you are. You can sell and move the proceeds into a company in the same sector, or even a mutual fund. The risk you take is that the stock you sold increases rapidly in value (and more than it's replacement) over the next thirty days and you aren't invested in it to participate. Typically, in funds and ETFs, if Fund A does well, chances are—if it is invested in the same asset class—that Fund B will do well too. Either way, if you really want to be invested in Fund A, (or stock A) you can buy it back after thirty days.

This might seem complicated, and I understand if you want to skip this opportunity. It doesn't have to overwhelm you, but you do need to be proactive and have a good system to implement the strategy. A lot of people think the only right time to sell is when the market is up, but as you can see from the above example, selling into a down market can also have some benefits—as long as you know what to do with the loss.

Asset Location

Placing certain types of investments in a retirement account and other types in a non-retirement account is known as *asset location*. For example, you could put all your taxable bond interest into a retirement account, while assets that receive capital gains treatment might make sense in a non-retirement account. Yet the reverse could be better for you, especially if you need cash flow. Remember the domino effect: Medicare premiums, capital gains rates, and even the amount of money you have in your portfolio will have an impact on this decision.

Deferred Compensation, Stock Options, and RSUs

Company-offered deferred compensation plans (also referred to as "deferred comp"[33]) are touted as a great way to push off taxes to a time when you might be in a lower tax bracket. What could be wrong with that? In theory, nothing. In practice, a few things. If you're deferring your compensation, you need to be fairly sure that the company you're working for is going to be around and on solid financial footing ten or twenty years from now when you want to access that compensation. Unfortunately, even the CEOs of these companies can't make a guarantee the company will be solvent down the road. Unlike 401(k) balances, deferred compensation accounts are considered assets of the company, so please be aware of this risk. If the company were to go into bankruptcy during that period, you would be in the same line as every other creditor. Deferred comp is great from a tax planning perspective, but it doesn't provide the same protections a 401(k) does, so always utilize that option first. A company failure doesn't often happen, but as we have learned, even something as unthinkable as a pandemic can happen and can take down even well-known household names.

If you're putting money into a deferred comp plan, you will also need to state when you want to take withdrawals and pay the taxes. You might elect to receive the balance all at once when you retire. If the assets have grown to a sizable amount, you might face a significant

---

33   Here's a random fact: Generally speaking, human beings want to shorten things. When I started Key Financial, a book I was reading had a chapter on naming a new entity. I didn't want it to be named "Brennan Something or Other," and a friend commented that when I wanted to emphasize something, I would always preface the statement with, "This is *key*." I learned that it's best to keep the name four syllables or less; otherwise, people will abbreviate or shorten it. For example, Kentucky Fried Chicken is KFC, the Internal Revenue Service is the IRS, and a deferred compensation plan is deferred comp. *Random, I know*, but you made it this far in the book.

tax liability in that year. To avoid that, you might want to look at staggering the payouts over a period of five or ten years. In essence, the deferred compensation becomes a new salary during retirement.

Stock options come in one of two forms: non-qualified stock options (NQOs) and incentive stock options (ISOs). Most mature companies are now issuing NQOs because it makes more sense from the company's perspective. Young companies, on the other hand, often issue ISOs to attract key talent. When deciding how you want to make these benefits part of your portfolio, you first need to know which kind you have and understand the difference.

NQOs give you the option of purchasing a specific number of shares (often referred to as a grant) in the company at a set price, no matter what the price is at the time of purchase. The option will have two time limits: a vesting period and an expiration period. While vesting periods vary, expiration periods can last up to ten years. As an example, Bill is granted the option to purchase 1,000 shares of company stock at $25 per share. It vests in one year, and he is given ten years to exercise the option. Bill watches the stock grow to $60 per share and decides to use his option to purchase 1,000 shares at $25 each. In an NQO, you typically buy and sell at the same time, so he doesn't need to have $25,000 on hand to exercise the option to buy 1,000 shares; it's considered a cashless transaction. Therefore, Bill will just pocket the difference, in this case $35,000. Non-qualified options are subject to ordinary income tax, so Bill will be taxed on the profit at his tax bracket.

ISOs can work a little differently. If Bill is exercising an incentive stock option, he will still pay just $25 per share for 1,000 shares of stock worth $60 per share (but he may not want to sell on the same day). Yes, he will have to come up with $25,000 to buy the stock, but he can reduce his tax liability by holding on to those shares for at least twelve months. If he does that, his profit will be considered a long-term capital gain rather than ordinary income. Let's assume Bill is in a 32% tax bracket, so instead of a $11,200 tax liability, his capital gains tax at 15% would be $5,250. Incentive stock options provide the opportunity to pay a lower overall tax on the gain[34].

To repeat a word of caution, don't let taxes be the sole driver of your decisions, especially with incentive stock options. The price of the stock is very important too, and while no one can predict stock prices, you want to be smart with your money. Many employees learned this tough lesson during the 2001 tech bubble and the 2008 financial crisis. They exercised their options and bought the designated shares with cash on hand, only to watch their profit—and some of the principal—evaporate over the next six months. Things got even worse when those employees realized they were subject to an Alternative Minimum Tax on profits that were no longer there. While there would have been a carry-forward tax credit for the extra tax they paid, the stock had to recover before they could take advantage of it. A tax professional needs to keep track of this credit as well.

Yes, it's nice to cut your tax liability, but it's far better to keep the profit.

Restricted Share Units (RSUs) are another form of compensation that has become popular for corporations. This structure grew out of the tech bubble, when employees saw their stock options grow at an exponential rate, only to watch them crash within a very short period. All that wealth evaporated into thin air, because if you don't exercise the option, it's not your money.

---

34   Be careful. Even under the tax law passed in 2018, incentive stock options are still a tax preference item for calculating alternative minimum tax (AMT). This could result in a large and nasty surprise the following April, and a tax bill on phantom income. So, at the risk of sounding like a broken record, always consult your tax advisor before implementing a strategy with tax implications.

RSUs take that uncertainty out of a stock option. Instead of granting an option that must be exercised, RSUs are a grant of units that represent actual shares of stock. So if Bill works for one of these companies, instead of receiving—for example—a grant representing 4,000 options to purchase shares at a "grant price," he might receive 750 actual shares of stock, but as the name suggests, they are restricted[35]. There is usually a vesting period before Bill can access those shares, and he won't receive dividends until he vests. If Bill leaves the company for another job or is subject to a downsizing and is let go, the shares that were not vested are typically forfeited. For now, let's assume Bill is happy and retains his position, and will vest a third of the shares next year, a third the following year, and the final third in the last year. It's kind of a golden handcuff. When RSUs vest, it's a taxable event. They're considered a form of compensation, and the company is required to sell some of his shares to pay the withholding tax. In this example, a third of the shares granted, or 250 shares, will vest in year one. Approximately fifty shares will be sold to cover withholding tax, and Bill will retain the balance of the stock. He will then start receiving dividends on the remaining 200 shares, or he could choose to diversify this holding, knowing he has more of these same shares vesting in subsequent years.

Sometimes, companies give employees the choice as to whether they would prefer to receive their stock incentive plan in the form of stock options or RSUs. Ultimately the decision will come down to your tolerance for risk, the need to capture that income for other important objectives, and your tax situation. Once vested, the stock granted in the RSU is yours whether you continue to work for the

---

35   If you have RSUs, an 83(b) election might apply to your situation. If this is the first time you are hearing about an 83(b) election, be sure to speak with your tax and other advisors.

company or not. It is the more conservative of the two types of plans. Stock options tend to leverage the performance in the company stock and may have a better tax outcome if it's an ISO, but you could also walk away with nothing, because the stock price *has to grow* from whatever the price was when it was granted.

Health Savings and Flexible Spending Accounts and the Tax Advantages of Social Security[36]

In addition to utilizing traditional retirement accounts, such as IRAs, and strategically structuring the sale of assets to manage your tax liability, there are several other ways you can keep more of what you earn. Consider leveraging a Health Savings Account (HSA), a Flexible Spending Account (FSA), and good old Social Security.

Corporate employers typically have several options when it comes to medical insurance. Many employees naturally gravitate to low-deductible traditional plans, but a high-deductible plan, when paired with an HSA, might be better in the long (or even short) run.

A high-deductible health plan (HDHP) is a plan with a deductible of at least $1,400 for individuals and $2,800 for families. Total yearly out-of-pocket expenses (including deductibles, copayments, and coinsurance) are capped at $6,900 for an individual and $13,800 for a family.

The high-deductible plan is a little scary for many people because they see the exposure of the deductible and wonder if they can afford to pay that much for their healthcare. But those numbers don't tell the whole story. First, premiums for the high-deductible plan are signifi-

---

36   Yes, Social Security is tax-efficient.

cantly lower than for traditional plans, which gives the employee extra money each month to put into an HSA. Whether you're obtaining medical insurance through an employer or through the Afford- able Care Act (ACA) exchange, there are out-of-pocket maximum payments that can range from $4,000 to $9,000. There are different types of high-deductible plans; some require in-network physicians and encourage generic prescriptions, while others are more flexible— with the higher premiums to go along with them. Nonetheless, the out-of-pocket maximums will limit exposure to the big bad bills.

Here's the real advantage of an HDHP: the ability to fund a Health Savings Account. The money is contributed through payroll deductions on a pre-tax basis as with a 401(k), it grows tax-deferred, and if it is used for qualified medical expenses, withdrawals are tax-free. It doesn't get much better than triple tax-free.

A Flexible Spending Account (FSA) has the same tax advantages as its cousin, the HSA, and can also be used for medical expenses, but the maximum pre-tax contribution is $2,850, and all but $570 must be used *within* the year. The $570 can be rolled into the next year, but it must be used typically in the first three months *or forfeited*. It's a great option for those who want to eke out every tax advantage, but given how busy people can get, be aware of the risk of forfeiture.

HSAs never expire, and there is no limit to how much you can roll over each year. An individual can deposit up to $3,650 each year, (subject to potential increases for inflation, this is as of 2022), while the family max is $7,300 (with a catchup contribution limit of $1,000 for people over age 55). Since we don't know what potential increases will average, let's just assume a level contribution of a contribution of $5,000 per year earning 5%. In this example, the HSA could grow to $62,889 in 10 years, $165,329 in 20 years, and $332,194 in 30 years.

In addition, many companies encourage the use of high-deductible plans by depositing money into every employee's HSA each year.

There are very few examples of a free lunch, *but this is one of them.* If your HSA is used for healthcare, insurance, or even Medicare premiums, the money comes out tax-free. You don't pay taxes going in, the account is tax-deferred, and you don't pay taxes coming out. Thus, an HSA is more powerful than any other savings vehicle. As wonderful as the tax-free growth might sound, a Roth IRA does not provide the up-front tax deduction that you get with the HSA. 401(k)s and traditional IRAs give you a tax deduction up front, but you are taxed—often on a higher dollar value—when you make a withdrawal.

Funding an HSA can be a big deal at any age, especially if you start early. Considering that healthcare and retirement are the biggest concerns of Americans today, having an HSA account can be instrumental in reducing overall cash flow needs in retirement, since the capital can be pulled out tax-free.

Is Social Security really a tax-efficient vehicle? Everyone wants to begin collecting Social Security at some point, regardless of their net worth. It's understandable: you made the contributions and so did your employer, and you want what is owed. But determining when you should begin taking payments isn't as easy as you'd think.

For retirees who don't need to dip into their retirement accounts and have after-tax savings or investment accounts, waiting until age 70 to start receiving Social Security can pay big dividends over the years.

Let's take Jack as an example and assume he had steady earnings at the maximum level starting at age 22. According to Social Security Administration(.gov), if he retired in January of 2022, his social security statement says that he would receive $2,364 at age 62, $3,240 at his FRA (66 and 6 months) or $4,190 at age 70 (Social Security Administration, "Workers with Maximum-Taxable Earnings").

Although the numbers look fine, it is important to look under the hood, especially when it comes to Social Security.

First, the statements include estimates only, and assume Jack works up until the age when he claims his benefits. The benefits are calculated based on the average of the highest 35 (capped at 35 years) years of earnings history, so his later years might have more impact on the benefits than when Jack was in his 20's. How does Jack feel about working beyond age 66 or to 70? Sure, he could retire, and get cash flow needed from other sources (savings, investments or retirement accounts), but what are the investment and tax implications of doing so? Is Jack married? If he takes it early, and since there is typically a breakeven age, how is his health? If Jack is married, would his spouse qualify for their own benefits or receive 50% of Jack's, and how is his or her health? If he died, his surviving spouse would see a drop in their cash flow because they can only receive the higher of the two benefit amounts. What other resources would they have to live on and would there be a significant shortfall? If Jack decides to wait, is using his investments to live on worth the stress?

Although just doing the math might look easy, nothing is ever black-and-white when it comes to financial decisions.

Waiting might make sense if Jack is able to pay bills and enjoy the beginning years of retirement without dipping into his retirement accounts. This is especially true if he's healthy and his parents lived well into their eighties. But if he's going to have to use money from his 401(k) or IRA for cash flow during those years leading up to age seventy, it might be better to take Social Security as soon as he reaches full retirement age.

The reason he'd rather take Social Security than dip into his retirement accounts is that Social Security is very tax efficient. Even at the highest incomes, only 85% of the benefit is included as taxable income. On the other hand, 100% of tax-deferred distributions are taxed as ordinary income. For example, if Jack receives $3,000 per month, or $36,000 per year, and is at the highest includable tier of 85%[37], he is paying taxes on $30,600 of his Social Security instead of the entire amount that he's receiving from the IRA.

If he is in a 24% tax bracket, the tax savings on the $5,400 difference is real money saved each year. *In other words, the $1,296 in taxes Jack is not paying on his Social Security needs to be factored into the Social Security election decision.*

One more thing. Many Americans are concerned about Social Security in general. They worry about the solvency of the system and whether they will ever get the benefits promised to them. Unless Congress acts by 2035, the trust funds in Social Security will be depleted, and continuing taxes will only be enough to pay about 75% of the obligations promised to current—and future—disabled workers and retirees.

This is not the first time the solvency of the Social Security system has been threatened. For years 1973 through 1983, the trust(s) (OASI and DI Trust funds) were operating with a negative cash flow that was depleting the reserves toward exhaustion. Amendments made in 1977 and 1983 made substantial modifications including a change in the way benefits increase each year, gradual increases in the retirement age from age 65 to age 67, and the introduction of taxation of benefits with revenue that would be credited back to the trust fund(s). It seems as leaders lacking political will is not a new phenomenon: both amendments occurred as trust fund assets were approaching exhaustion.

---

37   Depending on your Provisional Income, you may be required to include only 50% of Social Security, *or even none of it*. Talk to your advisor about ways to reduce your MAGI, as well as Social Security claiming strategies still available today.

Yet even then, these changes were phased in. For example, while the increase in normal retirement age was amended in 1983, the change was phased in for individuals reaching age 62 in the year 2000, 17 years after enactment, with full increase in normal retirement age to 67 not complete until 2022.

There have been 27 legislative proposals in the last three years to create a more sustainable retirement program for Americans, each with its own nuances. One proposal would add social security tax to investment and business income and smash the tax cap for people earning $250,000 or more. The tax cap, which in 2022 was $147,000, means any income above that amount is not subject to this payroll tax (also referred to as FICA) (Picchi, *One Way to Fix Social Security?*). Clearly, repairing Social Security is a politically charged issue. Theatrics aside, Democrats seem to agree on raising taxes on the wealthy and expanding benefits, while less unified Republicans favor delaying retirement to age 70 and shrinking benefits for the affluent.

If Congress waits until 2035 to take action until the trust fund becomes exhausted, the Social Security Board of Trustees project that changes equivalent to an immediate reduction of benefits of between 13 and 15% or increased in the combined payroll tax from 12.4% to 14.4% would be required to allow full payment of the scheduled benefits for the next 75 years. Past legislative changes suggest that a combination of changes phased in will have the best chance of getting through political deadlock.

While some people don't want to count on Social Security at all, I think this is a mistake. Excluding Social Security income in the plan could create unnecessary angst and a delay of enjoying life's true wealth—freedom. Sure, run scenarios to determine the impact of a reduction or even elimination, but don't make decisions based on that alone. Doing so would fall into the category of: "Creating a problem that doesn't exist, yet," and an assumption that a solution won't be agreed on for a well-known issue far in advance of it's negative impact.

Leveraging Payments to a Continuing Care Retirement Community

Certain life events can create wonderful tax planning opportunities. For example, a number of age-in-place retirement communities require a large down payment of several hundred thousand dollars to move in, plus monthly fees. If the community provides continuing care, a certain percentage of the lump sum and fees would be considered a medical expense. Let's say Joe pays $400,000 as an entry fee to move into his dream retirement community. To keep things simple (which, as you are learning, *they rarely are*), let's assume that one-third of that fee, or $130,000, could be a tax-deductible medical expense over and above the 7.5% of Adjusted Gross Income (AGI) requirement.

Depending on his AGI, Joe can now include what could be upwards of $100,000 as an itemized deduction to reduce the amount of taxes he's paying. If he doesn't have the $100,000 of income, Joe might take $100,000 from his IRA and do a Roth conversion, with the medical expense (over an AGI of 7.5%) creating a direct offset to the taxes that would have been due on the Roth conversion.

Keep in mind that all this *must* be done in the year the deductible payment is made to the continuing care community.

I was talking with a couple who had moved into one of these retirement communities the previous year. As I was reviewing their tax return, they said they were so pleased because they didn't have to pay *any* income taxes that year. After reviewing the return, I looked up and said, "I am so sorry to hear that."

"Why?" the husband asked.

The problem was that they had taken a $130,000 tax deduction but didn't have any income to offset it. *So that deduction was totally wasted,* and there was no way to recapture it.

They were sick about the lost opportunity, and the $32,500 (or more) they would have saved on taxes.

For example, they could have converted $130,000 of their IRA to a Roth IRA, still avoided paying *any* taxes that year, and avoided having to take Required Minimum Distributions—and paying taxes on the RMDs in the future. Instead, assuming the converted money remained in the Roth for a period of five years, the entire account and all growth could be distributed tax-free.

Something else to keep in mind is that in addition to the lump-sum fee due upon entering the community, a portion of the monthly fee is also tax-deductible, so make sure there is taxable income to offset those deductions. And remember not to confuse taxable income with cash flow. In order to pay this monthly fee, you may need a monthly deposit into your bank account, but it doesn't have to be taxable.

Saving Taxes While Doing Good

The next chapter will outline several charitable giving strategies that can be applied to save a bundle of income and estate taxes, but the most important driver of these strategies is charitable intent. You are giving away your money—either right away or at some point in the future—to a nonprofit entity, and it's an irrevocable decision. While these strategies save money today, they might mean leaving less to future generations. For example, Charitable Remainder Trusts allow you to contribute low-cost-basis investments, sell them in the trust tax-free to avoid the capital gains tax altogether, and create a stream of income from the trust that pays you for the rest of your life. As the donor, you also receive a wonderful tax deduction up front, and when you (and your spouse, if you're married) pass, the balance goes to named charities. Charitable Lead Trusts and Charitable Annuities are additional techniques addressed in a later section, and each has its pros and cons. It's important to understand that these tools can reduce the amount you leave to your heirs, so charitable intent is key.

Revisions to the tax code passed in 2018 have changed the way you might want to donate to charity. Instead of donating $10,000 each year for three years, it often makes better financial sense (from a tax perspective) to donate $30,000 in a single year. Under the prior law, anyone who itemized could likely get a tax deduction for what they donated to charity. Under the law in 2022, however, the standard deduction for joint filers is $25,900 (with a $1,400 boost for those over age 65), and $12,950 for single filers. In addition, the amount you can deduct in various categories has been reduced. While you can itemize and deduct all of your mortgage interest, the state and local tax deduction has been capped at $10,000. Also, certain miscellaneous items, such as casualty losses and financial fees, are no longer deductible, and only the amount of medical expenses over 7.5% of your AGI are includable as an itemized expense. That all means that for the vast majority of people, the standard deduction will be higher than itemizing.

If you aren't itemizing, you aren't going to get a tax benefit for your charitable contributions. Or can you? The answer is yes. People who are 73 years old with retirement accounts can use their required minimum distribution (RMD) to do a qualified charitable distribution (QCD) and make tax-free donations. For example, let's assume retiree Bill has a $30,000 required minimum distribution. He is also charitably inclined and makes a $10,000 donation each year. Typically, Bill has his RMD deposited into his bank account and then writes a check to the charity. This year, however, Bill will be taking the standard deduction on his tax form, so he is not able to itemize the charitable deduction. His church certainly benefited from his generosity, but he is no longer getting a tax benefit.

Let's go with Plan B. Instead of having the entire $30,000 deposited into his account, Bill could have $10,000 sent directly to the charity by the IRA custodian. The $20,000 balance (less the tax withholding) would be deposited into his bank account as usual. If he does this, he satisfies his $30,000 RMD but only pays taxes on the $20,000. Even better, he still gets the full standard deduction.

Another idea could be for Bill to use (up to $50,000) his RMD to fund a Charitable Gift Annuity. He makes the donation, and then the charity can pay him an annuity income of about 7% on the contribution for the rest of his life. Keep in mind that like other annuities, he has lost access to his principal, and the income (usually) ends at his death.

A third way to get a tax deduction is to bunch several years' worth of deductions to make itemizing the better choice. If you normally donate $10,000 a year, you can reach the itemization threshold by donating $30,000 every three years.

Finally, you could set up a donor-advised fund (DAF). These accounts work like a foundation, without the legal fees and onerous recordkeeping. In this case, you donate $30,000 in a donor-advised fund and take the deduction up front. Then you can donate it out over that same three years as you have been doing in the past. You don't get a tax deduction in the second and third year because you've already claimed that benefit, but the $20,000 left in the fund can be invested and continue to grow until you are ready to contribute it to a charity. There are administrative fees for these accounts, but most charities are thrilled to benefit from your generosity.

Why Bother Working If It Increases Your Tax Bracket?

This is a question that can come up when both spouses are working or a more lucrative job opportunity arises. It is important to consider quality of life today and in the future. Keep in mind that even if your marginal tax rate increases to another bracket, you still have that after tax increased cash flow coming in. What would it be like if you didn't have it, and what are the longer-term implications on your career and ability to save (or stay out of debt)? Is it worth it?

Just don't make the decision based on taxes or your tax bracket alone. Net after-tax cash flow *is still* cash flow.

Bottom Line

Ben Franklin once wrote, "Our new Constitution is now established, and has an appearance that promises permanency; but in this world nothing can be said to be certain, except death and taxes."

He was right that taxes are certain, but how much you pay can vary greatly depending on what strategies you use to manage what you pay. Before making any major financial decision—when to take Social Security, how to structure deferred compensation, whether to enroll in an HDHP, how to structure charitable donations, etc.—stop and analyze how each scenario will affect your taxes. Chances are, there are more tax-efficient ways to do what you want to do.

Benjamin Franklin is also credited with saying, "A penny saved is a penny earned"[38]. In this case, a dollar saved through tax-efficient strategies is better than a dollar earned because you have the dollar—and the taxes you didn't pay—to invest and compound.

---

38 Translated into today's language, this quote may be misattributed to Benjamin Franklin. He did write that "A penny saved is two pence clear" in the 1737 Poor Richard's Almanack.

CHAPTER 6

The Unexpected and the Inevitable

How do you transfer risks to others and assure a seamless inheritance for the people you love? In the last chapter, we looked at several tax strategies that can help you hold onto more of your savings. We now turn to two other legs of wealth preservation: insurance and estate planning. Just as we did when we examined tax strategies, we are going to concentrate on several insurance and estate planning strategies that can make an oversized difference in preserving your wealth.

The Unexpected - Lawsuits and Liability

Assets may be lost through acts of God, such as fires, tornados, and floods. They can also be lost through lawsuits. Before you say that this could never happen to you, stop and look around. Do you have teenagers or young children who will become teenagers? As the mother of four children, including one who had several fender benders and accidents in his first two years behind the wheel, I know that anything can happen at any time.

While my kids seemed to exercise good judgment, let's remember that teenagers, whose frontal lobes are still developing, often make bad choices. They look at a text, or drink and drive, and the unthinkable happens. They are in an accident, and they kill someone. If it was your child, you own the car and insure it, so depending on the state you live in and the incident itself, you could be liable even though you weren't anywhere near the accident when it occurred.

Your assets are now subject to a multimillion-dollar lawsuit. And even if you don't have significant assets or wages, the threat alone will be stressful. Before you wave this off by saying you don't have kids (or yours would never do this), think of some other scenarios. What happens if your spouse pulls an all-nighter finishing up an important project, goes to work in the morning, and then falls asleep at the wheel on the way home? What happens if you hit an errant golf shot and it strikes someone walking down the street? You need to be prepared for the unexpected.

First, in most states, it is important to understand what happens when you title your accounts and assets. When establishing a joint non-retirement account, JWROS (joint with rights of survivorship) is nearly always the default. It simply means that both you and whomever else you choose own the asset jointly. If one of you dies, the asset transfers to the survivor automatically. Tenancy by the entirety (TBE), works exactly the same way in that both parties have access to the account and it transfers to the survivor, though it is only available between spouses. There is an additional major difference, however, which is why you should discuss both forms of ownership (and all of this) with an attorney.

Let's go back to the example of one of the spouses falling asleep at the wheel and causing a fatal accident. If assets are being held in a joint account, they are at risk. It doesn't matter which partner is being sued. If you hold your asset in tenancy by the entirety, both tenants (spouses) need to have done something wrong for those assets to be attachable in a lawsuit. Yet only one person can drive a car. Depending on your state of residence, tenants by the entirety can provide an important barrier to predators, and their attorneys.

The next tier of protection is an umbrella liability policy. Please consider purchasing an umbrella liability policy that covers what homeowners and car insurance do not. A $1,000,000 policy can easily be added for about $400 more per year. It can be an inexpensive premium to preserve what you've worked so hard to build.

Long-term Care Insurance

Let's say you've done the best financial planning in the world, achieved important investment objectives, and set up a retirement plan based on tax-efficient cash flow that you will never outlive. In spite of these wonderful planning strategies—if you or your spouse becomes ill and needs home healthcare, assisted living, or nursing home care--that can wipe away everything.

Unfortunately, there is no way to predict who will need long-term care and who won't. We can look at family health history to give us a bit of insight, but in general, many people are just rolling the dice. And it can be a very big gamble if you play the odds and lose.

Not everyone needs long-term care insurance. The first thing to do is run the numbers to see if you can be your own insurance company. In other words, you can self-insure: "If it does happen, we have sufficient resources, whether from income or savings to cover the added costs, and we can cross that bridge if and when we come to it." Be conservative in your estimates and include worst-case scenarios. This might mean assuming that someone who is paying for long-term care themselves will need $150,000 each year for eight years. Most claims are not this high, and the average need is less than three years, but if dementia or Alzheimer's runs in the family, these illnesses can skew the averages upward. If you're married and you see that the costs can be absorbed without impacting the financial well-being of your spouse, you might choose to assume this risk yourself instead of transferring it to an insurance company. The advantage here is that if the money isn't needed for long-term care, it will remain part of the estate to support both of you and may even be passed to the next generation. Leaving a legacy is not just for married people, so this same principle might apply across the board. Just remember that long-term care insurance can be expensive, but it can be a better option than hoping for the best if you don't have the funds to cover the cost of care yourself.

When my dad retired, the issue of failing health later in life came up, and he and I discussed funding a potential need for long-term care with insurance. Dad was the patriarch, and while he thanked me for bringing it to his attention, he said he was not the least bit interested. Unfortunately, my father was diagnosed with bladder cancer when he was sixty-three. It wasn't long before he needed twenty-four-hour care, which my parents could not afford. We had an aide come in for the morning shift to get him up and ready for the day, Mom took the second shift, and each child covered one night per week. There are seven of us, so it worked out well, with out-of-state family members doing their part. It was still a patchwork of care, but I was never so happy—and proud—to be one of seven children devoted to our parents. I was almost eight months pregnant with my son Jack, and we just found a way to make it work.

Even with family filling in for two-thirds of the time, I was shocked by how fast money was going out the door. Whatever was spent on Dad's care was money deducted from Mom's future finances. My parents were the same age, and she was only sixty-six when he passed.

Meanwhile, the side effects from radiation meant that Dad had to sleep upright in a chair at night, which was also the toughest part of his day. It was my turn to care for Dad one night, and I had fallen asleep on the extra mattress on his floor. When he woke up, he needed to use the commode, which was right next to his chair. He was very weak. I wrapped my arms around him and rocked him back and forth to get some momentum. I pulled him forward, and he flopped back in the chair. We tried again. And again. After the third attempt, he looked up at me and said, "I am so sorry."

"Sorry for what?" I asked.

"I am so sorry I didn't get that long-term care insurance you told me about. If I had, you wouldn't be here at three o'clock in the morning, eight months pregnant, trying to get me to the darn commode."

With tears in my eyes (even as I write this) I said, "Dad, you couldn't keep me away right now. It's payback time. This is my time to say thank you for sending me to Georgetown when you had three other kids already in college, and for all the sacrifices you and Mom made over the years."

That was my heart talking, and I still feel that way. But the fact of the matter is, *he* didn't want me there. He was the patriarch of our family. He lost something that night that all the money in the world can't replace: His dignity.

That's what long-term care insurance can do. It can give a person the kind of care they want, need, and deserve, and it lets them age with dignity without having to feel like a burden to their family and friends. It can also prevent bankrupting the family.

My father died not long after that, and Mom lived to be eighty-three years old. It was tough toward the end of her life, as money was really tight for her. If we'd had to pay for 24-hour care for my father, she would have run out of money in her early seventies. This was one of many times that I was so happy to be from a large family, but most patients do not have seven children and a healthy spouse who can all pull together and provide care.

If you decide to get long-term care insurance, do so hoping it's the biggest waste of money you ever spend[39].

Don't Carry Insurance You Don't Need

Now that you're thinking about adding insurance you've never had before, I want you to look at some of your standard insurance policies and make sure you still need them. Paying for something you don't need means you have less to save, invest, and pass on to those you love.

There will be periods when carrying life insurance is an example of not paying for something you don't need. The purpose of life insurance is to create money where it doesn't yet exist. A young couple, for example, probably doesn't have $1,000,000 in investments or in a 401(k), so they get a $1,000,000 life insurance policy in case one person dies. However, once they have saved a critical mass of savings, they may not need as much (or even any) life insurance.

---

39   There are now hybrid policies that can provide a partial or full return of premium, and as always, speak to a professional before you integrate it into your plan.

Also think about your auto insurance. If you're retired, are you still driving as many miles each day as you did when commuting to work? You can lower your premiums by readjusting your annual mileage estimate. Dr. Joseph Coughlin's research at MIT's AgeLab (see Chapter 1) has shown that auto-related expenses are the second-highest expenses in retirement. Many people are finding that ridesharing services like Uber and Lyft are not just convenient and safe but possibly more cost-effective. I know a man who will never drive again due to Parkinson's disease accompanied with dementia, but he likes to look out the window at his car parked in the driveway, so his wife is still paying for insurance coverage on that car. The best option for her is to sell the car and put the money toward her husband's care, but if she can't bring herself to do that, she could reduce the insurance coverage to the bare minimum required by her state. Better yet, she could let the registration lapse and cancel the insurance completely. If this sounds familiar, just make sure you hide the keys.

You might even be able to save money on your health insurance without reducing benefits. For example, if you're thinking about retiring before age sixty-five, you might be able to extend your group insurance for eighteen months, but don't rule out insurance provided by the government. The Affordable Care Act (commonly referred to as "Obamacare") offers tiers of coverage and depending on the sources and level of your income, you may even qualify for a subsidy. Here's something many people don't know: *the amount of money you've saved is completely irrelevant* because the subsidies are based on income only. Keep that in mind before you apply for Social Security.

The bottom line is to be responsible and purposeful. Don't skimp on insurance to save money. The risk is too great. Just be aware of what you're paying for, and don't pay for what you don't need.

The Inevitable Passing on Your Estate: Wills, Probate, and Trusts[xxiii]

If the COVID-19 pandemic taught us anything, it's that even relatively healthy people can succumb to a virulent strain of a microscopic murderer. We never really know when our time on earth is going to be over, and we also can't live in fear of that uncertainty, but we can—and should—control what happens to our estate when we are no longer around to make decisions. Each state has default provisions if someone dies intestate—that is, without a will—and the actual distributions vary depending on the deceased person's domicile, which is determined by where they reside more than 50% of the time. You've worked hard your entire life for your money. Don't let the laws of intestate succession determine what happens to your estate and who inherits your assets in the absence of a will. Planning for this can also save heirs from having to pay more taxes and probate fees than necessary[xxiii].

The hardest part of estate planning is having the conversation. While it's not nearly as fun as talking about a dream home, it's just as important, and when it's done, you'll be comforted knowing that your assets are accounted for, and how they will be distributed.

I had a meeting with a client's son, who happened to be a CPA and the executor of his parents' estate. As I was explaining some of the strategies that his parents had implemented, he just shook his head in awe. "I can't believe my parents did all this for us, they really thought things through. I just wish they were alive to see how much we all appreciate it." I knew his parents well, and I found myself saying, "Oh, Tom, believe me: they know."

Estate planning is one of the most unselfish things you will ever do, because you really don't get any benefit from it. It's common for younger, married clients to think that they don't need to consider estate planning because they don't have an estate yet, but many younger clients who are also parents have a very important and emotional decision to make. Where would their children go if they were to die simultaneously in an accident? And how should their care be paid for? Most parents would not feel comfortable making the children's guardian the beneficiary of an insurance policy to spend as they wish. As an alternative, the death benefit can be paid into a trust account that can only be used for the benefit of the children. How would you want college expenses to be handled? At what age would the children gain access to the trust income? How about the principal? So many questions, and so many viable answers because each family is different.

Although everyone can benefit from an estate plan, most conversations about estate planning tend to be with middle-aged or older couples. This is the time when they understand how important it is to make sure everything continues seamlessly for the surviving spouse. And then, when the second person passes away, the assets are distributed with as little tax and cost as possible.

It's important to ask yourself what you want to accomplish with an estate plan. What do you want to leave a surviving spouse? How about your children? When would you want them to have full access to their inheritance—if ever? How old are your beneficiaries? Are there charities you want to support? Do you have any concerns about the stability of your children's marriages and any prospects of divorce? Do you have grandchildren with special needs?

Also, it might be helpful to have the (somewhat morbid) "warm hands versus cold hands" discussion. Do you want to begin distributing your estate while you're still living? If you do want to start gifting in a significant way, just make sure you do the math and don't give away assets you might need later in life. A gift of any kind is an irrevocable decision, and there is nothing worse than a healthy eighty-year-old saying, "I wish I hadn't."

To protect your wealth and ensure distributions are made based on your wishes, you need to have a few documents in place.

Wills

A will is the legal document that distributes your assets to your intended beneficiaries. A letter of instruction attached to a will can include last words, instructions about burial, and who should take care of the cat. A will only controls those assets that do not already have a designated beneficiary. *Read that again* because it's very important: a will does not control jointly held assets, the distribution of retirement plan assets, insurance, annuities, or any account that might have a Transfer on Death or Payable on Death (TOD, POD) designation. These beneficiary designations always supersede the instructions in a will.

In other words, anything that has a beneficiary designation—life insurance, IRAs, 401(k)s, and pretty much all retirement accounts—does not have to go through probate. These accounts go directly to the named beneficiary. Also, anything held in joint with rights of survivorship (JWROS) or tenancy by the entirety (TBE) will go to the other person free of probate. You do not have to be married to put assets in JWROS but be very careful when doing so with anyone other than a spouse. First, there are important income tax considerations, and once the account has that person's name on it, they can take out whatever they want, whenever they want, as if they owned 100% of the account. Anyone can title an asset jointly with rights of survivorship.

Another option to avoid probate is a transfer on death account (TOD). This is an account at a bank, brokerage firm, or mutual fund that includes a beneficiary designation. You can even do it with real estate, by changing the title on the deed. For example, I could have a mutual fund in my name but list my husband as the beneficiary. The account would automatically be transferred (without probate) upon my death.

This might be the most important thing you need to remember when putting together or updating a will. Married couples often leave everything to the surviving spouse. Sometimes, early on in marriage, a couple will take out an insurance policy to provide for their children's care, with a children's trust named as the beneficiary. When they update the will years later, they decide to delete the trust because the children are now adults. Having forgotten about the original designation, they never change the beneficiary on the policy. So, who receives the insurance proceeds? Having encountered this situation more than once, I can tell you: *it's a mess.* Years of filings and attorney's fees could have been avoided by reviewing all of the beneficiary designations. *In other words, assume nothing.* If this is a second marriage, make sure a former spouse isn't named as the beneficiary on a prior employer's 401(k), which will save your heirs from future problems. Update beneficiary designations and wills after the divorce is settled to prevent any possibility of confusion—even if you want to leave a former spouse as a beneficiary. If the form is updated to a new date after legal documents have been signed, intent probably won't be questioned.

It is important to remember that when it comes to life insurance, retirement accounts, annuities, and transfer on death accounts, what you have in your will is irrelevant. Make sure these designations and the titling of the assets reflect what you want and are coordinated with what you have in your will.

Outdated Wills That Establish Mandatory Trusts

Approaches to avoid federal estate taxes have changed dramatically over the last twenty-five years, yet too many people have not updated their estate plans to reflect these new developments. For example, under prior rules, it made sense for married couples to include instructions for the executor of their will to set up a trust at the first death for the surviving spouse. These trusts were often referred to as "bypass" or "credit shelter" trusts. This arrangement would optimize the tax credit each spouse is entitled to, which would offset any federal estate tax due. The surviving spouse would have access to the income and principal under certain circumstances as outlined in the trust, with the proceeds distributed to the named beneficiaries when the second spouse dies. Under current law, this arrangement is no longer absolutely necessary, although it still makes sense for some families. This is another reason why reviewing your estate planning documents and the outlined strategies with your estate planning attorney is important. In this example, this mandatory—*and irrevocable*—arrangement would have to be executed at the first death.

What Exactly Is Probate, and Should It Be Avoided?

We've all heard horror stories about the cost and time involved in probate. Each state has its own rules and procedures—some more onerous than others. For example, in Pennsylvania, probate is not an expensive process. In fact, if you're an executor and you go to a probate office in my town, you don't even sit down anymore. You would stand at a counter, provide identification, and present the original will. Typically, a check under $500 would be due and you (as the executor) would receive what is called a *Short Certificate*. This gives you the legal authority to follow what was written in the will.

It's not a court proceeding, and you don't need an attorney. Nonetheless, it is still advisable to obtain an attorney's help to settle the estate; there are some things you need to do irrespective of probate. For example, federal estate and state inheritance tax returns may need to be filed, especially if you are married and want to preserve the deceased spouse's tax credit (more on that later). Announcements notifying creditors need to be made in certain publications. It's also good to have an expert help you interpret some of the legalese found in wills and trusts.

Other states can be a different story. My uncle was a Florida resident, and we thought he had everything titled in the name of his Revocable Living Trust (see below), but after he died, we found $5,000 in a separate account. It cost $3,000 in fees to probate a $5,000 account, plus the cost of flying back and forth to Florida three times to get the matter resolved.

Regardless of the state you live in, there are several things you can do to make sure your executor doesn't end up spending unnecessary time and money administering your estate.

One possibility is to set up a Revocable Living Trust, which includes the same type of instructions you might include in a will, with additional language to avoid the probate process. Once that is done, you can populate the trust with your assets (that extra step my uncle missed on the bank account) which need to be titled in the name of the trust. The advantages of this approach are that your estate doesn't go through the court process; it's private, and the heirs avoid those costs and delays. Since it is a revocable trust, you can change its terms up until the date when you can't—which is when you die (or become incapacitated.) The tax identification number (Tax ID) is your Social Security number, and the trust is taxed in the same manner as it would be if you owned the assets outside of the trust.

For example, if Janet Smith has investments that create taxable dividends and capital gains, and if she transfers them into an account titled in the name of "The Janet Smith Revocable Living Trust," dated February 20, 2021, those taxable earnings are reported on Janet's tax return just as they were before. Even though the assets are owned by the trust, it's as if she owns them personally. Establishing a Revocable Living Trust satisfies the goal of avoiding the probate process while also allowing you to keep control of the assets and adjust the terms in the document if circumstances warrant.

Creating a Revocable Living Trust (also referred to as a "living trust") is relatively simple. Think about a will or trust as a letter to an executor or trustee. Whatever you would have written in a will, you simply write into a living trust. However, the one mistake people make over and over is that they don't title their assets correctly. To be effective, the living trust must be populated by (typically non-retirement) assets and real estate so they are owned by the trust. If you skip that step, the trust is useless; since the accounts are still owned by you as an individual, the executor will have to set up an estate and go through the probate process. Having a living trust does not impact income or estate taxes in any way; the assets simply avoid probate, assuming that's a worthy goal in the state where you reside.

There may be one more advantage. Keep in mind that a will only applies at death. If you become unable to manage your affairs while you are still alive, your family might need assets for your care that they can't access. The revocable trust avoids this rare but not unheard-of situation. Keep in mind that you are the primary trustee of your revocable trust. The successor trustee you've chosen just steps into your place and is able to pay your bills and manage your financial affairs as if they were you. It is a huge responsibility for the person taking over, and they must only use the assets for your benefit. If a

Revocable Living Trust seems like overkill in the state where you live, this can also be accomplished with a Power of Attorney. Either way, the person you choose doesn't own the assets, you do. As such, they are a fiduciary, and they are bound both legally and ethically to act in your best interest[40]. Upon your death, assets in the living trust are distributed in the same manner as they would have been with a will, except without that walk to the courthouse.

Let's not make probate a bigger deal than it really is and remember to be careful when changing the title on accounts or real estate. There could be significant unintended consequences. For example, let's assume clients named Scott and John are married and live in a state where probate is a process worth avoiding if possible. They own stock worth $50,000 with a very low cost basis of $5,000 in a joint account. If Scott gets a diagnosis that makes it probable that he will predecease John, a better tax outcome would result if they put that account in his name only, even if it had to go through probate. Under current law, if Scott passes, the cost basis steps up to the fair market value as of the date of his death, which in this example is $50,000. A better idea still might be for Scott to keep the stock in his name but set up a TOD account, naming John as his beneficiary. This way, upon Scott's death, John would receive a full step-up in cost basis *and* still avoid probate. If the stock was held jointly (avoiding probate) and John sells it after Scott's death, only 50% of it gets the tax benefit.

With a transfer on death (TOD) designation, the taxable gain is either minimized or eliminated entirely[41]. You can elect to move assets

---

40   Trust me, it's no joke to be held to that standard.

41   In 2020 there was a tax proposal that would eliminate this benefit entirely (the full step-up in cost basis at death), and that was not the first time the government had proposed closing this loophole. There are several things that could be radically different if certain proposals are adopted in the future, requiring a fresh set of eyes on your overall financial plan.

into this TOD structure at any time, but there is one caveat. In the case of a terminal diagnosis, assets can be transferred into the name of the ill spouse and potentially save the surviving spouse a significant amount of income taxes, but the sick spouse has to live for twelve months after the transfer in order for it to be effective. There really isn't a downside, though; it's a "heads you win, tails you break even" decision. If the sick spouse does pass before twelve months, it's as if you didn't make the transfer, but you aren't any worse off. This type of maneuvering can make people uncomfortable—it feels a bit like jumping the gun or dancing on the grave, and I certainly understand that. As long as the subject is broached with sensitivity and care, I have found terminal patients to be clear-eyed and practical when it comes to finances.

And there may be a better option. A few years ago, we were helping one of our new clients transfer their accounts when the husband called from the hospital. His wife had just been diagnosed with liver cancer and was in intensive care. At that point I took a deep breath and said, "Joe, I know this is probably the last thing you're thinking about, but we should consult an attorney and consider moving assets into a marital trust. There could be significant tax benefits if Pam were to predecease you."

"This is why I have you here," he said. "I want you to think about these things."

It was clear that Pam wasn't going to live the full twelve months necessary for Joe to get the full step-up in cost basis if we transferred assets into her name, but if we moved them into a marital trust for his benefit, he would! With the help of his estate attorney, we went ahead and took care of things, so they didn't have to think about finances at such an important time. Sure enough, she did predecease him, and that change of retitling those assets saved him more than $150,000 in taxes, without removing his access to them.

Keep in mind that a professional can often facilitate steps and take action when one spouse (or any family member) is facing end-of-life decisions. Upon such a diagnosis, reaching out to your advisors would not be your first or second call, but it could be your fifth or sixth call. That gives each professional a chance to review the situation and determine if anything needs to be restructured for the best financial outcome. It certainly helps if there is a trusted relationship beforehand.

Now, putting the assets in the dying spouse's name isn't always the best move. If assets have gone down in value, you would want the (healthy) surviving spouse to keep the original high-basis assets in their name. That's because if the asset is in the deceased spouse's name, the *cost basis would step down* to the fair market value as of the date of their death. Valuations can be done as of the date of death, or six months later, whichever is more favorable from an estate and income tax planning perspective. Let's say that you bought 1,000 shares of Great Deal Stock three years ago at $100,000. Let's assume a bear market occurs and the price of the stock drops 20%, so the value is now $80,000. If you're in poor health, you would want to sell that stock while you're still alive so that you get the income tax benefits or transfer the account tax-free to your spouse to retain the higher cost basis. In other words, just as the cost basis can step up as of the date of death, it can also step down. If heirs inherit it, they will receive an asset valued at $80,000, which becomes their new cost basis, and that $20,000 capital loss deduction would be lost. At a tax rate of 15%, this $3,000 benefit may be worth preserving.

Trusts for Minor Children (and Adults)

Wealth-busting predators just seem to flock around estates and inheritances like vultures circling prey. A well-written trust works like a vault when it comes to protecting assets from taxes, probate, bad marriages, lawsuits, bankruptcies, and other minefields. Even situations like addictions can be addressed with a substance-abuse clause. *While it sounds intimidating,* a trust account simply has a different title and separate tax identification number. It's similar to a business entity like a corporation or LLC with its own investment objectives and bylaws. A trust can ensure there are assets left to control. It can also protect your assets while you are still living.

You don't need to be a millionaire to warrant incorporating a trust into your estate plan. You only need to want to hold your assets in a form that is most beneficial for you and your heirs.

When it comes to leaving your wealth to the next generation, it's important to take their maturity into account. Sometimes kids are ready to receive it, *and sometimes they're not.* Trusts can solve that problem. You probably wouldn't want to give your children access to $1,000,000 when they turn eighteen, but you can set up a schedule of payments that makes sense. For example, in addition to distributions from the trust for their health, education, and overall support, you could stipulate that they will receive 10% when they're twenty-five, 30% when they're thirty, and the balance when they're thirty-five. This way they can learn how to handle money and won't have the opportunity to blow it all at once.

Trusts can even be set up to encourage a specific type of behavior. Some trusts will pay for education but not for a car. Some will provide a down payment for a house but not for speculative investment. Some will pay for living expenses so that a beneficiary can afford to work a low-paying job helping others—pro bono legal work, for example—but won't pay living expenses for heirs without jobs. One couple believed that it was important for a parent to stay home with young children, so they set up an incentive trust. If one of the parents stayed home with their children, the trust would pay them the equivalent of a $50,000 salary. The goal was to replace what they would have earned in the workplace. It wasn't a mandate, but it provided an incentive to encourage a certain behavior that was consistent with that family's values.

The key to a good trust is to make it as flexible as possible without including language that could negate the intended benefits it can provide.

Trusts provide barriers against other outside forces that could negatively impact an estate, such as bankruptcies and lawsuits, but the area that concerns many parents is the potential for even seemingly happily married children to end up in a divorce one day. If a trust for them is written correctly, it—and therefore the assets it contains— never becomes a marital asset, so in the event of a divorce, none of that money is included at the bargaining table. Similarly, if one partner is a doctor and gets sued for malpractice, those assets can't be reached. *Remember those kids with the yet to be fully developed frontal lobes?* At the age of eighteen they're considered adults, so if they make a mistake and cause a fatal accident, the assets in a trust would be protected from a lawsuit.

Anyone (especially those with minor children) would be well advised to have legal documents drawn up and stashed in a safe place: a current will or Revocable Living Trust, which might include trusts for children[42]. Most probate offices will not accept copied documents.

A will contains a set of instructions to your executor that outlines to whom you want your assets to go to and how, either in outright

---

42 *And please* tell someone where the original documents are held.

distributions or by placing assets into a trust for the benefit of your heirs. When death occurs, a will is a once-and-done type of deal.

A trust is different. It is a legal entity that explains how the money is to be handled on an ongoing basis, including the amounts and times of distribution. It is particularly important to have assets go into a trust if minor children are the beneficiaries of an estate. First of all, in most states, minors cannot inherit real estate or sell financial assets without an adult custodian or trust in place. As soon as the minor's signature is required to open an account, sell, refinance, or transact other business, a court would have to get involved to protect the child's interests. This is an expensive, time-consuming process that you want to avoid at all costs. At the very least, the decisions made in court may not reflect your values, or even the unique circumstances of each child. Either way, in most states at age 18 the entire inheritance is theirs.

A better option is to set up a children's trust in your will or Revocable Living Trust and name someone to manage the inheritance. This will also give you the ability to designate when your children will have full access to the assets. Most parents who establish trusts want their children to be several years older than eighteen—legal adulthood in many states—when they receive their inheritance. We have found that most eighteen-year-olds would spend money differently from twenty-five or thirty-five-year-olds. Maturity develops at different ages, and priorities change. A testamentary trust that is written as a contingency plan in the will does not come into play unless it is necessary. In fact, most testamentary trusts are never launched, because the thing we were worried about—both parents dying at an early age and leaving minor children—never happened.

But it can.

Estate planning should not be a set-it-and-forget-it process, even though it often is. For this reason, a good estate planning attorney will try to anticipate contingencies and make the language in documents provide as much flexibility as possible. Be careful, though, because one word can change an outcome dramatically.

Let's take an example. When an attorney is drafting a trust or any legal document, words have consequences. "A trustee" is very different from "a corporate trustee;" the former could be a relative or friend who knows the family, while a corporate trustee is typically a bank or trust company that may not. Also, the words "shall" and "may" carry very different meanings in the world of trusts, especially if you want to protect your children's inheritance. "The trustee *may* pay income" *is very different from* "The trustee *shall* pay income." One word in the document can change the dynamics of the trust itself, as well as those between the trustee and the beneficiaries. The objective is to protect the assets so that no one can pierce that trust wall and put a claim on the money intended for your loved ones.

Let's assume you have two sons in their late twenties. One is married, one is dating someone. You love your daughter-in-law but aren't as enamored with the girlfriend. We can't pick our children's spouses, and even wonderful marriages can go sour when the pressures of life become divisive. So, with the help of your estate planning attorney, you might set up trusts for your children with staggered distributions based on each son's age while leaving some discretion with the trustee in case the relationship (or marriage) has taken a dark turn. The goal of a trust is not to keep the money from your children (although a spendthrift trust is a great tool to help save them from themselves), it is to protect your children from others. With guidance from your attorney, you can decide whether the trustee "shall" (i.e., must) or "may" pay out all or some of the trust income and principal as the children reach specified age. The "may" option gives the trustee discretion in holding up a payment if outside circumstances, such as a divorce, a malpractice suit, a substance abuse issue, or a bankruptcy, make it an unwise time for that payment. Since the trustee will be making these decisions in your stead, the selection of the trustee (and their successor) is one of the most important decisions you will make on a trust.

Inherited IRAs: Land Mines to Avoid

IRA accounts can be inherited, just like any other financial account. The problem for heirs, however, is that the assets in the account haven't been taxed yet, so it will be up to the beneficiary to take care of that liability. Managing the tax impact on an inherited IRA typically involves more than just cashing out the account and paying all the income taxes at once. This is rarely the best option. Spouses can roll the inherited account into their own IRA, but if there is a significant age difference between them, that may not be the best course of action because the surviving spouse might be able to use a different table. *Remember when I said RMDs are complicated?* This is an area with lots of ifs, ands, or buts, so proper legal and tax counsel is appropriate at this time.

One word of caution. If your existing will or trust includes language for an "IRA Trust," with the asset protection a trust can provide, a recent piece of legislations called the SECURE Act (and SECURE Act II) warrant a reexamination of that document. In an attempt to protect a beneficiary for a period of years, such a trust might inadvertently expose them to a higher tax rate, yet another reason why a periodic review of your financial and estate plan is so important.

Avoiding Estate and Inheritance Taxes: A Worthy Goal or Overkill?

Married couples do not pay a federal estate tax at the first death irrespective of how many zeros are in their net worth. Further, estate and gift tax planning have become less of a priority because of the tax legislation passed in 2017. As of 2021[43], the total amount that each spouse can gift or leave to non-spouse beneficiaries without incurring any estate or gift tax liability is $11,700,000. This is referred to as the "exemption," and in the spirit of making things as complicated as possible for all of us, each person receives a tax credit that happens to equal the taxes that would otherwise be due on an estate of about $11,700,000. That means a couple would need to have a taxable estate over $23 million (under current law as of 2021) before estate taxes are triggered.

A few caveats. First, individual states might have an estate or inheritance tax, so there still might be some tax considerations over and above the income tax planning I've talked about so far. I'm not going to get into the generation-skipping transfer (GST) tax rules, a complicated area of estate planning that warrants proper counsel.

Probably even more important is the fact that leadership in Washington attempted to pass several dramatic changes in tax law over the past few years, and for some people none are as important as those in the estate planning area. Even though this legislation did not go through, the current tax law with the higher estate exemptions is scheduled to sunset in the year 2025, which means that the exemption would revert to what it was before the law was changed. ($5,500,000 adjusted for inflation) The sunset provision means that income and estate tax changes put into place in 2017 would revert to what the law was before. These changes could have profound implications in many areas of income and estate tax planning.

---

43   You are probably reading this book a few years later, because it has taken me that long to write it. Just keep in mind that while the numbers may be different (higher and more favorable to you), the concepts remain the same—until the year 2026 if the sunset provision kicks in. That's when a new edition of this chapter will be needed.

Gift taxes are usually included in the discussion of estate taxes because the amount exempted from tax can be used either while you're alive or after you die. Under current law, you can give $15,000 per person per year (which increases each year) to as many people as your heart desires (and your pocketbook can afford). Only the excess over that amount to each person would be subject to a gift tax. That does not mean you're paying that tax with cash; you're using some of the exemption (the $11.7 million dollars) today instead of waiting until death. It's the warm hands approach. For example, let's assume Joan has two children. Joan can gift $15,000 to each child each year, or $30,000 total, and there is no need to file a gift tax return. This money is not considered taxable income to the children either; it is literally a gift. This year, she wants to give them $100,000 each for a down payment on a home. The first $15,000 is free, so Joan would have her CPA or tax attorney file Form 709, which essentially reports the gifts, reducing her exemption at death by $170,000 (the additional gifts, or $85,000 to each child). If Joan dies, the amount excluded from tax would be about $11.5 million, instead of $11.7 million.

Are you with me so far?

For another case study, let's take this one step further. Let's assume their neighbors, Bob and Sue are in their early sixties and own a small business they love. Let's assume it's the year 2026[44] and the value of their estate including retirement plans, real estate, life insurance, and their business is $25,000,000.

Under current law and after certain deductions and discounts, there would be little to no estate tax, but assuming the law doesn't change again between now and the end of 2025, the amount each of

---

44   Which it might be by the time I get this book finished. To keep things simple, I will
       use 2021 exemption figures, which will increase by inflation until (or if) the sunset
       provision becomes law.

them can leave estate tax free is scheduled to go back down to about $5,500,000 (indexed for inflation). There is sad truth about broken hearts: Losing a spouse increases the likelihood the other will follow *within a year* is 30 to 90% (Elwert and Christakis, "The Effect of Widowhood on Mortality by the Causes of Death of Both Spouses"). Assuming Bob and Sue died tragically in the same year (2026) and the sunset provision kicks in, they will be able to leave about $11,000, 000 between the two of them, but $14,000,000 is now exposed to being taxed at a rate of a 40%, and their heirs will owe about $5,600,000[45]. That's great if there are liquid assets, not so great if the value of the business is $20,000,000 of the $25,000,000 (or 80% of the total). The children will either have to borrow the additional money needed or sell the business to pay the tax. When there is a tax deadline, look out for the bottom feeders.

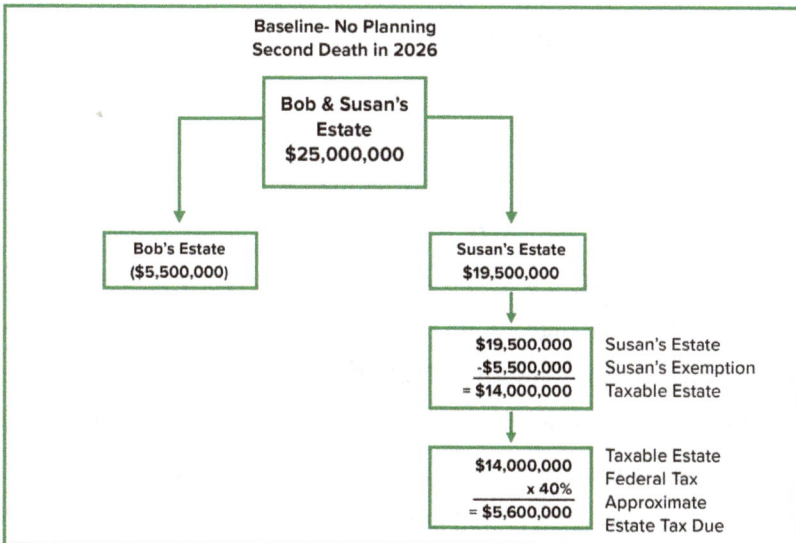

Baseline- No Planning
Second Death in 2026

Bob & Susan's Estate
$25,000,000

Bob's Estate
($5,500,000)

Susan's Estate
$19,500,000

$19,500,000	Susan's Estate
-$5,500,000	Susan's Exemption
= $14,000,000	Taxable Estate

$14,000,000	Taxable Estate
x 40%	Federal Tax
= $5,600,000	Approximate Estate Tax Due

---

45   An important note: this is a simplified overview only. Estate tax calculations are actually very complicated, changing year to year, and estate planning is worth a book of its own.

What is a potential solution for Bob and Sue? The optimal estate plan will depend on the actual composition of their net worth. As I write this, we have identified about 54 viable options and some might work better than others and have strings attached. Examples of what might influence the choice include amounts invested in retirement accounts versus non-retirement accounts, how much of Bob and Sue's net worth is comprised of illiquid assets such as real estate or a closely held business, and the cost basis of invested money, to name just a few important considerations.

One solution might include establishing a Spousal Lifetime Access Trust (SLAT), which is basically a trust for children and other heirs—*eventually*. Instead of waiting until death, a SLAT involves using that juicy estate and gift tax exemption of $11,700,000 available now. In this example, Bob can place up to $11,700,000 of his exemption into the SLAT for Sue's benefit while she's alive, to go to their children only when she passes. Remember, Bob is still alive, but this is an irrevocable trust. Sue has lifetime access; she can receive the income from the trust assets, and she has access to the principal, or both. If the law changes, Bob and Sue have already removed a total of $11,700,000 from the taxable estate. I'm a big fan of solutions that create a "heads you win, tails you break even" outcome. In this case, heads, this family wins. If the law doesn't change, either through new legislation or because it doesn't revert to prior law after 2025, the estate tax situation is about the same with or without the SLAT, so with the exception of attorney's fees to set it up and administer, it's tails—they break even.

And by the way, they will have saved the federal estate tax of 40% on *at least* the excess over $5,500,000 if the law does revert under the sunset provision in 2025. At 40%, that equates to $2,480,000 saved. Remember, after 2025, Sue would be able to leave up to $5,500,000 estate-tax-free upon her death, but the excess over that amount would be subject to tax. Once Bob places the assets in the in the Spousal Lifetime Access Trust, the assets grow outside of *both* taxable estates.

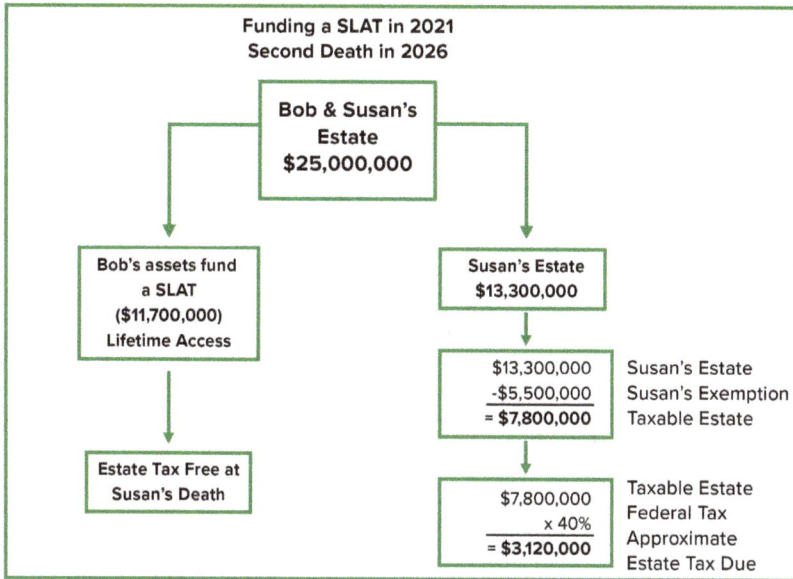

It gets better. Let's assume Bob lives 10 years and Sue lives for 20 years. Depending on the couple's cash flow needs, using other assets to pay expenses in retirement allows the assets in the SLAT to compound and then be transferred to the next generation or heirs without federal estate tax. If we assume a 7% rate of return where money doubles about every ten years, $11,700,000 would double to $23,400,000 in ten years. Based on that assumption, if Sue passes in year twenty, almost $47,000,000 is transferred to the children free of federal estate tax. Depending on the laws, at 40% that could save almost $17,000,000 in federal estate tax!

One caveat: the assets do not receive a step-up in cost basis at either Bob's or Sue's death. Therefore, it may be important to be selective in choosing which assets should fund the trust, and discuss a substitution clause with your attorney.

Can Sue do a SLAT also? The answer is: maybe. They have to be very careful to work with an estate attorney who understands how to avoid certain land mines if each spouse sets up a SLAT for the other. This is intended to be a high-level overview of this technique[46], but if your estate might benefit from the tax savings, don't be intimidated. There are excellent law firms specializing in the latest estate tax planning techniques that can save your heirs a significant amount of money.

Transfers of Family Businesses

What if the value of Bob and Sue's business comprises a significant percentage of their estate? In the example above, if the business isn't an appropriate asset to put into a SLAT, are there other options?

Yes! They might be able to apply for a minority discount[47] by transferring a certain percentage of the business to each family member in a Family Limited Partnership (FLP), an Intentionally Defective Grantor Trust (IDGT), or other tools. The key is determining whether Bob and Sue plan on keeping the business, need the cash flow from it, or want to involve the children in the enterprise. This can get tricky if there are some children who work in the business, while others do not.

Insurance Trusts

One of the least complicated ways to save significant estate tax is to have an insurance trust. Since most people are named as the owner

---

46   These are simplified examples of certain tools, and the estate tax system in general, which in reality changes year to year.

47   A minority discount recognizes that the value of a business (or any entity) is reduced for tax purposes because even the IRS recognizes that partial ownership of something is not the same as full or majority ownership. For example, 25% of an illiquid asset that the person has no control over is not worth the same as 51% or more of an asset where the decisions they make cannot be contested and are final.

of a policy on their life, the death benefit is included as part of the decedent's taxable estate. If life insurance is owned by a well-drafted trust, it is not included in the insured's taxable estate. The proceeds can remain in trust for the benefit of the surviving spouse, and upon their death, whatever is left goes to the beneficiaries of the trust completely estate-tax-free. If you gift an existing policy, there is a three-year lookback, so if death occurs in that period, it's as if it was never put into a trust. Any cash value in that policy put into a trust is considered a gift, as are future premiums if the insurance is funded by the insured. In order to qualify for the annual gift tax exclusion, there are important annual notices that the trustee must send to the beneficiaries each year. Once the system of sending the notice is set up, it is easy for the trustee to follow.

Other Tools to Save a Bundle of Taxes

To use another (high-level) example, Matt and Cathy, ages sixty and fifty-eight, own a home in New Jersey worth $1,000,000. They wish to bequeath the home to their two grown children, who've expressed a desire to use the home as a vacation getaway for their families. Matt and Cathy set up a Qualified Personal Residence Trust (QPRT) and transfer the home into the trust for a twenty-year term, i.e., "retained income period." During that time, they continue to live in the home and enjoy it. Using tables from 2021, the future gift (20 years later) is valued at a discounted "present value" (PV) of $361,230, because, according to the IRS discount rate for such transfers (about 2.4% as of this writing), that is the present value of a future transfer (twenty years from now) of $1,000,000. If interest rates increase, this discount is even more enticing.

Even better, in this example, we've gotten the house and all future appreciation out of the estate, at a deep discount, using only $361,000 of the $11.7 million exemption.

At the risk of sounding like a late night informercial *("But wait, there's more!")*, what happens at the end of the term? At that point, Matt and Cathy's children would technically own the home, but what if Matt and Cathy want to continue to use it? They can pay "rent"[48] to their children, removing more money from their taxable estate, without those payments being considered gifts for tax purposes. There are many considerations for this type of vehicle, and a qualified estate attorney can guide you appropriately. Most areas of estate planning include a gift in one form or another, and some strategies allow you to do so at a deep discount. A Qualified Personal Residence Trust might be funded by gifting a residence or vacation home into a trust that you'd like to keep in the family.

There is no shortage of estate planning techniques currently available, all with their special acronyms. (Note the word "currently." Legislation proposed at any given time could close these loopholes.) There are GRITs, GRATs, and IDGTs, and each one of these has a different application. Some are more useful when interest rates are high (such as a QPRT), others are more effective when they are low (A Charitable Lead Trust). I do not believe in trying to solve a problem that may not exist, so work with a professional to understand the implications. While there may be an issue now, many people will find their estates declining in value later in life because they are living on the assets. Others might simply use the convenient $15,000 per year

---

48   Be careful of non-financial implications here. Depending on family dynamics, paying rent to the kids (and their spouses) may not be a great experience for Mom and Dad. While it could be a good way to get additional money out of the taxable estate without the rent being considered a gift, there could be some unintended consequences.

gift tax exclusion to children and grandchildren so they can see them enjoy some of their inheritance while they are alive.

My point is this: no overkill. Most trusts to save estate taxes are irrevocable, so it is important to know how they work, understand potential unintended consequences, and assess whether the strategies meet your overall objectives.

Charitable Giving

We touched on the income tax benefits of charitable giving in chapter 5. Without knowledge of various strategies, many charitably inclined people simply name a nonprofit in their wills and leave it at that. But there are more tax-efficient ways to donate while still receiving tax benefits.

An underutilized method of charitable giving is a charitable annuity. These are similar to standard annuities, except instead of giving a lump-sum payment to an insurance company, you donate a lump sum of money, stocks, real estate, or other income-producing assets to a nonprofit organization you want to support. In exchange, the nonprofit agrees to pay you a predetermined set amount every month for the rest of your life. After you die, the charity keeps whatever is left of the donation, which they have presumably invested to cover part or all of the monthly payments. Just as with a standard annuity, you can set charitable annuity payments to stop at the end of your life or continue as long as your spouse is alive, too.

Charitable annuities have several advantages that make them worth considering. Aside from supporting a cause you believe in while receiving annuity payments, you get to take a tax deduction in the year you make the donation. You can also avoid capital gains taxes on appreciated stock if you use it to fund the charitable annuity. There is no limit to the number of charitable gift annuities you can set up: one for your church, one for your alma mater, one for a local foundation, one for a national charity, etc. And they don't need to be huge donations. While a large donation will typically result in larger monthly payments, smaller donations to local nonprofits might be appreciated more by the organization. Since you will be relying on the monthly payments for retirement income, you just want to make sure the organization is financially solid. You can't take your gift back if the nonprofit runs into trouble.

Another option for donating to your favorite charity while still receiving income is a charitable remainder trust (CRT). In this case, you place whatever assets you want to donate to the charity into an irrevocable trust. Again, you'd ideally transfer highly appreciated assets, and you'd get a tax deduction for the donation. There are limits to the amount you can deduct against income each year, although unused portions of the deduction can be carried forward for five years. The trust then pays you a specific percentage of the assets each year. For example, if you place $100,000 into a remainder trust, you can set the terms so that it pays you 5% each year, meaning that you'd receive $5,000 the first year. Normally, the assets would be invested and generating returns, so if the rate of return was also 5%, the payments would be relatively the same each year. If the return on the trust investments was 7%, the trust would retain the extra 2%, but next year you'd get the 5% on $102,000, or $5,100. These payments would continue until you (or both spouses) die, at which time the charity would receive the balance of the trust assets.

The reverse of a charitable remainder trust is a charitable lead trust (CLT). Like the charitable remainder trust, the CLT should only be considered for those who are charitably inclined already, and this option really sizzles in a low-interest-rate environment and in a year when you have a large capital gain. The tax deduction is based on a formula applied the year of the donation, so keep the CLT on your radar if you ever sell a business, a piece of real estate, or any investment that triggers a capital gain. This strategy pays an income to the charity for a term, typically a period of years, and at the end of the term, whatever remains in the trust account can revert back to you, or—better yet—your heirs. If the latter, and if designed accordingly, there is no impact on your estate and gift tax exemption, and they could receive this remaining balance tax-free. Just make sure you understand the specific strategy before implementing it, and work with a team of professionals who understand you and your intent.

Powers of Attorney

Even after completing your will, you aren't done. Naming a financial power of attorney works the same way that naming a successor trustee of a living trust does; they are fiduciaries you have designated to conduct your financial affairs if you aren't able to. You may have been in a car accident or had surgery, and this person can step in and make sure bills are paid and financial institutions are notified.

A healthcare power of attorney is a whole different animal. Most of the time, if you're working with a qualified estate planning attorney, they will include this as part of the documents. If you're sick or get hurt and cannot make decisions for yourself, this allows the person you designate to consult with medical professionals and authorize treatments. If there is no hope for survival, you can provide guidelines for end-of-life decisions.

Also, don't forget that in most states, once a child turns eighteen years of age, they are an adult. They need a financial power of attorney for any accounts they have in their name, and perhaps even more importantly, a healthcare power of attorney.

This is where I hope you'll learn from my own potential mistake.

My Son's Traumatic Brain Injury

One weekend, Ed and I were in New York City about to attend a formal gathering for a nonprofit organization. I was on the phone with my daughter, Carrie, wishing her a happy birthday, when I saw another call coming in on my phone. Not wanting to interrupt our birthday chat, I told Carrie it was her younger brother Jack and that I'd call him after she and I were finished.

For whatever reason, on the fifth ring I asked Carrie to hold and swiped to the other call. Jack said he'd fallen off his skateboard and asked if I could come home from the office. When I reminded him that we were away, he said he'd be fine *but in a drifted-off kind of way.* The mom and ICU nurse in me didn't like that answer, which started a flurry of activity to prevent him from going up to bed and to get him to the hospital.

I didn't realize it at the time, but Jack had not one *but two* brain hemorrhages, two skull fractures, and a clot resting on his lower spinal cord that could have rendered him paralyzed for life. Intuition told me we needed to get home from New York fast, which was not an easy task, as the Pope was about to drive by the front door of our hotel. While we were scrambling, Jack stopped breathing, was put on a ventilator and was being medevacked to the Hospital of the University of Pennsylvania. It was September of his senior year in high school, and my nursing background made me painfully aware of the consequences of traumatic brain injuries.

Fortunately, this story has a happy ending. Jack recovered and graduated from college with high honors and no residual effects except for a permanent loss of smell. The cranial nerve that gives us our sense of smell forks off the same nerve involving taste, which was severed in the upper root. Jack is able to savor burgers and Mexican food as he did before the fall, but he will always miss the smell of turkey in the oven and the piney scent of Christmas tree in December. I later learned he was riding a skateboard at forty miles per hour down a long, steep hill without a helmet. And while I did want to kill him when I found out, I was so grateful that it wasn't worse.

Why am I telling you this story? Jack was exactly seventeen years and nine months old. If he were eighteen, he would have been an adult, and under the rules for HIPPA, the hospital would not have been in a position to give us information or authorize the brain surgery he may have needed. As far as the hospital was concerned, I would have been "some lady on the phone."

So here is the solution: get healthcare powers of attorney for your adult children. If they're going to college, get it done before they leave. They probably don't have much money yet, so the financial power of attorney or a will isn't as important. A healthcare power of attorney however, is important, even if they're married.

I've had several scares with my children, and this detail is the last thing you want to be dealing with in a crisis. If Jack had been 18 years old, that would have been a heartbreaking mistake.

PART THREE: HIJACKS

CHAPTER 7

15 Mistakes People Make Over and Over Again[49]

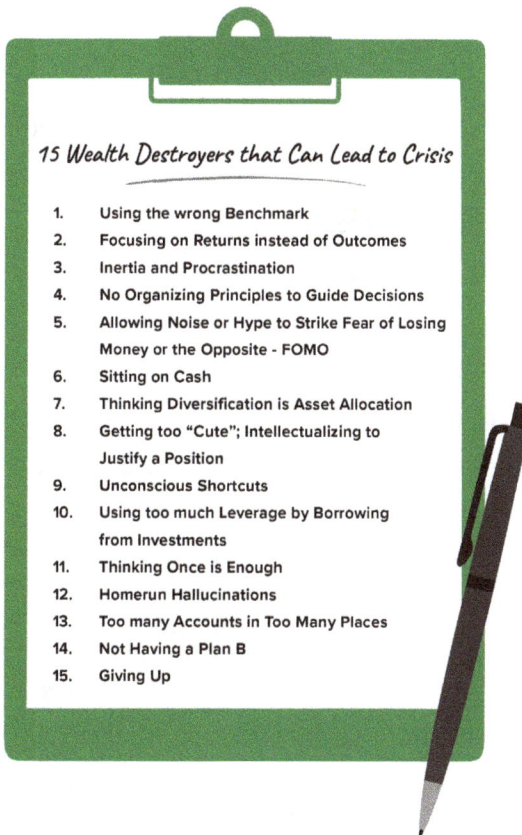

15 Wealth Destroyers that Can Lead to Crisis

1. Using the wrong Benchmark
2. Focusing on Returns instead of Outcomes
3. Inertia and Procrastination
4. No Organizing Principles to Guide Decisions
5. Allowing Noise or Hype to Strike Fear of Losing Money or the Opposite - FOMO
6. Sitting on Cash
7. Thinking Diversification is Asset Allocation
8. Getting too "Cute"; Intellectualizing to Justify a Position
9. Unconscious Shortcuts
10. Using too much Leverage by Borrowing from Investments
11. Thinking Once is Enough
12. Homerun Hallucinations
13. Too many Accounts in Too Many Places
14. Not Having a Plan B
15. Giving Up

---

49   Beware! There are wealth destroyers that can lead to financial demise.

Speaking of mistakes, we're all human, and we're going to make them. But given the choice, I have always favored learning from other people's mistakes, so I don't have to live through the consequences personally.

Some of what follows may feel repetitive from earlier chapters. *That is by design.* After more than thirty years as a financial planner, I've pinpointed fifteen of the most common errors people make over and over again, and frankly, sometimes hearing important concepts more than once can make the difference.

1. USING THE WRONG BENCHMARK

This is probably the most common mistake, *and it's a big one.*

People who track the S&P 500 (or any unmanaged index) often cause themselves unnecessary stress. They compare an index to their portfolio, wonder why their portfolio isn't earning a better rate of return, feeling like they aren't keeping up.

There are indeed times when less really is more.

We have already discussed the math of compounding and the impact of timing when returns are generated (see Mistake #2 and the sequence of return risk). There will be times when a 6% average annual return on one portfolio and a 6% return on another portfolio end up with very different values.

CHAPTER 7

Why Bronze Winners are Happier than Silver Winners

As the sister of a two-time Olympian, I found this comparison fascinating, and another example of how perspective can give us joy or *take it away*.

You might be wondering what the Olympics have to do with one of the most common mistakes people make in personal finance. Bear with me. Some years ago, I came across an article by James G. Goldman in a Scientific American blog, and the title immediately grabbed me: "Why Bronze Winners are Happier than Silver Winners" (Goldman, *The Thoughtful Animal*). Goldman begins with a quotation from a classic book by William James, *The Principles of Psychology*, written in 1892.

It is well known in psychology that a person's achievements matter less than how that person *judges* those achievements. For example, one employee might be thrilled with a 5% raise, until they learn that a colleague got 10%. But when that person with the 5% raise *expected* a 3% boost while the one who got the 10% raise *expected* 15%, the former is clearly happier than the latter, despite the lower outcome. In athletic competition, there are clear winners and losers. In the Olympics, one might expect that the athlete's happiness would mirror their achievement; with the gold medalist being the happiest, followed by the silver, and then the bronze. But as my ecstatic sister would have told you, this was not her experience at all. (She won bronze medals in Barcelona and Atlanta in Ten-Meter Diving.) This phenomenon—in athletic endeavors or just life in general—can be explained by a concept called "counterfactual thinking," or *imagining the outcome that didn't happen.*

This means that people compare their objective achievements to "what might have been." The most obvious (counterfactual) thought for the silver medalist might be to focus on *almost* winning gold—nailing the dive perfectly with no splash, allowing the water to envelope her body. Not being on the top stand feels like she lost. The bronze medalist, however, might focus her thoughts downward towards fourth place, and realize she came very close to not winning a medal *at all.* The categorical difference between being a medalist and not winning a medal does not exist for the comparison between first and second place.

We tend to bucket our thoughts, and it's because of this "apples to oranges" comparison that the bronze medalist—who is *objectively* worse off—would be more pleased with herself and happier with her achievement than the silver medal winner.

The article then quotes William James: *"So, we have the paradox of a man shamed to death because he is only the second-best pugilist or the second greatest oarsman in the world. That he is able to beat the whole population of the globe—minus one—is nothing; he has pitted himself to beat that one other person, and as long as he doesn't do that, nothing else counts"* (James, 1892)[50].

Most people reading this book aren't going for a gold medal in finance, yet this very human tendency to make comparisons can be seen in many areas, not just financial planning. We have seen how the math of returns can impact actual wealth accumulation, making comparisons to benchmarks like the S&P 500 irrelevant. Indices also make poor benchmarks because they rarely line up with your portfolio. To be a credible benchmark, the index and portfolio must have similar assets, the same cash flows in and out, similar holding periods, and similar weightings in various sectors. It's important to compare apples to apples. There are many factors that can make a personal portfolio different from a general index. Indices are 100% one asset class or another: for example, all equities, all bonds, or all commodities. Your portfolio will be more diversified, with bonds, money market accounts, stocks listed in the U.S. and abroad, and perhaps some real estate and other inflation hedges.

When I refer to cash flows, you're likely adding money to invest or withdrawing money to live on, *so some of the money wasn't invested for the entire year.* The index you are comparing it to is fully invested all year. Your portfolio might contain some cash-equivalent holdings, as well as some higher-risk assets. You may be more heavily weighted in one asset class than another. An index, however, rarely rebalances its holdings. It isn't overweighting or underweighting investments in companies, and it certainly isn't including cash in its calculations. The index is fully invested starting January 1; the 401(k) to which you and your employer are contributing is not. This makes comparing your portfolio to an index meaningless because the index isn't reflecting the type of assets and the amount of time you are invested in it.

---

50 Take note of the date of that book: Proof that human nature hasn't changed.

Here you might be saying, "Well, I'll just invest in an S&P index fund anyway, and then I really will be getting the benefit of that index." That sounds great on the surface, but be careful; it still might cause asset depletion far too soon. Take a look at the S&P 500 Envy chart below, an idea first prepared by BlackRock. We're looking at two $100,000 portfolios. One of them follows the S&P 500 exactly. The other is diversified among various asset classes and follows an asset allocation model that's right for this client. During bull markets, the S&P 500 portfolio returns more than the diversified portfolio. During bear markets, the diversified portfolio still loses money, though not as much as the market-based portfolio. Diversified investors never seem happy (check out the emoji faces next to the quotes to the right) as they see their portfolio first lose money, then trail the market benchmark. However, when all is said and done, it is the diversified portfolio that wins.

TIME PERIOD	S&P 500 INDEX	DIVERSIFIED PORTFOLIO	EMOTION	RESULT
DIVERSIFICATION CAN WIN EVEN WHEN IT FEELS LIKE ITS LOSING				
THE ANNUAL RETURNS OF THE S&P 500 FROM 2000-2022 REPRESENTED A PERFECT "S&P ENVY" MARKET				
2000 - 2002	-37.61%	-8.15%	:(	"I LOST MONEY'
2003 - 2007	+82.86%	+88.94%	:)	"DIVERSIFICATION WORKED"
2008	-37.00%	-26.87%	:(	"I LOST MONEY"
2009 - 2019	+351%	+223.91%	:|	"I DIDN'T DO AS WELL AS THE S&P..."
*Q1 2020	-30.43%	-23.01%	:(	"I LOST MONEY"
*Q2 2020 - 2021	+100.20%	+66.71%	:|	"I DIDN'T DO AS WELL AS THE S&P..."
2022	-18.11%	-15.66%	:(	"I LOST MONEY"
TOTAL RETURN	+305.89%	+341.17%	:D	"DIVERSIFICATION CAN WORK EVEN WHEN IT FELT LIKE IT WASN'T!"
GROWTH OF $100K	$405,892	$441,166		

Performance is from 12/31/2019 to 3/23/2020. +Performance is from 3/24/2020 to 12/31/2020. Diversified Portfolio is represented by 25% S&P 500, 19% Russell Mid Cap Index, 7% MSCI EAFE Index, 5% Russell 2000 Index, 4% FTSE Emerging Stock Index, 25% Bloomberg U.S. Aggregate Bond Index, and 15% Bloomberg U.S. Corporate High Yield Index. Past Performance does not guarantee or indicate future results. Index performance is for illustrative purposes only. You cannot invest directly in the index. Diversification does not guarantee a profit or protect against a loss in a declining market.

That final statement, "Diversification can work even when it feels like it's losing," might be one of the most profound statements in this book[51]. Try not to beat the S&P 500 or compare your return to a benchmark. The return you need to meet your goals *is* the benchmark.

---

51   Credit to the folks at BlackRock for this statement.

Over time, you either meet them or don't. If a portion of the portfolio is underperforming, understand why and whether the underperformance could be temporary. Rebalance and make course corrections to align that portion with the original plan design. Eventually, with some attention and tweaking from time to time, this process should bring returns to the level needed to meet your objectives.

In a quote widely if dubiously attributed to him, Einstein once said, *"If you judge a fish by its ability to climb a tree, it will live its whole life believing that it is stupid."*

People do this to themselves when they measure their progress based on a benchmark such as the S&P 500. *That's like the fish who felt like a complete loser because he couldn't climb a tree.* As we learned from the example of S&P 500 Envy, be careful what you ask for. Measuring your progress against something you probably shouldn't want—a concentrated portfolio in one sector or asset class—may not just be counterproductive, *it may also make you feel like the silver medal winner at the Olympics.*

Stop doing that to yourself—and your advisor.

2. FOCUSING ON RETURNS INSTEAD OF OUTCOMES

This mistake is similar to using the wrong benchmark, but it's a little different. It has to do with sequence of return risk, where two investments with the same average rate of return end up with different ending values. The ultimate goal of a portfolio is to provide cash flow and insure the growth of cash flow over your lifetime. Especially in a very low interest rate environment, the key is cash flow, not income.

As discussed in Chapter 3, there is a big difference in returns depending on how they are calculated. There are arithmetic returns and geometric returns, time weighted rated of return (TWR) and internal rates of return (IRR). If you work with an advisor, they are probably going to report your internal rate of return, which takes into consideration cash flows in and out of the portfolio, accounting for when each investment was made during the year, after of all fees and expenses, and when money was taken out. This is considered the most accurate measure of how your portfolio performed.

But if you manage your own portfolio or 401(k), be careful how you calculate returns and make decisions. Let's take a simple example. In the chart below, the following information is purely hypothetical and is presented for illustrative purposes and in no way is to represent a particular investment or a guarantee of future performance of any kind. This hypothetical example assumes a beginning account value of $10,000 and an annual contribution of $10,000 added to the account at the beginning of years two and three. *Three columns show different rates of return, but the outcomes are less than intuitive.* Each portfolio starts out with $10,000 and earns a return, and then the investor adds another $10,000 to the closing value at the end of each year. If we apply simple math to the equation, the first investment earned a three-year average return of 5%, while the second one earned 12% and the last one generated an impressive 20% return. In spite of these significant differences, the sequence of when these returns were earned creates a very different (and unwelcome) outcome. In this case, comparing the three-year average rate of return calculated this way does not tell you which of the three investments provided the highest accumulation of money, which can lead to decisions made with the wrong information that sabotage the strategies and overall plan. At the very least, you could end up not achieving the outcome you intended: less money and a lot more stress[xxiv]!

WHEN A 5% AVERAGE RETURN IS BETTER THAN A 20% AVERAGE RETURN

	5%	10%	20%
AVERAGE RETURN:			
YEAR 1 RETURN	-35%	30%	45%
YEAR 2 RETURN	25%	-10%	45%
YEAR 3 RETURN	25%	10%	-30%
ENDING PORTFOLIO VALUE:	$38,281	$33,770	$31,868

HOW IS THIS POSSIBLE?

YEAR 1 STARTING VALUE	$10,000	$10,000	$10,000
YEAR 1 RETURN	-35%	30%	45%
YEAR 1 ENDING VALUE	$6,500	$11,000	$14,500
YEAR END CONTRIBUTION	+$10,000	+$10,000	+$10,000
YEAR 2 STARTING VALUE	$16,500	$21,000	$24,500
YEAR 2 RETURN	25%	-10%	45%
YEAR 2 ENDING VALUE	$20,625	$23,100	$35,525
YEAR END CONTRIBUTION	+$10,000	+$10,000	+$10,000
YEAR 3 STARTING VALUE	$30,625	$33,100	$45,525
YEAR 3 RETURN	25%	10%	-30%
YEAR 3 ENDING VALUE	$38,281	$33,770	$31,868

In his book *Simple Wealth Inevitable Wealth*, one of my favorite authors, Nick Murray, tells the story of two retirees sitting on a bench feeding ducks (Murray, *Simple Wealth, Inevitable Wealth*). The first one says, "My portfolio did really well last year. I earned over a 6% rate of return." The second retiree says, "That's nothing. My portfolio came in at more than 11%!" What both of them fail to realize is that neither portfolio is doing well enough to prevent them from running out of money. The first retiree might run out at the age of seventy-two while the second one hangs on until he's seventy-five, but they're both going to be destitute by the time they're eighty.

Instead of asking what rate of return you ended up with, a better question might be, "Will this portfolio provide enough cash flow to cover my rising expenses until I die?" That's a far better metric for a successful strategy. If a portfolio isn't covering all your expenses, it's not doing its job, *no matter how impressive the return.*

3. INERTIA AND PROCRASTINATION

People often think that making a mistake is a proactive endeavor, but one of the most common mistakes people make is not doing anything.

It's natural for people to be afraid of making a mistake. It's also natural for them to postpone investments or delay putting a financial plan in place. Remember: a financial plan is simply a set of action items integrated to help you accomplish the goals that are most important to you. You might see yet another apocalyptic headline warning you how awful things are, which seems to justify the need to wait. Spoiler alert: There is no perfect time, and everything is easier the sooner you start. *Just start from where you are and get going.*

It's also easy be lulled into complacency, to believe that your portfolio doesn't need to undergo a periodic review, or to assume you have accumulated enough resources to live the life you've envisioned. If you aren't using a scoreboard to measure progress and make sure you're on the right course, *you might be kidding yourself.*

The 4 Disciplines of Execution, Chris McChesney and Sean Covey tell the story of a high school football team in New Orleans (McChesney and Covey, *The Four Disciplines of Execution*). The team always played to a full house as the entire town turned out for the Friday night games, until Hurricane Katrina blew through, leaving a path of destruction. Katrina destroyed the scoreboard and bleachers, but miraculously, the football field was still playable. So it was decided the game would be played the next Friday, despite the damage to the stadium. Without the scoreboard, however, the supporters in the stands found their attention drifting. Instead of watching the game, the fans were talking among themselves, and there wasn't nearly as much cheering or enthusiasm.

What made these devoted fans, crazy football fanatics with face paint, team jerseys, and loud noisemakers, **fall prey to apathy?** They were losing sight of what was happening because *they had no idea* how much time was left on the clock or even what the score was. They needed a scoreboard to keep track, to stay focused and engaged in the game.

We all need the same type of scoreboard to make sure we're hitting the mark. In many areas of life, whether it's setting goals for your business, your career, or your financial plans, it's really important to keep track of the score. Just make sure you're using the right benchmark (see Mistake 1).

Nearly twenty years ago, a couple came in for an initial consultation. They were clearly not on track. We talked about doing a financial plan to give them specific action steps to get to their destination. Life got busy for them, as it often does for people with jobs and families, and they never followed through with our recommendations. Twenty years later, they returned. They were then in their early sixties, and even though they had a seven-figure portfolio, they were feeling hopelessly behind. They'd paid more for their home than it was worth, mortgaging almost half of it, and they'd leased and replaced cars far too often. They hadn't accumulated enough savings for their lifestyle, and we needed to address deficiencies in their portfolio and play catch-up fast.

Because they'd waited so long, the couple had to modify their goals. There was no way they were going to be able to retire when they were sixty-five years old. They had to face the very unpleasant fact that they were going to have to continue working beyond the age they had envisioned. Eventually, they were able to work part-time and then retire, but they had to sell their home and make some changes in their lifestyle. All of that could have been avoided had they made some of the easier decisions along the way and monitored the progress of their investment portfolio and financial plan.

Remember: You get what you measure, and over time what you measure can improve. Having a scoreboard—a *real* financial plan—is key to avoiding this mistake.

4. NO ORGANIZING PRINCIPLES TO GUIDE DECISIONS

Anyone can control their financial health, but to do so, you need to concentrate on the things you can control and ignore what you can't.

Too often, people spend a tremendous amount of time and energy analyzing their holdings—and then wonder why they still aren't reaching their goals. Analyzing an individual stock or the movement of the stock market can give you a false sense of security because, try as we might, we can't control stock prices. No one has been able to consistently predict the economy, interest rates, the markets, or to control the fallout from unexpected economic movements. Your best bet is to stop wasting time analyzing the health of the butterfly flapping her wings in China when you're trying to predict the next tornado in Kansas. Control the things you can.

Principles under your control include deciding how important each goal is and prioritizing resources accordingly. How important is it for you to live for today vs save for the future? How about risk management and risk transfer, the amount and types of insurance you have, or how much is enough to educate your children. Do you want them to have skin in the game?

These are not easy questions to answer, and sometimes it's easier to organize principles and priorities once you have an idea of how things look currently. We're back to that "You are Here" sticker on the map at the mall from Chapter 2.

5. ALLOWING NOISE OR HYPE TO STOKE FEARS OF LOSING MONEY, OR THE OPPOSITE: FOMO (Fear of Missing Out)

During the tech bubble and recession in the early 2000's, several of our clients nearly lost everything because they made decisions based on emotion. During the first year of the recession, clients understood that bear markets occur, and they didn't panic. Then came September 11th, and that was a disastrous event, not only for our country, but also from an economic and financial perspective. Markets were shut down for a "cooling off" period, and no one knew what to expect, but clients still hung on. Then along came 2002, and some capitulated, saying, "This is not over, I am not sleeping, and I can't take it anymore."

In most cases, I was able to ease their immediate concerns, refocus their energy, and help them keep their eyes on the goals for their allocation and longer-term financial plan. But there were seven clients during that final year of the recession who said they were *"done"*. In two of the seven cases, we sold all of the stock funds. In the other five, we sold half. As an experiment, we kept a record of where the Dow, S&P 500, and international indices were on the days when they capitulated.

Initially, all seven clients felt vindicated because the market continued to fall. But then, seemingly out of nowhere *and while the news was still awful*, the market began to rise. Long after the market soared past the initial level at which they sold, all seven clients called with their own version of, "Hurry up, get me back in!" They were as panicked on the upside as they were on the downside because they were so worried that they were going to lose the opportunity to recover their losses. In reality, they already had.

Even though the market was going down, they had not actually lost any money until they sold.

To sell during the bear market was not rational. This may sound counterintuitive, but risk is actually lower when prices are lower, because the value you get for each dollar spent increases. Think about a 50% (wicked) bear market in terms of buying a sedan. It's the same car, just half the price. It's easy to get caught up in really scary and dramatic commentary and react to short-term fluctuation. What happens during a down market is not relevant to someone retiring ten years or longer from now, not if the financial plan has a sound foundation.

If you are already retired, please keep in mind that you are probably not 100% exposed to that kind of volatility. When you organize the asset allocation to work with the cash flow projections in your financial plan and you've set up the Three Pools of Money, you have created firewalls to reduce your chance of becoming a victim of impulse or emotions. The market volatility is probably affecting only a portion of your portfolio, and you aren't going to need all of it at once anyway. As difficult as it might be, try to ignore the noise.

The other side of this is to allow hype (or sentimentality) to affect decisions. There are often very good reasons to sell a holding, even at a loss. If a stock has fallen because of weak company fundamentals, and not just as part of an overall market decline, it might be time to abandon that investment and look for a better one. Let's assume you invested $50,000 in a stock and now it's only worth $35,000. It's human nature to want to hold on at least until you've recovered your principal, even when presented with rational reasons to sell. You may have a sentimental attachment to that investment, or you don't want to experience a loss, which is not a great feeling. Remember: that stock has no idea what you paid for it, and the company could care less as well. Each investment you own is simply a means to an end.

A great way to overcome this irrational but very human thought process is to ask yourself, "If I had $35,000 in cash today, would I be buying that investment?" If the answer is yes, hold it. If the answer is no, get rid of it. That's the rational approach.

6. SITTING ON CASH

More often than not, when someone comes into a lump-sum windfall, they just feel in their gut that investing it slowly over time is better than all at once. A lot of this comes from fear.

Fear is the cousin of inertia, but it's hidden in a wonderful rationale: "The market is at an all-time high, earnings are going to disappoint," or "The yield curve is going to invert, so I'm just going to wait until the market goes down and then invest." The money just sits in the bank account, often for a long period of time, because the market didn't quite go down enough. Unfortunately, while it remains in a cash account, chances are high that it is not even keeping pace with inflation.

This is when there can be real advantages to dollar averaging, which is a strategy of dividing up the dollar amount you want to invest into periodic purchases—for example, monthly—to reduce the impact of volatility on large purchases of financial assets such as equities. This can be an effective brain hack because it establishes a system for automatic investing that you can stick with.

But studies done by Vanguard have shown that when there is a lump sum of cash available, about two thirds of the time it's better to invest in one fell swoop (Guadiano, *Investing a Lump Sum All at Once*). Even more striking, researchers found that lump-sum investors saw annual returns average 2.3% higher than those who used a dollar averaging model. That might not seem like a lot, but who wouldn't want a 10.3% return versus an 8.0% return? And over the years, the difference can be substantial.

Of course, not everyone is comfortable with seeing their windfall invested all at once. Sleep is important too, and hopefully you don't have to squeeze out every ounce of portfolio return that a diversified approach can provide. To see the potential impact on your financial future, stress-test your financial plan with a lower rate of return, just to understand the implications.

7. CONFUSING DIVERSIFICATION WITH ASSET ALLOCATION

Asset allocation methodology is used to achieve a rate of return goal. Diversification is how you get there.

In Chapter 4, we compared asset allocation and diversification to a baseball team. The various "asset classes" of players include pitchers, base players, and outfielders. You can't win a game with only pitchers because they are typically not great at bat. And a coach knows that players go through slumps, so he "diversifies" his pitchers, maintaining a deep bench with the hope one of them can pitch a no-hitter.

A financial plan helps determine the rate of return you need to accomplish the objectives you've set. What is the internal rate of return you need to average over time (*not every time*) to accomplish the objectives you've identified? All of this is based on the resources you have and will accumulate (after taxes to provide cash flow) over time. The asset allocation then focuses on percentages in various investment classes to help you achieve that return with the least amount of risk (fluctuation) you can tolerate.

The last step involves diversification of the investments within each asset class. The specific assets you choose within the broader asset classes is very personal. It will depend on your risk tolerance, return objectives, and other investments you might already own. For example, the founder of a tech company will probably not want to invest in other tech firms because his or her net worth is already so tied to the tech industry. Instead, they might allocate capital to other industries, such as healthcare, utilities, or blue-chip offerings, to diversify both the industry and the risk. Your asset allocation may change as your goals change and you get closer to retirement. The diversification of your portfolio, however, is typically consistent.

Diversification isn't just for your investments, it's also for *how* you invest. Think about using the Pools of Money approach to align your portfolio with your cash flow needs and overall financial plan. Once you've identified how much you'll need to withdraw each year and when, you set up your portfolio based on the previously discussed three investment horizons—short-term, medium-term, and long-term. By diversifying your investments according to when you need the money, you will have enough capital to see you through the down times while retaining plenty of money to invest for longer-term opportunities. There is also value in diversifying among the five tax buckets: taxable, tax-free, capital gains, tax-deferred, and Roth. This helps to optimize your net after-tax returns for the best outcome and can make your money last longer.

8. GETTING TOO "CUTE": INTELLECTUALIZING TO JUSTIFY A POSITION

Sometimes we see this when events are unfolding, such as presidential elections. We don't know who is going to be elected or what they will attempt to accomplish when they're elected. Nor do we know how markets will react.

We also see intellectualizing cloaked in words like "tactical allocation" or "technical investing" based on economic predictions or charts. Irrespective of the rationale, the objective of these approaches is to get out of equities before a certain amount of loss becomes larger, with the hope of getting back in at much lower levels. While the intention may be genuine, the problem is that we are all painfully human. Real, permanent losses can occur when we forget that fact.

We learned earlier the fallacy of thinking we can beat the odds in poker, even though the gambler might score big occasionally. Eventually the house will win, and the same outcome occurs with investors who try to time the market.

The COVID-19 pandemic crisis is a perfect example of this phenomenon. On March 12, 2020 (in the heat of the crisis), a newsletter recommended moving into safer, high-quality bond investments with the rationale that this was sound and reasonable, especially given a worldwide economic lockdown and the uncertainty created by the pandemic. The entire world was confined to their homes, markets were crashing, and comparisons with the Great Depression were grabbing headlines. Of course, there was no mention in this newsletter of cash flow needs, when to reposition, or how long the investor was supposed to remain conservatively invested. Nor were there warnings of the capital gains the reader would have to pay the following April. After all, it was a newsletter.

Everyone who took that advice sold that day and probably rested comfortably that night (and maybe even every night for months). The market plummeted and they cut their losses (at least temporarily). Even the traders were patting themselves on the back as markets continued its downward spiral, from a Dow Jones Industrial index average of 21,200 on March 12 to a low of 18,591 on March 23: "Whew, we dodged a bullet," they sighed in relief, but they didn't get back into the market. Just when people think they've outsmarted the unpredictable market, the house cleans them out.

And a temporary loss becomes a permanent one.

It is critical for you to know that as quickly as markets plummet, they can pivot, recover, and then go back down again! Before he retired, Don Connelly of Putnam Investments compared an investor's constant obsession with the market to a kid holding a yo-yo while walking up a flight of stairs. If you hyperfocus on the movement of the toy, you might lose sight of the fact that whether the yo-yo is up or down on the last step, eventually that child is at the top of the stairs. There will always be something to worry about, and if it isn't obvious, some pundit will probably make something up. If (when) the markets correct again, continue to harvest losses for tax benefits to lessen the pain on the other side, and rebalance *into* the volatility as opportunities present themselves.

Don't succumb to anyone pretending that they know what's going to happen in the next month, year, or three years. No one does.

9. UNCONSCIOUS SHORTCUTS

As I keep saying, we are all human. No human is immune to unconscious errors or biases. It's simply how our brains are programmed. We use shortcuts all the time to make decisions when we don't have time to analyze every situation. For example, if no one is eating the casserole at the potluck dinner, we might assume there's something wrong with it and pass it by. There is no harm in following the crowd unless it leads us to poor investment decisions. The best way to overcome these unconscious biases is to recognize we have them and work to make decisions based on objective metrics.

One experiment that highlights the surprising if predictable irrationality of financial decisions was first done with graduate students at an Ivy League university. The professor announced that he was going to auction off a $100 bill, with bidding progressing in $5 increments. The one difference between this auction and a standard auction was that the losing bidders would have to pay the amount of their last bid. The students were excited—an easy gain in a short amount of time! Five dollars was quickly followed by ten dollars, fifteen, twenty. Bidding accelerated, with even sixty dollars meaning a profit of forty dollars! At this point, however, the students realized that they had to keep going to avoid having to pay their last bid amount and get nothing in return. At ninety-five dollars, the bidding took on a feverish pitch. One hundred dollars soon followed and then. . . silence. The student who shouted, "$105!" recognized that it was better to lose five dollars than the ninety-five dollars he had pledged minutes before.

But it didn't end there. Where do you think the final bid landed[52]?

Irrational, right? This is just one example proving that many people, even MBA students at an Ivy league university, will do more

---

52 *$240.*

to avoid a loss than to obtain a gain. Awareness is the key to sidestepping these natural tendencies.

10. USING TOO MUCH LEVERAGE BY BORROWING AGAINST INVESTMENTS

People will try to boost returns via leverage—borrowing money to juice up returns. They reason that if a little is good, a lot will be better.

A little leverage can be a good thing, especially if it's used to purchase something you'll be able to use in the meantime, like a home. But too much, especially if an investment portfolio is being used as the collateral, can be devastating. Just as it can enhance returns, it multiplies losses when things are going down. It was leverage that caused the debt crisis in 2008 and is often a leading indicator for an impending recession. Just as it brought the financial world to its knees in 2008, using too much debt to achieve goals can sabotage an individual portfolio and destroy a financial plan.

11. THINKING ONCE IS ENOUGH

Remember, it's called planning, not a plan (that is set in stone).

As the years progress, you and your circumstances will undoubtedly change, and you'll want to tweak things. Life happens, and goals are often adjusted. Think about this process as you'd think about driving to a new destination. Back in our parents' days, they would look at a paper map while driving. There was no way to know if there was an accident up ahead or an alternative route without tolls. Effective financial planning is more like GPS. By continually monitoring your portfolio and how it's tracking against your goals (there's that scoreboard again), you can make sure you don't drift too far off track.

When monitoring, try to remain focused on the long-term implications. Short-term glitches are going to appear, but they shouldn't derail your efforts. Don't despair! In addition, you don't want to go down a rabbit hole chasing an opportunity that promises short-term gains but comes at the expense of your long-term security. Keep your eyes on the prize, your Three Pools of Money full, and let time take care of the rest.

12. HOME RUN HALLUCINATIONS

While procrastinating can be damaging to your financial health, hurrying can be just as problematic.

Too often, people try to go for the home run or fall for the hot tip they picked up at the neighborhood barbecue. They think it's much more exciting to try to get it all now than to set up a staid, consistent strategy. The hot tips, however, are often immature concepts offered by untested managers and riddled with fees, if they're credible at all. And those home runs? Yes, some games are won on a roaring walk-off homer, but the vast majority are won using small-ball tactics—get as many players on base as possible and move them around. As one of my mentors, Roy Diliberto, said many years ago, "Small things, done consistently, over time, create major impact." Don't blow your chance on those wild swings.

13. TOO MANY ACCOUNTS IN TOO MANY PLACES

Many people confuse the expression "Don't put all your eggs in one basket," which is intended to encourage portfolio diversification, with putting their eggs in a lot of different account baskets. They want to have a certain amount with one broker, another account somewhere else, and their 401(k) and retirement accounts self-managed separately.

You might want to do this yourself, but keeping accounts all over the place usually defeats the purpose. Not only is it difficult to keep track of everything, but this also usually leads to unnecessary taxes, lopsided allocations, redundant holdings, and gaps in the asset allocation. Most advisors charge based on assets under management and splitting it between two (or more) firms will create the issues mentioned already, plus higher fees. It's a left hand/right hand issue, and it's really time consuming! Try to consolidate accounts by titling— one retirement plan account (if married, one per spouse), maybe a Roth IRA, and an individual or joint brokerage account all held at the same custodian or under the care of one trusted advisor.

14. NOT HAVING A PLAN B

Change is often difficult. People lose spouses, jobs, a community if they are forced to move, their memories, half of their retirement funds in a financial crash, or their ability to take care of themselves. Be prepared. No one likes to think these things can happen to them, but they can, and they do. Always have a Plan B, even before you implement Plan A.

Devising a Plan B is often a painful exercise and may seem irrelevant because we don't want to think about the types of things that could derail our lives. Having a Plan B will force you to come up with a contingency plan before you need it. The very worst time to make major decisions is when you're stressed and in the middle of a crisis. When you prepare for a crisis, you eliminate a lot of unnecessary worry. If you know in advance what Plan B is going to be, the crisis doesn't have to keep you up at night, lead to impulsive decisions, or derail your future.

15. GIVING UP

There is always hope. It's worth it because <u>you're</u> worth it.

Earlier in this chapter I talked about the couple who put off getting their financial lives in order. When they came back to my office 20 years later, they were embarrassed that they hadn't handled their financial life better and were scared that they were going to run out of money. We worked out a plan that gave them more clarity and confidence. It isn't the life of their neighbors or friends, but it is full and comfortable. It is their life.

Sometimes people give up because they fear the cure is worse than the disease. Not making the changes you need to make is like avoiding your doctor when you know you're sick. As a former oncology nurse, I saw this all the time. People didn't want to hear they might have cancer because they feared the effects of chemotherapy. Yes, the side effects are unquestionably bad, but you know what? It's the short-term awfulness that gives you hope of living a longer life.

On a podcast with Tim Ferriss in February 2022, author Anne Lamott referred to fear as "Future Events Already Ruined" (Lamott, *Taming your Inner Critic*). If you haven't been taking care of your financial affairs, you might have to cut back on things you like doing or sell things you like having. *It also might not be nearly as bad as you might have feared!*

Instead of focusing on the problem, focus on the solution, and never, ever give up.

CONCLUSION

Three Types of People and Important Takeaways from Patti

There is always hope, but hope is not enough.

Over the years, I have learned there are three categories of people.

1. Those who are not tracking well, and they know it.

2. Those who don't know how they are tracking.

3. Those who have plenty of capital and don't care how they are tracking.

People can reach their fifties or even their sixties without the portfolio needed to see them through their retirement years. They throw up their hands and figure they'll just see what happens. That's not a good solution; there is almost always something that can be done to make life better, no matter how bleak things may feel at the time.

Others just have no idea where they are and are either too busy or too afraid to face the facts. I love working with this group of people until they are able to realize that they are actually doing really well.

Even those with a high net worth, who are very comfortable financially and assume that their legacy is preserved, may find that their financial situation is not optimized, and they are exposed to litigation or taxes that are completely unnecessary. The key is to take that first step, and then a second. It's a journey, and it can begin wherever you are at the moment.

A Summary of Steps

Here are ten steps to monitor your financial future, enhance your family's future, and leave behind a true intergenerational legacy.

1. Dump the filing cabinets—the ones in your house, your computer, and your brain. Start prioritizing information so it is usable and retrievable.

2. Understand your resources and organize your financial affairs—as they are today.

3. Create a visualized future, rich with specifics. Have fun with it!

4. Run the numbers to help with decisions. Stress-test alternatives. No guessing.

5. Design a structure for purposeful savings aligned with your vision.

6. Apply strategies to accelerate your progress. Be smart. Find smart. Do smart.

7. Automate savings, but not your bill paying. Pay bills the old-fashioned way.

8. Limit damage from taxes, the unexpected, and the inevitable: death.

9. Monitor your financial plan on an ongoing basis and adjust as necessary.

10. Enjoy the process. Reward yourself along the way. Otherwise, this probably isn't going to work.

An Important Takeaway: Legacies Can Mean More Than Just Money

At the start of this book, I acknowledged that many of the concepts and philosophies I'm writing about are a culmination of what I've learned from many wise people both in and outside the industry. I don't remember every source, but I will never forget something Ron Carson, founder and CEO of Carson Wealth Management, shared with me: "An Inheritance is what we give to someone; a legacy is what we *put into* them."

Several years ago, a conference I attended offered a breakout session on estate planning. The speaker asked the audience of about five hundred CFP® professionals to raise our hands if we knew the first names of our grandparents. Most of us did. When he asked how many of us knew the first names of our great-grandparents, only a few people raised their hands. Then the speaker made a statement that has remained with me ever since: "Isn't it sad to think that one hundred years from now, our own families aren't even going to remember our names?"

How's that for a reality check? It's a harsh one, as if you don't die just once. But it doesn't have to be that way for you.

One Christmas, a letter written by my husband's father surfaced. It was a note to his sister (Ed's aunt) when he was in the army in France just after D-Day. There wasn't much to it, but to see his father's handwriting and realize what he might have been going through at the time brought Ed to tears. As I watched this man in his sixties read the note from his dad, I realized how meaningful a handwritten note could be. Here's an idea:

In an age of instant gratification, Facebook, and unrealistic story lines filled with euphoric pictures of fake fun or brief moments in time, your perspective and wisdom can be priceless. Think about writing a letter, *by hand,* to children, grandchildren and/or others you care about, and be real with them. You know *they live in a world where anxiety, depression, and suicide are at record highs and self-medication with drugs and alcohol is rampant.* In 2019, for the first time in over fifty years, life expectancies in America actually went down. Suicide and the opioid crisis are two obvious culprits, with alcoholism not far behind.

As you write your letter, *let them know that whatever challenges they might face <u>are normal</u>.* Talk about your values and your great memories, *but also about the difficult times, and maybe even one or two when you were scared.* We've all had struggles, times when we worried whether we could make a payment, fund a tuition or could lose a job, when wanted to provide everything in the world to the people we love and weren't sure we could. Tell them your stories, what you might have been thinking at the time, how you dealt with those seemingly endless days of uncertainty as you plugged through. *Acknowledge that their experiences will probably be very different but that things are not always as they seem.* The goal here is <u>not</u> to hash out how hard life was for you, *it's to tell them they are not alone* and to give them tools.

One of my favorite tools is the "brain dump." I've taught my children that when they're especially anxious, they should sit down with a blank piece of paper and write down everything—and I mean *everything*—they're worried about. They keep writing until they're exhausted and have gone fifteen minutes without putting pen to paper. Then comes the most important step: when they're done, *they put the paper in an envelope and tuck it away for six months.* When they reopen it, *they will find that 99% of the things that kept them awake at night never happened and the 1% that did weren't nearly as bad as they'd feared (or even turned out to be blessings in disguise).* Sometimes it took two or three brain dumps for them to realize (up front) that worry is just a waste of energy, and to use that energy to focus on solutions instead of problems. This is simply a technique that has worked for our family; the key is to share what you've learned from the school of hard knocks you attended, and what helped you to get through.

Our children and loved ones are going to have tough times, and when they do, *they can look back at your letter and be reminded that they can be just as resilient as you were* and get to the other side. As they face the future, they might need your perspective, and they will never forget your handwritten words of wisdom and encouragement.

Don't just give them money. Share your values and give it to them straight. Share what worked for you and what made you truly successful, not just living a rich life but a full one. A handwritten letter can be your true legacy, more valuable than any trust fund. Give them perspective; give them truth; give them hope. No matter what they might face, remind them *there is always hope,* but hope is not a strategy. If they keep those goals close to their heart, follow up with inspired action and adjust as necessary, *anything* can become their reality.

Like it was for Mom.

Much of this book has been about a process. The Four Keys for Life lay out the steps behind planning, and the Six Key Force Multipliers can accelerate your progress. There are many tactics and ideas in the book to help you save money on taxes and get better outcomes so you can accomplish your objectives. It's important to think strategically and always be on the lookout for ways to weave different concepts together to result in a better outcome than if you took those same actions independently (like the brick wall stacked for strength).

But in the end, it's not just about achieving goals. Yes, that's the "what and how" behind real financial planning and wealth management. The "why" for most people *includes a feeling of being organized and in control, knowing you are taking care of yourself and the people you love so you have more time to leverage your gifts and pursue your purpose in life.*

To me, that is the definition of true happiness.

Seth Godin talks about the resistance we often feel when faced with a daunting task; writing a book amidst everything else (and my tendency to *over-tweak*) contributed to a *long* process. When I began writing many years ago, interest rates were low to the point of vanishing, there was no looming debt-ceiling crisis, no COVID-19 pandemic, no war in Ukraine. Things have changed radically since then, which is a cautionary note to keep in mind. The winds of change will always blow, but no one can know with certainty for how long or in which direction. But that doesn't mean you can't insulate yourself with a strategic financial plan that will mitigate the effects of whatever change may come. You can do that with the help of a CFP®, or you can do it for yourself, perhaps using the guidance in this book. *That was my aim in writing it, and for those who have asked for a book that is truly different:* written in layman's terms with valuable content that is actionable. It can be used as a guide for individuals, families, and the many professionals at my firm (and outside) clamoring for a better way to add value to other people's lives. It has been a labor of love, and if you are one of those people, I thank you for the nudge.

Mostly, I hope this book was everything you were looking for, and maybe…even more.

Patti Brennan, CFP®

GLOSSARY AND DISCLOSURES

The Dow Jones Industrial Average (DJIA) is a price-weighted average of 30 actively traded "blue chip" stocks, primarily industrials, but includes financials and other service-oriented companies. The components, which change from time to time, represent between 15% and 20% of the market value of NYSE stocks.

The S&P 500, or the Standard and Poor's 500 Index, is a market-capitalization weighted index of the largest publicly traded companies in the U.S.. It is widely regarded as the best gauge of large cap U.S. equities, but that is all it is: a gauge. It is a proxy to represent this class of companies that are domiciled in the United States.

Indices are unmanaged and investors cannot invest directly in an index. Unless otherwise noted, performance of indices does not account for any fees, commissions or other expenses that would be incurred. Returns do not include reinvested dividends.

Mutual Funds and Exchange Traded Funds (ETF's) are sold by prospectus. Please consider the investment objectives, risks, charges, and expenses carefully before investing. The prospectus, which contains this and other information about the investment company, can be obtained from the Fund Company or your financial professional. Be sure to read the prospectus carefully before deciding whether to invest.

Diversification does not guarantee a profit or protect against a loss in a declining market. It is a method used to help manage investment risk.

Rebalancing/Reallocating can entail transaction costs and tax consequences that should be considered when determining a rebalancing/reallocation strategy.

Past performance may not be indicative of future results. Different types of investments involve varying degrees of risk. Therefore, it should not be assumed that future performance of any specific investment or investment strategy will be profitable.

Investing in alternative assets involves higher risks than traditional investments and is suitable only for sophisticated investors. Alternative investments are often sold by prospectus that discloses all risks, fees, and expenses. They are not tax efficient and an investor should consult with his/her tax advisor prior to investing. Alternative investments have higher fees than traditional investments and they may also be highly leveraged and engage in speculative investment techniques, which can magnify the potential for investment loss or gain and should not be deemed a complete investment program. The value of the investment may fall as well as rise and investors may get back less than they invested.

Hedge Funds are unregistered private investment partnerships, funds or pools that may invest and trade in many different markets, strategies, and instruments (including securities, non-securities, and derivatives) and are NOT subject to the same regulatory requirements as mutual funds, including mutual fund requirements to provide certain periodic and standardized pricing and valuation information to investors. Hedge Funds represent speculative investments and can involve a high degree of risk. An investor could lose all or a substantial portion of his/her investment. Investors must have the financial ability, sophistication/experience, and willingness to bear the risks of an investment.

Fixed annuities are long term insurance contracts with a fixed return, carrying a surrender charge generally between the first 5-7 years. Withdrawals prior to age 59 ½ may result in a 10% IRS penalty, in addition to paying ordinary income tax on the gain if held outside of a retirement account. If in an IRA all withdrawals are subject to both, not just the gain. Any guarantees of the annuity are backed by the financial strength of the underlying insurance company. They are not FDIC insured.

Variable annuities are annuities whose benefits may change based on market conditions and the underlying subaccounts chosen by the investor. Be sure to consider the investment objectives, risks, charges, and expenses carefully before investing in variable annuities. The prospectus, which carries this and other information about the variable annuity contract and underlying investment options can be obtained from the insurance company or your investment professional. Read the prospectus fully before deciding whether to invest. The investment return and principal value of the variable annuity investment options are not guaranteed. Variable annuity sub-accounts fluctuate with changes in market conditions. Be sure to understand the underlying annual fees on variable annuities as they can be significant over time. The principal may be worth more or less than the original amount invested when the annuity is surrendered.

Unless stated otherwise, when "average" returns are discussed in this book or the mathematics are shown, I am using **time weighted geometric (compounded) returns.**

Dollar cost averaging may help reduce per share cost through continuous investment in securities regardless of fluctuating prices and does not guarantee profitability nor can it protect from loss in a declining market. The investor should consider his/her ability to continue investing through periods of low-price levels.

Bear markets—losses of 20%, 30%, or even 50%—are predictably unpredictable. If you have money in stocks or funds that invest in equities (and even bonds which tend to fluctuate less), please understand that bear markets happen. They are completely unpredictable in terms of when they will occur, how deep they will be, and how long they will last. They key is knowing how they might affect you financially.

Active portfolio management, including market timing, can subject longer term investors to potentially higher fees and can have a negative effect on the long-term performance due to the transaction costs of the short-term trading. In addition, there may be potential tax consequences from these strategies. Active portfolio management and market timing may be unsuitable for some investors depending on their specific investment objectives and financial position. Active portfolio management does not guarantee a profit or protect against a loss in a declining market.

Any tax advice contained in this communication is not intended to be used, and cannot be used, for purposes of illegally avoiding taxes or penalties imposed under the United States Internal Revenue Code.

ADDITIONAL DISCLOSURE INFORMATION

Patricia ("Patti") C. Brennan, CFP® is the founder and Chief Executive Officer of Key Financial, Inc. ("Key Financial"), an investment adviser registered with the United States Securities and Exchange Commission, located in West Chester, PA. The book content is for information purposes only and does not provide any personalized advice from the author to the reader that is based upon the reader's specific situation or objectives. To the contrary, no reader should assume that this book serves as the receipt of, or a substitute for, personalized advice from the investment and/or other professionals of his/her choosing. The author is not a lawyer or accountant. No portion of the content serves as personalized investment, legal, accounting, tax or insurance advice. Please remember that different types of investments involve varying degrees of risk. Therefore, it should not be assumed that future performance of any specific investment or investment strategy (including the investments and/or investment strategies referenced and/or recommended in the book), or any non-investment related content (including financial planning topics), will be profitable, equal any historical performance levels, be suitable for a reader's individual situation, or prove correct. Certain portions of the book may reflect positions and/or recommendations as of a specific prior date, and may no longer be reflective of current positions, recommendations, or laws. Moreover, any case studies illustrate the hypothetical experience of a fictitious client based on a scenario that an actual client might experience. The scenario is designed to help illustrate recommendations Mrs. Brennan might provide to similarly situated clients. Keeping in mind that no two clients, situations, or experiences are exactly alike, and no case study should not construed as an endorsement of Mrs. Brennan or Key Financial by any of its past or current clients, nor any assurance that Mrs. Brennan or Key Financial may be able to help any client achieve the same satisfactory results. To the contrary, there can be no assurance that a client or prospective client will experience a certain level of results or satisfaction if Mrs. Brennan or Key Financial is engaged, or continues to be engaged, to provide investment advisory services. Please Note: Limitations. The achievement of any professional designation, certification, degree, or license, membership in any professional organization, or any amount of prior experience or success, should not be construed by a client or prospective client as a guarantee that he/she will experience a certain level of results if Key Financial is engaged, or continues to be engaged, to provide investment advisory services. In addition, no ranking, award or recognition should be construed as a current or past endorsement of Key Financial by any of its clients, or any assurance of a future satisfactory experience. Please see the participation criteria/methodology published by the ranking or awarding organization at www.keyfinancial.com/awards. Please Also Note: Mrs. Brennan offers securities through Osaic Wealth, Inc. ("Osaic"), a separately owned, registered and operated FINRA/SIPC member. Key Financial is not affiliated with Osaic. All advisory and insurance services are provided by Key Financial and Mrs. Brennan, respectively. Patti Brennan and her firm, Key Financial, Inc. are not associated with or endorsed by the Social Security Administration or any other government agency.

This book contains general information that may not be suitable for everyone. The information contained herein should not be construed as personalized investment advice. **Past performance is no guarantee of future results.** There is no guarantee that the views and opinions expressed in this book will come to pass. Investing in the stock market involves gains and losses and may not be suitable for all investors. Information presented herein is subject to change without notice and should not be considered as a solicitation to buy or sell any security. Patti Brennan and her firm, Key Financial, Inc. do not offer legal or tax advice, and nothing contained in this book should be used as personalized advice of any kind. Please consult the appropriate professional regarding your individual circumstance.

The case studies provided do not reflect actual clients. Any reference to securities is based upon historical data that is public sourced. No statement made herein is to suggest stock market performance or future performance is guaranteed in any way, and no case study is used to imply future performance. The case studies are intended to illustrate concepts or approaches utilized by the adviser and is no way to be taken as advice. Actual results will fluctuate with each person and market conditions and will vary over time.

Representatives from Key Financial, Inc. do not offer legal or tax advice. Please consult the appropriate professional regarding your individual circumstance. Key Financial, Inc. is a federally registered investment advisor with the United States Securities and Exchange Commission. Securities offered through Osaic Wealth, Inc., member FINRA/SIPC. Osaic Wealth, Inc. is separately owned and other entities/marketing names, products or services referenced here are independent of Osaic Wealth, Inc. Insurance services offered through Patti Brennan are independent of Osaic Wealth, Inc. Advisory services offered through Key Financial, Inc, a registered investment advisor not affiliated with Osaic Wealth, Inc. and do not offer tax advice or tax services. Please consult your tax specialist for individual advice.

BIBLIOGRAPHY

Aliaga-Diaz, Roger. "Here's Why Bonds Still Belong in Your Portfolio." Vanguard, June 7, 2017. https://personal.vanguard.com/us/insights/article/bonds-portfolio-06201?SYND=RSS&Channel=IPF.

Bessembinder, Hendrik. "Do Stocks Outperform Treasury Bills?" Journal of Financial Economics, September 2018.

Board of Governors of the Federal Reserve System. "Economic Well-Being of U.S. Households in 2022." May 2023. https://www.federalreserve.gov/publications/files/2022-report-economic-well-being-us-households-202305.pdf.

Carlson, Debbie. "9 Facts to Know About Stock Market Corrections." U.S. News & World Report, January 17, 2019.

"Costs." Medicare. March 30, 2023. https://www.medicare.gov/basics/costs/medicare-costs.

Duckworth, Angela. "*GRIT, The Power of Passion and Perseverance.*" Page 149. Scribner Press, 2016.

Ellis, Charles D. "The End of Active Investing?" Financial Times, January 20, 2017.

Elwert, Felix and Christakis, Nicholas A MD, PhD, MPH. "The Effect of Widowhood on Mortality by the Causes of Death of Both Spouses." U.S. National Library of Medicine, November 2008. https://www.ncbi. nlm.nih.gov/pmc/articles/PMC2636447/#:~:text=Recent%20longi-tudinal%20studies%20put%20the%20excess%20mortality,and%20 around%2015%%20in%20the%20months%20thereafter.&text=Th-is%20longitudinal%20study%20of%20373%20189%20 elderly,the%20causes%20of%20death%20of%20both%20spouses.

Fadlon, Itzik, Shanthi Ramnath, Patricia K. Tong, and Lisa Crammer McKay. Federal Reserve Bank of Chicago, Chicago Fed Letter No. 438. "Financial Life After the Death of a Spouse." May 2020. https:// www.chicagofed.org/publications/chicago-fed-letter/2020/438.

Fischer, Michael S. "Here's How Much Americans Think They Will Need to Retire." ThinkAdvisor.com, May 24, 2022.

"Fixed Income Outstanding." SIFMA. https://www.sifma.org/resources/ fixed-income-chart/. Accessed May 5, 2022.

Goldman, James G. "The Thoughtful Animal." Scientific American, August 9, 2012.

Goss, Stephen. "The Future Financial Status of the Social Security Program." Social Security Bulletin 70, no. 3. 2010. https://www.casact.org/sites/ default/files/presentation/annual_2011_handouts_g3-goss.pdf.

Guadiano, Anora M. "Investing a Lump Sum All at Once Is What Research Says—but That Isn't Always the Best Plan." Marketwatch, April 26, 2018. https://www.marketwatch.com/story/investing-a-lump-sum-all-at-once-is-what-research-saysbut-that-isnt-always-the-best-plan-2018-04-26.

"Guide to Stock Market Recoveries." Capital Group, July 19, 2023, www. capitalgroup.com/advisor/insights/articles/guide-market-recoveries. html. Accessed June 30, 2023.

BIBLIOGRAPHY

"Income Taxes and Your Social Security Benefit." Social Security Administration. www.ssa.gov/benefits/retirement/planner/taxes.html. Accessed July 19, 2023

Internal Revenue Service. "Seniors & Retirees." IRS. Last modified January 10, 2023. https://www.irs.gov/individuals/seniors-retirees. Accessed July 19, 2023

James, William. *The Principles of Psychology.* 1892.

J.P. Morgan Asset Management. Guide to the Markets. https://am.jpmorgan.com/us/en/asset-management/adv/insights/market-insights/guide-to-the-markets/. Accessed March 30, 2021.

J.P. Morgan Asset Management. Guide to the Markets. https://am.jpmorgan.com/us/en/asset-management/adv/insights/market-insights/guide-to-the-markets/. Accessed December 31, 2021 and 2022.

Keller, Gary, and Jay Papasan. *The One Thing: The Surprisingly Simple Truth Behind Extraordinary Results.* Bard Press, 2012.

Lamott, Anne, host. "Taming your Inner Critic, Finding Grace and Why Perfectionism is the Voice of the Oppressor." The Tim Ferris Podcast, July 9, 2021.

"A Long-Term Perspective on Market Downturns." AMG Funds, June 1, 2023, www.amgfunds.com/research-and-insights/keep-calm-and-remain-diversified/longterm_perspective_on_market_downturns/. Accessed September 26, 2023.

"Lump-sum Investing versus Cost Averaging: Which Is Better?" Vanguard, April 21, 2023. https://investor.vanguard.com/investor-resources-education/news/lump-sum-investing-versus-cost-averaging-which-is-better.

McChesney, Chris, and Sean Covey. *The Four Disciplines of Execution; Achieving Your Wildly Important Goals.* Page 66. New York Free Press, 2012.

Murray, Nick. *"Simple Wealth, Inevitable Wealth."* Sixth edition, 2019.

"Number of Jobs Held in a Lifetime." U.S. Department of Labor, Bureau of Labor Statistics. https://www.bls.gov/nls/home.html. Accessed March 30, 2023.

Picchi, Aimee. "One Way to Fix Social Security? 'Smash the Cap.'" Moneywatch, March 3, 2023.

Portnoy, Brian. "The Geometry of Wealth." Harriman House Limited, June 11, 2018.

Ptak, Jeffrey. "Setting the Record Straight on Our Fund Ratings." Morningstar, Inc., October 26, 2017. www.morningstar.com/funds/setting-record-straight-our-fund-ratings.

Social Security Administration. "Workers with Maximum-Taxable Earnings." https://www.ssa.gov/oact/cola/examplemax.html. Accessed October 7, 2024.

Swedroe, Larry. "Individual Investing Involves Risk." Advisor Perspectives, September 17, 2019.

Welsh, Josh. "GenXers will not Retire Comfortably, Schroders finds." Investment News, December 14, 2023. https://www.investmentnews.com/retirement/news/gen-xers-will-not-retire-comfortably-schroders-finds-247126#.

ADDITIONAL DEFINITIONS AND DISCLOSURES

i   The charts and graphs represented in chapters one and two are printed with permission from eMoney, a comprehensive financial planning system used by professional advisors. There are several companies offering software to advisors today; this is the one we rely on. My goal here is not to endorse software; it's simply to demonstrate the power of using technology to help model potential outcomes. You've probably heard the saying: garbage in… garbage out. Even professionals can misunderstand or misuse software, creating unrealistic expectations. Trust but verify.

ii   Converting an employer plan account or Traditional IRA to a Roth IRA is a taxable event. Increased taxable income from the Roth IRA conversion may have several consequences including but not limited to, a need for additional tax withholding or estimated tax payments, the loss of certain tax deductions and credits, and higher taxes on Social Security benefits and higher Medicare premiums. Be sure to consult with a qualified tax advisor before making any decisions regarding your IRA.

iii   Private investments are subject to special risks. Individuals must meet specific suitability standards before investing. This information does not constitute an offer to sell or a solicitation of an offer to buy. As a reminder, hedge funds (or funds of hedge funds), private equity funds, real estate funds often engage in leveraging and other speculative investment practices that may increase the risk of investment loss. These investments can be highly illiquid and are not required to provide periodic pricing or valuation information to investors and may involve complex tax structures and delays in distributing important tax information. These investments are not subject to the same regulatory requirements as mutual funds; and often charge high fees. Further, any number of conflicts of interest may exist in the context of the management and/or operation of any such fund. For complete information, please refer to the applicable offering memorandum.

iv   A 529 plan is a college savings plan that allows individuals to save for college on a tax-advantaged basis. Every state offers at least one 529 plan. Before buying a 529 plan, you should inquire about the particular plan and its fees and expenses. You should also consider that certain states offer tax benefits and fee savings to in-state residents. Whether a state tax deduction and/or application fee savings are available depends on your state of residence. For tax advice, consult your tax professional. Non-qualifying distribution earnings prior to 2024 are taxable and subject to a 10% tax penalty. Beginning in 2024, unused 529 plan funds may be rolled into a Roth IRA assuming the following conditions are met: 1) must have owned the 529 plan for 15 years, 2) can only convert funds that have been in the 529 plan for at least 5 years, 3) rollover amount cannot exceed $35,000 and 4) rollovers must be made to a beneficiaries Roth IRA.

v   Asset Allocation does not guarantee a profit or protect against a loss in a declining market. It is a method used to help manage investment risk.

vi   Hedge Funds are unregistered private investment partnerships, funds or pools that may invest and trade in many different markets, strategies and instruments (including securities, non-securities and derivatives) and are NOT subject to the same regulatory requirements as mutual funds, including mutual fund requirements to provide certain periodic and standardized pricing and valuation information to investors. Hedge Funds represent speculative investments and can involve a high degree of risk. An investor could lose all or a substantial portion of his/her investment. Investors must have the financial ability, sophistication/ experience and willingness to bear the risks of an investment.

vii   Rebalancing/Reallocating Asset Allocation does not guarantee a profit or protect against a loss in a declining market. It is a method used to help manage investment risk. and can entail transaction costs and tax consequences that should be considered when determining a rebalancing/reallocation strategy.

viii   Historically, market capitalization, defined as the value of all outstanding shares of a corporation, has an inverse or opposite relationship to both risk and return. On average, large-cap corporations—those with market capitalizations of $10 billion and greater—tend to grow more slowly than mid-cap companies. Mid-cap companies are those with a capitalization between $2 billion and $10 billion, while small-cap corporations have between $250 million and $2 billion.

ix   Diversification does not guarantee a profit or protect against a loss in a declining market. It is a method used to help manage investment risk.

x   The S&P 500, or the Standard and Poor's 500 Index is a market-capitalization weighted index of the largest publicly traded companies in the U.S.. It is widely regarded as the best gauge of large cap U.S. equities, but that is all it is: a gauge. It is a proxy to represent this class of companies that are domiciled in the United States.

xi   Indices are unmanaged and investors cannot invest directly in an index. Unless otherwise noted, performance of indices does not account for any fees, commissions or other expenses that would be incurred. Returns do not include reinvested dividends. Past history is no guarantee of what you can expect in the future.

Private investments are subject to special risks. Individuals must meet specific suitability standards before investing. This information does not constitute an offer to sell or a solicitation of an offer to buy. As a reminder, hedge funds (or funds of hedge funds), private equity funds, real estate funds often engage in leveraging and other speculative investment practices that may increase the risk of investment loss. These investments can be highly illiquid and are not required to provide periodic pricing or valuation information to investors and may involve complex tax structures and delays in distributing important tax information. These investments are not subject to the same regulatory requirements as mutual funds; and often charge high fees. Further, any number of conflicts of interest may exist in the context of the management and/or operation of any such fund. For complete information, please refer to the applicable offering memorandum.

Cryptocurrency is a digital representation of value that functions as a medium of exchange, a unit of account, or a store of value, but it does not have legal tender status. Cryptocurrencies are sometimes exchanged for U.S. dollars or other currencies around the world, but they are not generally backed or supported by any government or central bank. Their value is completely derived by market forces of supply and demand, and they are more volatile than traditional currencies. Cryptocurrencies are not covered by either FDIC or SIPC insurance. Legislative and regulatory changes or actions at the state, federal, or international level may adversely affect the use, transfer, exchange, and value of cryptocurrency.

Purchasing cryptocurrencies comes with a number of risks, including volatile market price swings or flash crashes, market manipulation, and cybersecurity risks. In addition, cryptocurrency markets and exchanges are not regulated with the same controls or customer protections available in equity, option, futures, or foreign exchange investing.

xii   Rebalancing/Reallocating can entail transaction costs and tax consequences that should be considered when determining a rebalancing/reallocation strategy.

xiii   Dollar cost averaging may help reduce per share cost through continuous investment in securities regardless of fluctuating prices and does not guarantee profitability nor can it protect from loss in a declining market. The investor should consider his/her ability to continue investing through periods of low price levels.

xiv Fixed Annuities are long term insurance contacts and there is a surrender charge imposed generally during the first 5 to 7 years that you own the annuity contract. Withdrawals prior to age 59-½ may result in a 10% IRS tax penalty, in addition to any ordinary income tax. Any guarantees of the annuity are backed by the financial strength of the underlying insurance company.

xv Please consider the investment objectives, risks, charges, and expenses carefully before investing in Variable Annuities. The prospectus, which contains this and other information about the variable annuity contract and the underlying investment options, can be obtained from the insurance company or your financial professional. Be sure to read the prospectus carefully before deciding whether to invest.

The investment return and principal value of the variable annuity investment options are not guaranteed. Variable annuity sub-accounts fluctuate with changes in market conditions. The principal may be worth more or less than the original amount invested when the annuity is surrendered.

xvi This is a hypothetical example that is demonstrating a mathematical principle. It does not illustrate any investment products and does not show past or future performance of any specific investment.

xvii Fixed income securities are subject to increased loss of principal during periods of rising interest rates. Fixed income investments are subject to various other risks, including changes in credit quality, liquidity, prepayments, and other factors. REIT risks include changes in real estate values and property taxes, interest rates, cash flow of underlying real estate assets, supply and demand, and the management skill and creditworthiness of the issuer.

xviii Indices are unmanaged and investors cannot invest directly in an index.

The Bloomberg Barclays U.S. Aggregate Bond Index, or the Agg, is a broad base, market capitalization-weighted bond market index representing intermediate term investment grade bonds traded in the United States. Investors frequently use the index as a stand-in for measuring the performance of the U.S. bond market.

xix Active portfolio management, including and perhaps especially market timing, can subject longer term investors to potentially higher fees and can have a negative effect on the long-term performance due to the transaction costs of the short-term trading. In addition, there may be potential tax consequences from these strategies. Active portfolio management and market timing may be unsuitable for some investors depending on their specific investment objectives and financial position. Active portfolio management does not guarantee a profit or protect against a loss in a declining market.

xx Investments in commodities may have greater volatility than investments in traditional securities, particularly if the instruments involve leverage. The value of commodity-linked derivative instruments may be affected by changes in overall market movements, commodity index volatility, changes in interest rates or factors affecting a particular industry or commodity, such as drought, floods, weather, livestock disease, embargoes, tariffs and international economic, political and regulatory developments. Use of leveraged commodity-linked derivatives creates an opportunity for increased return but, at the same time, creates the possibility for greater loss.

xxi This is a mathematical example of the concept of compounding only. It does not represent actual investing. Past performance is never indicative of future results.

xxii Tax loss harvesting is a strategy of selling securities at a loss to offset a capital gains tax liability. It is typically used to limit the recognition of short-term capital gains, which are normally taxed at higher federal income tax rates than long-term capital gains, though it is also used for long-term capital gains.

xxiii This a reminder that while the information I'm giving you as a CERTIFIED FINANCIAL PLANNER™ (CFP®) includes detailed approaches, ideas and things to look out for, it is not legal advice. As always, it is important to consult a professional, in this case a qualified attorney specializing in estate planning to help coordinate your wills, related documents and titling on accounts.

xxiv This is a hypothetical example that is demonstrating a mathematical principle. It does not illustrate any investment products and does not show past or future performance of any specific investment.

www.ingramcontent.com/pod-product-compliance
Lightning Source LLC
Chambersburg PA
CBHW070703190326
41458CB00046B/6830/J